Twenty
on th

In Commemoration of
the Miller Center's 20th Anniversary

Edited by Kenneth W. Thompson

Volume I

UNIVERSITY
PRESS OF
AMERICA

The Miller Center

Lanham • New York • London

University of Virginia

Copyright © 1995 by
University Press of America®, Inc.
4720 Boston Way
Lanham, Maryland 20706

3 Henrietta Street
London WC2E 8LU England

All rights reserved
Printed in the United States of America
British Cataloging in Publication Information Available

Copublished by arrangement with
The Miller Center of Public Affairs,
University of Virginia

The views expressed by the author(s) of this publication do not necessarily represent the opinions of the Miller Center. We hold to Jefferson's dictum that: "Truth is the proper and sufficient antagonist to error, and has nothing to fear from the conflict, unless by human interposition, disarmed of her natural weapons, free argument and debate."

Library of Congress Cataloging-in-Publication Data

Twenty years of papers on the Presidency / edited by Kenneth W. Thompson.
p. cm. --(In commemoration of the Miller Center's 20th anniversary ; v. 1)
1. Presidents--United States.   I. Thompson, Kenneth W.   II. White Burkett Miller Center.   III. Series.
JK516.T88   1995   324.6'3'0973--dc20   95-24738 CIP

ISBN: 0-7618-0070-0 (cloth: alk:ppr)
ISBN: 0-7618-0071-9 (pbk: alk:ppr)

⊖™ The paper used in this publication meets the minimum requirements of American National Standard for Information Sciences—Permanence of Paper for Printed Library Materials, ANSI Z39.48–1964.

TO THE MEMORY OF
DEAN RUSK
FIRST MILLER CENTER NATIONAL ASSOCIATE

CONTENTS

PREFACE ix

INTRODUCTION xiii

I: President at the Miller Center

1. THE PRESIDENT AND POLITICAL LEADERSHIP 3
   President Gerald R. Ford

2. THE PRESIDENT AND CONGRESS 21
   President Gerald R. Ford

II: Advisers Extraordinaire to Presidents

3. PERSPECTIVES FROM THE WHITE HOUSE
   ON LEADERSHIP 39
   James H. Rowe, Jr.

4. POLITICAL LEADERSHIP: ROOSEVELT,
   JOHNSON, AND REAGAN 49
   Thomas G. Corcoran

5. THE "COMPLEAT" PRESIDENT:
   DWIGHT DAVID EISENHOWER 77
   Bryce Harlow

CONTENTS

III. Views from the Cabinet

6. THE PRESIDENT AND THE
   SECRETARY OF STATE REVISITED 101
   Dean Rusk

7. CABINET GOVERNMENT: AN ALTERNATIVE
   FOR ORGANIZING POLICY-MAKING 133
   Griffin Bell

8. WHAT DOES AN ATTORNEY GENERAL DO? 153
   Herbert Brownell

IV. Presidents and the Congress

9. PRESIDENTIAL LEADERSHIP:
   LYNDON B. JOHNSON AND THE CONGRESS 175
   Jack Valenti

10. A SENATOR REFLECTS ON A PRESIDENT:
    LAXALT ON REAGAN 189
    Paul Laxalt

11. THE PRESIDENCY AND THE CONGRESS
    IN THE CONSTITUTIONAL SYSTEM 209
    Richard Bolling

V. Presidents and the Future

12. THE PRESIDENCY AND THE FUTURE 231
    David Broder

13. THE SETTING: MORALITY, POLITICS,
    AND FOREIGN POLICY 243
    George F. Kennan

14. THINKING AND WRITING ABOUT THE FUTURE 257
    Paul M. Kennedy

VI. An Epilogue

15. PRESIDENT CARTER ON URGENT
    CONTEMPORARY PROBLEMS 275
    President Jimmy Carter

PREFACE

The study of the American presidency has been the focal point of Miller Center programs. The choice was made in response to the wishes of the donor, Burkett Miller, who in conversations and correspondence defined his vision for the Center. Mr. Miller held that the presidency had not functioned as the Founding Fathers intended. Witness Vietnam. It cried out for reexamination, and American colleges and universities had not taken up the challenge. No center was devoting itself primarily to presidential studies. Mr. Miller believed much could be gained from concentration. To paraphrase the late president of a leading foundation, Frank Keppel:
> In philanthropy as in baseball,
> you score runs by bunching hits.

My colleagues and I have responded to the challenge. A procession of former presidents, presidential assistants, Cabinet members, senators and congressmen, legislators, journalists, and presidential scholars have passed through the doors of the Center. Taken together, their public service extends over more than six decades. They represent shades of opinion across the spectrum in the major political parties. Out of hundreds of such visitors, some stand out for the insights they contribute on presidents and the presidency. Two in this volume can speak from firsthand responsibility in the Oval Office. The rest have been close to the center of the action in positions in and out of government.

It is difficult if not impossible to explain what sets the smaller group apart. It is clearly the product of unique experience. Their understanding reflects having served in an important capacity as president or a high-ranking official who was an intimate of a president and had earned his confidence. An important factor is political wisdom as the ancients described it but moderns are resistant to acknowledge. Political wisdom is the ability to deal with political realities on their own terms rather than viewing the political arena as a passing phase in the development of a rational and moral order. Political wisdom accepts the recurrence of conflicts of national and group interests whereas reformism and perfectionism associates such conflicts with an aristocratic and elitist age. The majority of the contributors to this volume assume conflicts of interest that can be ameliorated and composed but cannot be eradicated once and for all.

Further, not only have they operated within the American constitutional framework of separation of powers and checks and balance and not only do they take it for granted. As one reads their texts, it becomes apparent that most of them revel in the moral and political opportunities such a system provides. They see it as a broad avenue down which policymakers can move. It opens channels for communication and compromise and for give and take and accommodation and reconciliation. It is a system they accept as reality and not one that can be reformed out of existence.

Third, the authors of the essays are acutely aware of the risks of politics and government. They know what it means to seek influence and power, and in this area almost all have been successful at one time or another. They also know the hazards of politics, the perils of carrying responsibility, and the vulnerability of political actors. Most have tasted defeat. A few know what is involved to be identified with failed policies and condemned as spokesmen and defenders when the real architects of the policy had fled and abandoned ship. There is a tragic dimension to politics, and although few have the courage or the greatness to write in this vein, the inevitability of setbacks and defeats runs like a red thread through the history of politics. Weaker and stronger leaders grapple with intractable problems and suffer shipwreck. In this they are not alone in the history of politics, even though American truimphalism may not prepare the citizenry to live with both victory and defeat.

Finally, whatever the risks of politics, the majority of our contributors are remembered for having the courage to act. None are armchair philosophers nor are they addicted to abstract theorizing. Major American policies are identified with a few of them, not always in the context they intended them. The majority are initiative-takers, whether as advisers or decisionmakers. History's final judgment is not in on most of the policies they espoused. None would claim they were always right. To call them true believers would be questionable. The majority seem to have had if not a love for politics at least a respect for its requirements. No true student of politics need be embarrassed by quoting them in teaching or writing. Indeed, most would agree with a political scientist who wrote:

> There is no end to the praises that can be sung of politics. In politics, not in economics, is found the creative dialectic of offices. The true politician is a reforming conserver, a skeptical believer and a pluralistic moralist. Politics is lively sobriety, a complex simplicity, an untidy elegance, a rough civility, and an everlasting immediacy. It is conflict become discussion.

INTRODUCTION

One year into its programs on the American presidency, the Miller Center was pleased to have a visit from President Gerald R. Ford. In two separate Forums, he addressed themes that have become central in studies of the presidency. He discussed, first, the president and political leadership, including leadership of the party, the country, and the world. Each broad area requires a sense of changing circumstances and the conditions under which action is possible. Mr. Ford leaves the reader with the impression that he loved the job, and that impression distinguishes him from certain of his predecessors and successors. The President went on to analyze Congress and the presidency, a subject on which his experience of 25-and-a-half years in the Congress was greater than that of any 20th-century president. He warned against two extremes: domination by the president or the Congress. He concluded that there is no substitute for a president knowing how the Congress works and having lasting personal relations with the members with whom he must work.

James Rowe was intimately acquainted with presidents from Franklin D. Roosevelt to Lyndon B. Johnson. He was an administrative assistant to FDR for four years and then served in the Department of Justice. Few observers had the firsthand exposure to what FDR would and would not tolerate from an assistant. FDR never moved too far ahead of the American people in his political actions. Rowe suggests that John F. Kennedy had style and Johnson substance in politics, yet Kennedy was the best national politician since Roosevelt in attracting delegates. Rowe explains why. Johnson was the brightest president Rowe knew but also the most complicated and insecure. FDR's staff at the outset was composed of three secretaries and six administrative assistants. In the Truman administration, nine people did what Rowe did for FDR. Each president ends up with more staff than his predecessor.

INTRODUCTION

Rowe warns of presidential *hubris*, especially after a landslide election. Most presidents rely on men they have known, especially in their youth. They each have their mafia. When crises arise, they tend to take counsel mainly from their friends.

Thomas G. Corcoran was described as a new political type in the time of FDR. He not only drafted legislation for the New Deal but maneuvered it through Congress. He and Benjamin Cohen were key members of Roosevelt's brain trust. In his essay, Tommy the Cork compares FDR, LBJ, and more briefly, Ronald Reagan. Corcoran was *sui generis* as he spoke at the Miller Center. Alternately poetic, outrageous, and profound, his comments bring back the dynamic energy of a legendary political figure who was present at the creation of the New Deal.

Bryce Harlow ranks with the foremost analysts of the presidency in the 20th century. Scholars who shunned political observers looked to him as an oracle. He not only understood politics, but he wrote about it as few politicians or academicians could. He served in the Congress, was with General Marshall during the war, was on Capitol Hill with the Armed Services Committee of the House, and returned to Oklahoma City. When President Eisenhower called for him, he reluctantly returned to Washington as Ike's special assistant and speech writer. For Harlow, Eisenhower was the "compleat" president, the finest leader the nation ever produced. Interviewed in 1983 in his office in Crystal City, Harlow explains the reason for that judgment. In that interview, Ike comes alive with his Kansas grin, five-star sternness, and expression of billowing anger that for Harlow was like looking into a Bessemer furnace. Harlow describes Ike's various abilities from writing to making decisions. Before Fred Greenstein had been recognized for his revisionist view of Eisenhower, Harlow was speaking of Ike's grasp of politics and the fate of "a hot political speech" he drafted for him. Harlow's Miller Center interviews on Eisenhower and Nixon are two of the finest appraisals of American presidents in the literature of presidents.

Dean Rusk is the longest-serving secretary of state since Cordell Hull. His chapter is the first of three on the presidency by former Cabinet members. He compares some 20th century presidents to make the point that the United States has had a great

INTRODUCTION

diversity of leaders. Circumstances were important in determining the kinds of presidents who emerged. A president's foreign policy is also a product of America's constitutional system and the restraints on America's authority abroad. Rusk calls attention to the basis of executive power in Article II of the Constitution, power reserved to only one president but activated within a constitutional system of checks and balances. Mr. Rusk outlines the relation of the president to the Congress and the secretary of state. He mildly suggests that White House staff should be held in a staff relationship and not injected into the chain of command. Rusk's essay has much to say about the conduct of foreign policy and guidelines for action by the Department of State, congressional testimony by the secretary, domestic politics, and the need in foreign policy for politics to stop at the water's edge. Principles affecting the relationship between the president and the secretary, including confidentiality, receive attention. In revisiting his original *Foreign Affairs* article on the subject, Rusk brings his statement up-to-date, reaffirming but elaborating key points.

Griffin Bell was attorney general in the Carter administration. In chapter seven, he discusses Cabinet government. Cabinet government was invented by George Washington invoking Article II, Section II, which specifies that the president may require the opinion in writing of the principal officer in each of the executive departments. Judge Bell reviews the history, noting that Washington and Lincoln on contested policy issues allowed members of their Cabinets to vote. FDR used the Cabinet and the White House staff as he chose. In those days staff was small and there was no National Security Council. Bell suggests that it would be difficult to have Cabinet government today and cites "show and tell" sessions during Cabinet meetings in the Carter and other administrations as evidence of the difficulty. Not only have White House officials become virtually co-Cabinet members but the National Security Council assistant may play this role despite not having been confirmed by the Senate. Judge Bell once advised President Carter to transfer the National Security Council people to the State Department and make White House personnel who are exercising Cabinet powers subject to confirmation. Constitutionally, only judges, ambassadors, Cabinet officers, and a few others are

INTRODUCTION

subject to confirmation. Confirmation and restoring the role of the Cabinet are two problems that Judge Bell insists deserve investigation.

The final essay by a Cabinet member is Herbert Brownell's piece, "What Does an Attorney General Do?" In a lively and often humorous account of the role of President Eisenhower's attorney general, General Brownell chronicles his selection, the trip to Korea, constitutional questions that arose, his part in the defeat of the Bricker amendment, McCarthyism, and civil rights. The story of his confirmation is amusing. His analysis of the appointment of federal judges is still germane (the Miller Center's Seventh Commission is studying the problem of delay in the selection of federal judges). In a brisk question-and-answer period, General Brownell discusses the relation of the attorney general to the FBI, the 25th Amendment, the Bricker amendment, the 1996 campaign, the primacy of the Justice Department's role in the selection of federal judges, the end of the Dewey campaign, Eisenhower and Chief Justice Warren, and the political process.

Three essays follow on presidents and Congress. Jack Valenti was special assistant to President Johnson and returned with him on Air Force One after the assassination of President Kennedy. With the present controversy over violence in the movies, Jack Valenti, who is president of the Motion Picture Association, has become an embattled figure, leading some to forget the role he played in the Johnson administration. In this chapter, he describes President Johnson's agenda for the Congress, the legislation he passed, and his direction to his staff in their dealings with congressmen. Valenti offers a series of dos and don'ts for any president in working with Congress.

Senator Paul Laxalt was perhaps President Ronald Reagan's closest friend. He traces Reagan's rise to national political leadership and identifies his emergence with the speech he made for Barry Goldwater at the 1964 Republican convention in Los Angeles. Reagan used his gubernatorial office in California to try out some of the policies he was to introduce as president. Laxalt rehearses the famous Reagan-Bush debate in Nashua, New Hampshire, and his campaign in 1984 against Walter Mondale. Reagan embraced a few simple principles, such as believing the federal government was too big, tax cuts, and the defense buildup against Russia. Most of his actions stemmed from these principles. Laxalt agrees that Reagan's budget deficits are open to question and explains how they resulted, going back to conversations with Hubert Humphrey when he entered the Senate.

Congressman Richard Bolling served in Congress from the Fifth District of Missouri during the tenure of eight presidents. Considered by many to be the country's foremost authority on the relation of presidents to Congress, he compares various presidents. He states that of presidents from LBJ to Reagan, only President Ford understood the Congress and how to work with it. His chapter is a brilliant review of procedures and personalities who played the principal role in executive-legislative relations. His account may be the best single analysis of presidents and Congress in the presidential literature.

The final three essays are broader, more philosophical, and more future-oriented than those that precede them. David Broder is considered by many to be the most respected American columnist and journalist. He notes the sudden and far-reaching changes that have occurred in attitudes toward recent presidents. He suggests how unpredictable president-watching has become. The institution and the organization of the White House tends to become a reflection of a particular president. Broder is critical of the idea of moving the presidential system closer to the parliamentary system. He warns that people would do well to keep their fingers crossed over what each new president will bring to the office.

George F. Kennan is one of the nation's most highly regarded diplomat-historians. He discusses a central issue in American politics and diplomacy, namely, the role of morality. At the outset of his discussion, he responds to Solzhenitzyn, who had suggested that Kennan and others sought to separate morality and politics. First, Kennan seeks to explain what morality is not. It is not making moral preachments to other peoples and governments. It is not reproaching others for what we ourselves do. It is not criticizing others for reasons of domestic politics. It is not being critical of our enemies and overlooking the moral lapses of our friends. It is not urging courses of action on others when one cannot foresee the probable results. Thereafter, Mr. Kennan treats areas where morality and purpose are relevant, subject always to the limitations of actions beyond our borders.

Paul M. Kennedy is a Yale historian who has written with great insight on thinking and writing about the future. He suggests that in public and foreign policy the United States faces new problems and challenges involving the environment, population, and terrorism. Having turned back Malthus's prophecy that population would outrun resources, people may be lulled into a feeling of false confidence. In fact, with problems of overpopulation, the shrinkage of job opportunities, coupled with job displacement from the robotic revolution, our chances of survival may be more endangered than we realize. Kennedy's piece introduces a somber note to our thinking on presidents and the future.

We began this anniversary volume with two essays by President Gerald R. Ford. We conclude it with a conversation with President Jimmy Carter. During a visit to the University of Virginia, President Carter invited questions from a Miller Center audience. Many of the questions concerned urgent contemporary problems. Mr. Carter, in his characteristic fashion, answered each question in a straightforward, sometimes outspoken manner. In an era when political leaders train themselves to "bob and weave," President Carter's responses were direct, refreshing, and to the point. In the face of the many unanswered problems the country faces, his positive approach may be reassuring for the future.

I.

PRESIDENT AT THE MILLER CENTER

~ One ~

THE PRESIDENT AND POLITICAL LEADERSHIP[*]

President Gerald R. Ford

THE HONORABLE LINWOOD HOLTON: Mr. President, ladies and gentlemen, this is a continuation of the series of the White Burkett Miller Center Forums, a series of discussions relating to the office of the presidency that came about as a result of a dream, throughout his lifetime, of Burkett Miller, who was a graduate of the University of Virginia Law School in the class of 1914. Mr. Miller was a successful lawyer in Chattanooga and was in a position to see that his dream was implemented by the time he died. I had the good fortune during my term as governor to be associated with Mr. Miller and with representatives of the University of Virginia in creating, Mr. President, a Center of Public Affairs that would, if Mr. Miller's dream does come true, bring together the theoreticians and academicians and the action people, the people in public affairs who have the requirement to make the decisions that affect the course of our history.
    We are very pleased with the fact that the Center has done as well as it has. People have come here, people who have been leaders in the political life of our nation and in the academic life of our nation; and ladies and gentlemen, we are particularly fortunate today to have one who has had the experience of being in the position of the leadership of the free world. Certainly no president in our time as had a broader background and experience for the presidency and for the discussions that Burkett Miller hoped would

---

[*]Presented in a Forum at the Miller Center of Public Affairs on 11 October 1979. Reprinted from *The Virginia Papers on the Presidency* (Washington, D.C.: University Press of America, Inc., 1979), Volume II.

take place here. He took office under the most awesome of circumstances.

I happened to have been in the East Room when he was designated for the vice presidency—and in a very difficult context—largely among people who were his colleagues in the Congress when the then-President, playing his little game of mysteries that he was so fond of playing, came to the point of describing the background of his designee having 25 years experience in the Congress and then pointing to Gerald Ford. Not only was there a feeling of relief but a great feeling of respect and admiration that was immediately sensed throughout the room. Then later he went to the Office of the President and was confronted by the most difficult decisions.

He has described his most difficult problem as the problem of inflation, which is, of course, in our laps today. But I think his most difficult decision was the decision with which not everyone in this room would agree, but I feel it was the correct decision, the decision to see that Watergate was put to bed. That decision may well have cost him reelection, but I think that decision assured the future health of this nation as a more indivisible unit. It is with that background that he comes to this discussion, and it is with a warm feeling of personal friendship, Mr. President, and great anticipation that we, as Virginians and academicians, welcome you to the White Burkett Miller Center.

PRESIDENT FORD: Thank you very, very much, Governor Holton. Our relationship transcends titles. Our relationship is one of long-standing personal friendship, and I thank you very much for your more than generous observations and comments. I am delighted to be here at the Miller Center seminar and be a participant in this kind of a discussion. I thoroughly enjoy such an opportunity, and I am grateful for the invitation.

As I understand it, the session this morning is aimed at the president and leadership, political leadership. From my experience, both in the Congress and in the executive branch, I believe the president traditionally is supposed to have three hats. Number one is political leadership of his party. Second is his leadership from the point of view of the country. Third, because of our country's role in the world, the president has an obligation on a world leadership basis. Let me take each of those responsibilities of a president and give my impression of where we stand at the present time.

Over the years, a president was looked upon as the person who represented his party in a pure political sense, organizationally, as it related to the party itself. Second, observers emphasized the president's relationship with the Congress, its members, the House and the Senate that came from his political party. Today, because of the disintegration of political parties, a president's role as a party leader has been undercut. Political parties today, as I view them, are no longer the traditional organizations that carried out a particular role over the earlier history of our nation. Political parties, at the local, state, and national level are no longer the formidable creatures that used to have a tremendous impact. Speaking only for myself, I think that is unfortunate. I don't think anyone would like to go back to the old days where everything was done more or less in a smoke-filled room where nominees were selected and decisions were made by limited groups of individuals; but nevertheless, in our political history the two-party system has played a very important role, and I think it is desirable that political parties continue to have an impact. We certainly don't want to fall into the trap of a multiparty nation, and certainly we don't want to become a part of a one-party political system. So I strongly opt for the effective role of a two-party system, and the president ought to have the leadership in his particular political party.

There have been some factors that have tended to undercut that viable role of the party. I think the best illustration is the proliferation of presidential primaries. They have done away with many of the ways in which the party can be built. I think we can still support the primary system, but the party ought to have a greater role than it seems to have had in the last several elections. I for one think the president, after he is nominated, ought to merge his efforts with the party in seeking election. I think it would have long-range beneficial impact on how he is able to govern the country.

The first political leadership role of the president is his relationship with the members of his political party and the House

THE PRESIDENT AND POLITICAL LEADERSHIP

and the Senate. We traditionally expect that a president from one party who has majorities in both the House and the Senate ought to be able to make things work very smoothly. That hasn't been the case, and I am not referring to the current situation. I think a Republican president with a Republican majority would have many of the same problems that President Carter has, not because of the presidency, but because of the developments that have transpired in Congress itself. I was minority leader in the House for nine-plus years, and I began to see during that span of time greater and greater problems for leaders, Democratic or Republican, in the Congress. The way Congress is elected today has made it much more difficult for a leader, a speaker, a majority or minority leader, to control, if that is the right word, his party members.

Two things come to mind that have undercut party responsibility in the legislative branch. Number one, the expansion and proliferation of what we call single-issue problems. I will only mention two, but they are ones that are mentioned frequently. One issue is gun control. That transcends party philosophy, party platforms, and so forth. Another is abortion. That really has no relationship to the traditional political philosophy of the two major parties, but those are issues that have torn apart the legislative branch in many ways and destroyed the traditional party cohesion and allegiances. The net result is when a party leader goes to members of his party and seeks to get their help and support on a party issue, the members of Congress on both sides of the aisle are often reluctant to give that support because they now think of themselves as elected regardless of their party affiliation.

A great many members of Congress think of themselves as being elected totally on their own, not because they are a Democrat or Republican, but because of their own talents—television has an impact on that. So when the Speaker or the majority or minority leader goes to a member and says, "this is a party issue," the party member is more provincial, more parochial, more self-centered and less interested in what the party means. So the party leader can no longer, as was traditional, report to his president and say, "Mr. President, the party will support you," because there are always so many disaffections that have developed just because of their own individual personality, or why they think they got elected, and so

President Gerald R. Ford

forth. This handicaps very greatly the capability of a president to put through his program, whether it is good or bad. He can no longer, even though he has significant majorities in the Congress, expect that he can turn a switch and work with the leadership and get whatever results he might seek.

The second role of a president and leadership is the role of being a country leader, a national leader. This is a little more difficult for me to discuss in any depth perhaps, because I am not sure anyone can give you a formula in this day and age of how that is achieved. We have periodic readings of various thermometers, polls, and surveys, and it was not very encouraging to me on a number of occasions to look at that thermometer, and I have great sympathy for President Carter when he sees the ones he has to look at today. But, that is the way public perception is of whether you are a leader or not: how you stand in the polls. I would only make this observation, and I am not being personal in any way, but in my judgment, from the point of view of what is good for the country, it is more important for a president to be a leader in a substantive way rather than in a charismatic way. The public is going to give greater support to a president if they believe he is being substantive rather than superficial. An image does not really bring about public support. Substance is the way to achieve it.

Third, the last role of the president and leadership is how he exercises that leadership vis-à-vis the rest of the world. Whether we like it or not, the United States is one of the great countries in the world, and as a consequence, we have to undertake certain responsibilities. They may be onerous, they may be something that we would like to push off. But we are there, we had better assume them, and we had better do our duty. It is not pleasant sometimes.

Overall there have been some shifts in recent years. I can remember an early post-World War II period when, for two very good reasons, we were without question the leader in the world; we were supreme militarily and economically. As a consequence, our president was unanimously the leader around the globe. In the decade of the 1950s, there were never really any serious challenges to that. De Gaulle was a leader because of his personality and the role of France. Mao was a leader because of 600 million people, even though China was pretty much a self-contained nation. But

THE PRESIDENT AND POLITICAL LEADERSHIP

the President of the United States, regardless of the individual, was recognized as the leader.

I believe there is a change today. The United States still has the right to be a leader, but we've got some challenges. We have the strengthening of West Germany, no question about it. Helmut Schmidt is a very important leader in the world. To some extent President Giscard in France is a leader. And although we have lost Mao and Chou En-Lai in China, the current PRC leaders are bound to have a significant impact throughout the world. Brezhnev, because of the growing strength of the Soviet Union, is a leader who is competing with the United States. I suspect our leadership role in the future will not be a sole leadership or unanimous leadership but will be challenged by other great countries and other outstanding leaders.

So the president must consolidate his strengths at home, gain the support of the American people, and then seek to convince other people, particularly in the Western world, that the United States deserves and warrants a role of leadership in world affairs. It is not easy with the problems we have at home and the difficulties we see around the world. But I come back to what I said at the outset, whether we like it or not, the United States has the opportunity and the obligation to be a world-leading nation, and our president ought to carry that mantle. It's not easy, as many people have found—including myself. But it is a responsibility I think our people, our country, and our president must assume.

GOVERNOR HOLTON: Thank you, Mr. President. President Ford has indicated, ladies and gentlemen, that he would like most of this discussion to be a response to your questions, and I am not going to call on any of you save one. But Mr. President, before I go to the others, I am going to say to you that, while we have a very distinguished group here, we do not have any of your predecessors in that office present. On the other hand, we do have someone who, for more than 30 years, has lived very intimately with one of your significant predecessors, and I'm going to let him ask the first question. Dumas Malone is the world's foremost authority on Thomas Jefferson, and he's ours. (LAUGHTER)

President Gerald R. Ford

MR. MALONE: I am glad to avail myself of the privilege of seniority to ask a question. Mr. Jefferson, as you undoubtedly know but I will remind you, referred to the presidency as "splendid misery," and there has been a great deal of talk, as I am sure you have often heard, about the tasks of the presidency having become too great for any one person to handle them effectively. I think that we should be very interested, sir, to hear your comments on the assertion that the presidency has become an impossible job, and perhaps some comments about the ways in which it might be made more effective to perform what you correctly say is his chief function: effective leadership in substantive matters.

PRESIDENT FORD: First, I do not agree with the comment that you frequently hear that the presidency is an impossible job. I concede that there are some times when you are president, the misery seems to overcome the joys. But I firmly believe that a person can perform the constitutional responsibilities of the presidency effectively. Not that there won't be some minuses as well as some pluses for the country and for the president, but there is no reason why we should assume a defeatist attitude that under our system we cannot have a chief executive or a commander in chief who can do the job if he has the talent, if he has the kind of staff that the president ought to have, if he has the experience that is essential, and if he has the judgment.

It does not mean that you can do it all in eight hours a day, five days a week. Quite the contrary, it is a long, hard, work-a-day process. It does necessitate that the president assemble an outstanding group of individuals to advise him and to execute what decisions are made. I do not believe you can husband all of the power in the White House and personally monitor on a day-to-day basis what happens throughout the government. You have to have, and I use this as an example, a kind of a cabinet whose members are responsible for the day-to-day operation of their respective departments. They, in turn, have to have the total support of the president. They have to have rapport with the president so that there is a high degree of unanimity in philosophy and viewpoint, but if he picks the right people and has faith in their day-to-day operational responsibilities, the president can concentrate, not on the minutiae, but on the broad issues that have to be brought to him in the Oval Office.

The president has to assume, when he takes office, that there will be many, many unpopular decisions because he has more knowledge as to what the alternatives are and he has to be prepared to be unpopular because he happens to think he is right, and hopefully he is right. But for us as a nation to assume that our structure of government is so cumbersome and so big and therefore so inadequate that no individual can handle the responsibilities is a bad attitude, and I vigorously oppose it.

MR. MALONE: You did not find it "splendid misery"?

PRESIDENT FORD: Well, on some occasions! But there were enough days of joy to overcome the dark clouds, and to be very honest with you, I loved every day that I was working in the White House. It was a challenge, and in all honesty, I could not wait to get to the Oval Office every morning as early as possible and to get to the business of the day. I felt equally intrigued by staying and doing what I thought necessary at the end of the day. It was a wonderful experience for which I am deeply grateful.

QUESTION: I was interested in your dividing the leadership job into three parts, and I was wondering whether there wasn't a fourth part, the leadership of the executive branch of the government itself? I have two or three questions in this connection. Since Teddy Roosevelt, more particularly since Franklin Roosevelt, it has been generally accepted among academics, and I guess among politicians too, that the executive power of the president included the administration of the executive branch of the government. Accordingly, through the administrations since Hoover, there has been a gradual, if sometimes halting, increase in the powers of the president and the responsibilities of the president vis-à-vis the operations of the executive branch. I think by and large the expectations of the public have to do with what the executive branch does. They tend to hold him responsible for mistakes and errors. In the last several years, I think the last ten years—I think this pre-dates Watergate—there has been a movement, somewhat, in the other direction reflecting the view that the president should not involve himself too much in the executive branch, but should be more restrained in his powers by the Congress. He should be more flexible; instead of supervising everything that goes on, he should pick his shots and keep his time available. Now there is a considerable academic backing for the position that in this regard the president should move in the direction of more restriction and less power and less responsibility. I wondered what your response would be to this view.

PRESIDENT FORD: First, I excluded the president's role of leadership in the executive branch because I have a feeling that this was by law and tradition a recognized responsibility of the president. Having said that, let me add that because of our setup where the president actually appoints approximately 2,000 federal employees out of two million plus, the president's day-to-day control of the operations of the executive branch is severely limited. He can appoint Cabinet officers and sub-Cabinet officers, but underneath that very thin layer of 2,000 out of two million, the rest of the employees of the federal government are what we call career employees protected by civil service. They carry out the minutiae of policy decisions at the local, state, and regional levels. So a president can establish broad policy-making decisions, and they are supposed to be carried out by his political appointees. But, as I found and every president finds, the career people don't always have a sympathy for those viewpoints, and in one way or another they can undercut them. I can give you a number of examples that were not only true in my administration but are also true in subsequent or previous administrations.

The point I think that you make, maybe indirectly, is one that I would like to comment on, and that is what the Congress has done to the role of the president in his responsibilities as president under the Constitution. The Congress has encroached, in my judgment, greatly on the capability of the president to carry out his functions as the chief of the executive branch of the government. This is particularly true in foreign policy. For example, Congress, by legislative fiat, imposed on me, and very reluctantly they have changed it under President Carter, an embargo in military arms sales to Turkey at a very bad time and for very bad reasons, in my judgment. That ought not to be a responsibility of the legislative branch.

I also think the Congress has made a serious mistake in the enactment of the War Powers Resolution. I know this may be controversial, but I speak my piece. That is a very serious intrusion on the responsibilities of the president as commander in chief and the person who formulates and ought to execute foreign policy. The day will come when the Congress will regret that legislation.

In the domestic field, the Congress has done a number of other things in which it has sought to grab power and to handicap the day-to-day operations of the executive branch of the government. This, I guess, is part of the historical swing of the pendulum. There have been days when the executive branch was the dominant force among the three branches of government. Then it changed, and the Congress became the leading one of the three branches. It is my feeling that there is some recognition by the press, by academicians, and by others that the Congress is going too far in both domestic and foreign policy. I trust that the voters will reflect it and we will get back to a more normal relationship so the president can carry out his constitutional role as commander in chief as the person who handles foreign policy and does have greater influence in the execution of domestic policy within the executive branch as a whole.

GOVERNOR HOLTON: You do see some extraneous pressures. When I was working for you when you were working on that Turkish embargo bill, we had the leadership from both sides of the aisle and the entire weight of the executive branch behind the president's position. Yet out of 435 possible votes, we got 65. One of your former colleagues in Congress looked at me and said, "Lin, I haven't got a single Turkish restaurant in my district!"

PRESIDENT FORD: It was a very bad decision on the part of Congress.

GOVERNOR HOLTON: Now they're going to veto everything.

President Gerald R. Ford

PRESIDENT FORD: I was very pleased to get a call from President Carter while they were struggling with the same limitation, asking for my help to convince a few Republican members of the House and Senate to change their vote. And we were able to be helpful because it was the right policy. That embargo was very devastating to the things we had to do vis-à-vis NATO, and so forth.

QUESTION: Mr. President, you have said on several occasions that only history will tell whether the quiet diplomacy approach that characterized your administration will be better or less effective than the public diplomacy of certain other administrations. I think the consensus of the scholarly community has shifted considerably toward quiet diplomacy. But the question people ask themselves is how a president, using quiet diplomacy, can at the same time be a public spokesman as effectively as when he, at every press conference, offers comments or *obiter dicta* about current negotiations.

PRESIDENT FORD: The practicalities are that a president, for political purposes, oftentimes likes to plunge in with some public statement. More often he finds that the decision to speak publicly undercuts his efforts to achieve results. You have to hold your tongue, and that's not easy. In every instance that I can recall where we did not get involved in the public arena but used a variety of other techniques, other channels, we were infinitely more successful. I cite, without identifying the particular problem, one instance when we were very upset about certain actions that the Soviet Union was taking. We were tempted to make a public controversy or confrontation. We decided that we would play it cool and not get into the public arena. We did certain things that were not understood by some people at the time. We cut off some technical exchanges and cultural exchanges—we suspended them, we didn't cut them off—but this had an impact. We did it without going out publicly and developing a head-to-head confrontation. Face-saving would often have handicapped the ultimate solution that we sincerely wanted.

THE PRESIDENT AND POLITICAL LEADERSHIP

QUESTION: Mr. President, why is it in your opinion that most presidents seem to gravitate toward foreign policy issues? Is that an illusion? Why, when there are so many domestic issues, do presidents drift to foreign policy problems?

PRESIDENT FORD: Well, I agree with the latter. We had our share on the day I took office, as I am sure you will remember. I certainly do. On the other hand, because of the role the United States has in world affairs, the president has to be a participant in world conferences, world meetings with leaders of both our allies as well as our adversaries. He has no choice. We are no longer an isolated nation as we were before World War II when we had the Atlantic on one side and the Pacific on another and we could go merrily our own way and be oblivious to what the rest of the world did. It is a different ball game, and the president has to assume that this is part of his responsibilities. He cannot neglect, and obviously should not neglect, his duties domestically. However, the minute he projects himself beyond the shores of the country, this is, in many respects, a bigger news story. There isn't much drama in doing the day-to-day operations involving domestic policy. But it is a news story every time the president goes overseas or meets with a head of government or a head of state. So the perception is that a president is overemphasizing or being monopolized by foreign policy. In reality most presidents spend as much time on domestic policy, but it doesn't get the news coverage that his activities generate when he goes overseas and meets with the head of government or head of state.

QUESTION: Mr. President, how do you feel about the presidential press conference? Is that one of the less "splendid miseries" that go with the presidency or, said more seriously, is it a good instrument of communication from the president's standpoint?

PRESIDENT FORD: It is an institutionalized part of our government, whether it is good or bad. Under no circumstances could a president abandon it. I personally enjoyed the challenge of it. In the first place, I had superb personal relationships with the members of the White House press corps. I was very fortunate in

President Gerald R. Ford

that regard. I understood their responsibilities and they in turn understood mine. There was no confrontation on a personal basis, so it was an enjoyable experience for me. I used to prepare because I wanted to win! I didn't always win, but at least I thought I was prepared enough to take them on, if that is the right term.

QUESTION: Would you make any changes in the way it operates now?

PRESIDENT FORD: No, not the traditional White House press conference, but there are things that a president can do, and I think ought to do, to expand the relationship of the president with the press. Number one, we should not just assume that the electronic media is the more important part of the media. The writing press in my opinion is just as important as the electronic media. The net result is, a president—and we tried to do it—ought to bring in individuals from the White House press corps who are strictly in the writing press category, to have a little more give and take without the camera being focused on the interrogator as well as the responder. The television camera takes away some of the substance in the exchange between the two. Those meetings between a president and the writing press can develop a little more in-depth discussion of an issue or a problem.

Second—this may also be favorably accepted by you—a president ought not to believe in the exclusivity of the White House press corps. We have some very fine newspaper, local radio, and television people in the grass roots. We used to, and President Carter is doing the same, have press conferences in various communities throughout the country. The White House press corps would be there, but we would have local press, and we divided up the time. A question could come from one of the local media and the next question from the White House press corps. In that way you get an input, which I believe is constructive, from newspeople who are not just exclusively involved in the day-to-day operations of the White House. That is important because some of those questions throughout the country coming from responsible news media people reflect what the people in those areas think and what their concerns are. They aren't necessarily always the concerns of people who live and work in the nation's capital. The president ought to get that input.

QUESTION: There appears to be, if you look over the last 10 to 15 years, a growing gap between what we expect a president to do and the latitude we give to a president for fulfilling those expectations by substantive leadership, particularly in such fields as energy, controlling the cost of living, the inflationary spiral, and nuclear proliferation. Do you think that we have come to expect too much of a president, and what do you think future presidents, if you look at the next ten years, can do to try to close this gap?

PRESIDENT FORD: I believe there may be too much expectation. But on the other hand, the president ought to assume he should seek to achieve those expectations. For a president to assume that he can't do the job, whether it is domestically or internationally, is a defeatist attitude. Not that you would expect to score a touchdown every time you have the ball, but you, as president, better assume that you are going to make some gains, get a first down, another first down, and another one. The public expects it, and I think they ought to have that expectation, recognizing all of the reasons why he can't get the Congress to do this or the courts to intervene and a wide variety of other problems, including what some ally or some adversary in world affairs won't do. For a president to assume that these hindrances make the job impossible is wrong. The American people want a president who believes the job can be done. There are voids in areas where you don't do it, but that defeatist attitude is an anathema to me.

QUESTION: I had a great professor here when I studied American history, and I will quote a remark he made. He said, "The American people, in selecting a president, strive for mediocrity, and they usually succeed." Now, the question in my mind is, does our system, the political background we have necessarily in a selection of a nominee, plus the fact that maybe the average American wants someone in his own image to represent him, does that mean we are precluding selecting some of the finest people this country has produced and can produce over the years? We need them desperately in the future.

PRESIDENT FORD: I can exclude myself because I was not elected, so I don't fall in that category. I tried, but they didn't select me!

I don't think the system necessarily produces what he described as a result—although I may have to modify that. What does modify it is the decision to get involved in the process. A lot of our most talented people in other fields, whether it is business, the academic world, and so forth, don't want to dirty their hands in the political process. They have a nice life and want someone else to do the job, so they exclude themselves. The net result is that you get individuals who, for their own personal reasons, are interested in government and are concerned about the country or state or city and are willing to take maybe a less desirable day-to-day life. It is, as Linwood (Holton) knows, and as I know, because they have certain convictions or dedications. But there are many other people who are higher in IQ scores or on the academic level in rankings in graduating classes who won't get involved. So by the decision of the people who might fit that category, they have reduced the field. This is unfortunate. I would agree with the observation that we haven't necessarily had the most talented people throughout our history who might have done a better job in the execution of public responsibilities.

QUESTION: Do you have any thoughts as to how the president and the 2,000 persons that he appoints could have a better relationship with the two million people who have to carry out these policies?

PRESIDENT FORD: That's a very difficult prescription to try to write this morning, but it is a very important problem because 2,000 people cannot on a daily basis monitor what happens throughout the country, throughout the world, because we have people all over the world in the executive branch of the government. Let me say very firmly, I don't think that the two million are evil. They are good people. They're good Americans. They are dedicated to their jobs. But they subjectively have their own philosophy or their own viewpoint, and it may not necessarily coincide with the president's philosophy or viewpoint or that of the Cabinet officer. And so they, as they do their day-to-day work, interject their own personal subjective viewpoint, and whatever the president's views are, are not necessarily executed. The president cannot visit every local or state office of every department of the government to try to establish rapport. I honestly can't tell you how that spirit ought to be generated. But it's lacking, as I am sure my predecessors and successors have found. It is one of the serious problems we face, and yet I don't think I could write a formula to answer the question.

QUESTION: I wondered if, on reflection, you think anything could or should be done constitutionally to improve the effectiveness of the office? I have in mind such things as term and re-eligibility. What other matters may occur to you?

PRESIDENT FORD: I have mixed emotions as to whether we ought to go from two four-year terms to one six-year term. I can understand those who believe that if a president is elected for one six-year term then he doesn't take office with the immediate necessity of seeking to be reelected for the succeeding four-year term. There is no question, I don't care whether it is Democrat or Republican, that a president who enters the office with that objective is going to interject political decisions in his process of deciding what is right and what is wrong. So a six-year term might modify the political impact in the decision-making process. On the other hand, I also understand the objections of people who say, if we made a mistake, why do we have to live with it for six years? At least they cut it 50 percent.

For the same reason, I have traditionally objected to the extension or expansion of the two-year term for a member of the House. I understand all of the arguments, that it would be a lot easier for a person to get elected once every four years and theoretically he would be a better congressman because he would not spend too much of his time going back to the district and handling the mundane, provincial, parochial things that all congressmen do. But on the other hand, I believe the public ought to have an opportunity once every two years to have an impact on the national government and who is running it. We elected a president for four years, we elect senators for six; the public ought to have a chance to say, we did make a mistake; why wait four or why wait six years; we ought to have the chance toe make a change at the end of two years.

I can give you one illustration. I don't mean it on a partisan basis, but in 1964, President Johnson badly defeated Barry Goldwater and in the process the Congress, the House, and the Senate went overwhelmingly for the Democrats. We were decimated on the House side from 190 to 140. For all intents and purposes in the House of Representatives, we were outnumbered better than two to one; our impact on legislation was minimal. Then, during that two-year span there was a tremendous flow of legislation that went through, most of which is still on the statute books. It was the Great Society. But in the 1966 elections we made a net gain of 47 House seats, which was a very big gain from 140 to 187. We were still short of a majority, but this change in attitude from the 1964 election to the 1966 election did give people on a nationwide basis—and the gains were nationwide and not in a particular geographical area—an impact on what happened for the next two years and may have had an impact on the election in 1968. So my objection to a six-year term is based primarily on a belief that the public ought to have a chance more frequently than six years to decide if they want to have a change in government.

QUESTION: Mr. President, how can a president exercise substantive leadership if the Congress is recalcitrant and the party structures are no longer stable?

PRESIDENT FORD: That is a very difficult question. It is difficult to exercise leadership when the president and the Congress are controlled by the same party, as we now know. But it is even more difficult when the president is in one political party and the majority in the Congress is controlled by the opposite political party. It is my feeling that a major reform has to come in the Congress more than in the executive branch. The Congress has to get readjusted, if that is the right way to say it, to an affirmative role. Instead of

THE PRESIDENT AND POLITICAL LEADERSHIP

having 535 members of the House and Senate all more or less (this is an exaggeration) concerned about their own provincial and parochial problems, they have to understand that there are broader responsibilities than themselves and their reelections; that they are a part of a political party that has an obligation to the country. Plus, they have to have the feeling that their interests and their responsibilities transcend their own congressional district and their own state and are vital to the domestic and foreign welfare of this country.

As much as I love the House, and believe me, I have nothing but great, great memories of it, the House is unmanageable today. I feel sorry for Tip O'Neill as Speaker. I bet Tip O'Neill prays every night that he had the situation that Sam Rayburn or Joe Martin had. Those days are not there anymore. I read in the paper that Tip O'Neill was thinking about retiring, and I understand it. We have many differences, but if he had the same circumstances that existed when Sam Rayburn was Speaker, head of the Democratic party, he would be an outstanding Speaker. But the House has just disintegrated. It is sad. So I come back to what I said at the outset: The problem substantively is to get the Congress straightened out and then a president, whether the policies are right or wrong, at least would have a chance to develop them substantively.

~ Two ~

THE PRESIDENT AND CONGRESS*

President Gerald R. Ford

PRESIDENT FORD: The subject that was suggested for this afternoon's meeting was "The President and the Congress." There will be some inevitable overlapping between what I said this morning and what I may say this afternoon, but we will focus more specifically on the relationship between the presidency and Congress.

Let me present two extremes that I think we ought to avoid. I do not believe we want a presidency that is imperial nor do we want one that is imperiled. We do not want an overly dominant Congress nor do we want a submissive Congress. Neither the White House nor the Congress should have those extremes if there is to be a proper relationship between the executive and legislative branches. We have had what some people, particularly the press, have labeled an imperial presidency and we have had, to some extent, what I consider to be an imperiled presidency. We have had, during my 28-plus years in government, an era when the Congress was somewhat submissive, and we have had an era, which we are in today, where I believe the Congress is overly dominant.

So let's take the two extremes that I happen to think tend to exist at the moment—an imperiled presidency and an overly dominant Congress. The net result is that you have the two branches of government, the executive and legislative branches, at loggerheads. The best example of being at loggerheads on a critically important issue is the inability of the White House to get

---

*Presented in a Forum at the Miller Center of Public Affairs on 11 October 1979. Reprinted from *The Virginia Papers on the Presidency* (Washington, D.C.: University Press of America, Inc., 1979), Volume II.

from the Congress or the Congress to give to the White House an energy program. We have no real operating, potentially successful, energy program. Three presidents have tried to get one. There have been differences in the approach of Mr. Nixon and myself and Mr. Carter, but whether you agree with those programs or not, neither my predecessor, nor successor, nor I myself was able to get Congress to come up with an energy program. Congress is so dominant, in one sense overly so, or is so fragmented on the other side, that it is tied up with parochialism and provincialism and the net result is that the country has no energy program that can solve or make more solvable our critical problem. So, I would hope that somehow the pendulum could swing away from an imperiled presidency, but not over to an imperial presidency, and I hope the role of Congress will change so that it will not be an overdominant Congress, as I happen to think it is at the present time, at least to a degree. However, I don't want it to become a submissive Congress.

Now passing from those generalities to what I think is important for a good relationship between the president and Congress on a more direct basis I would like to make the following observation—and please understand I am not saying this because of any past experiences I have had, but I think it is essential for future presidents, if they are going to be successful in trying to rebuild a better rapport and working relationship between the executive and legislative branches. From my own 25-and-a-half years in the Congress, all but two of them in the minority, and nine months as vice president and two-and-a-half years as president, I strongly believe that a person who has had intimate experience with the Congress makes a better president. Now that doesn't mean I make a better president, but that means a former member of the Congress makes a better president.

I would like to now identify some points from personal experience. A president who is in the Oval Office, who is confronted with a legislative problem in the Congress, if he understands intimately from personal experience the procedures that are used in the Congress to effectuate legislation, if he knows what he is talking about when he says to his aides, "We'll get the leadership to use suspension of the rules," or "to get a closed rule,"

President Gerald R. Ford

or "to get the leadership to agree to this particular procedure," he has an advantage; it is only something you can acquire by having been there. You can read all the textbooks and listen to all the professors, but the only way you know about it is to have gone through it. For a president to understand the legislative process is important in achieving legislative benefits from a program that he submits. An outsider coming in just does not have the background, and it is a handicap. On the other side of the coin, having it is a benefit.

One other observation. Most members of Congress of either political party will tell you, and I firmly believe it, that over a period of 25 years as I had the opportunity, I developed friendships, as many good friends on the Democratic side as on the Republican side. Some of them were better than many of my Republican friends, who I obviously knew, but for personal reasons my Democratic friendships were as good, deep, and personal as my Republican friendships. There is nothing like that situation that an outsider can have coming to the White House. Nothing. You can be the best governor, as you were Linwood (Holton), but I will say to any governor coming in from the state house into a new ball game that he may have had a multitude of friends in the state from which he came, but it is a new environment and it is nothing like the capability of being able to call, as I fortunately could do, many of my Democratic friends and just lay it on the line and say I need your help as President, not as a Republican President, but as President. And almost without exception I got a favorable response, in 99.9 percent of the cases. You can't develop that relationship overnight. The only way you can do it is by living with people for a long time in the actual political environment in which the Congress exists. It is highly important for the implementation and the achievement of getting a good relationship between the Congress and the White House. Many people will discount that, but I will refute them with page and verse.

There are no substitutes for, one, knowledge of how the Congress works, and two, personal relationships. The president can be the smartest man, the most successful person, can read all the books, listen to all the lectures, and go up to Harvard after he is elected and go through that course they give you there on how to be a good congressman or maybe a good president, but there is no substitute for coming out of the Congress, in my judgment, for being a good president.

COMMENT: I have been studying a president who I find has all the qualities that you describe in terms of the ability to know people on the Hill and understand relationships, but he did not come from Congress; namely, Dwight David Eisenhower, who was someone who came from the executive branch and had sustaining contacts with the Hill, both directly and through his liaison people.

PRESIDENT FORD: I would make the following observations. President Eisenhower was a unique president, unique in this century perhaps. Second, Ike was no neophyte to Washington, D.C. Third, most people, and I will be interested in your comment on this, agree that Ike's second term was more successful than his first one. He developed a rapport with Congress in his second term that did not exist in the first one. As a consequence, Ike, even though he had Democratic Congresses the last six out of his eight years, because of the rapport he had and the knowledge that he picked up and because he was a quick learner, had a better batting average in the last four years than in the first. Fourth, President Eisenhower was dealing with a different kind of Congress. It was the era of Sam Rayburn and of Joe Martin. Sam Rayburn was Speaker six out of Ike's eight years and Joe Martin was the leader during Ike's first two years. That Congress was not a dominant, overreaching Congress. It was a Congress that, to some extent at least, was on the edge of being submissive, but it certainly was not the kind of a Congress as disorganized as we have today; that is, with no particular fault of Tip O'Neill or Bob Byrd, a leaderless Congress. So you had a different kind of president and a different kind of Congress, and the net result was a different environment, so I would not pick Ike as an outsider who came in who would violate the general principle that I espouse.

QUESTION: How about Franklin Roosevelt?

President Gerald R. Ford

PRESIDENT FORD: Well, he got his political start as secretary of the Navy. President Franklin D. Roosevelt had been secretary of the Navy and then eventually went to Albany as governor of New York. Of course, he came in at a unique time, too.

COMMENT: I think your argument is quite valid, but I also think in a sense that experience in Congress, in the complexities of today's world, is certainly valuable to a president *if,* as he makes the shift as you did, he can put away the background of not having to make the decisions. You were a very fortunate former legislator. You could put that away and say, yes, I now have to make the decision, and I will make it. Many people with legislative backgrounds simply cannot bring themselves to that, and your argument is enhanced by the current president's apparent disregard—I would almost say lack of understanding, but I cannot believe it is that—of the system. It is a checks and balances system that involves an executive leadership and a legislative check, and he seems to have ignored that for three years.

PRESIDENT FORD: I would add to the arguments that you are making against what I proposed; few legislators run their offices very efficiently. They are not historically good administrators. But if they have good common sense as president, they can hire good administrators who are Cabinet officers and other people in the executive branch.

COMMENT: Since others are raising exceptions, I will raise one. Woodrow Wilson was no laggard in dealing with Congress.

PRESIDENT FORD: I must confess I am not a historical expert on Wilson's administration, so I am really not competent to talk about the details of his relationship with the Congress, but one comes to mind. I guess the one thing that he wanted most of all was to get the Senate to ratify the League of Nations, and in that he was unsuccessful.

COMMENT: I'm talking about the first six years. After six years, not many of them do very well.

THE PRESIDENT AND CONGRESS

PRESIDENT FORD: As I recall, he was quite ill at that time.

COMMENT: Theodore Roosevelt was no laggard either, although he had had experience in Washington.

PRESIDENT FORD: But I would respectfully say that the situation is a different environment today than it was in the early days of this century, for a wide variety of reasons. In the first place, Congress is in session many more weeks and months today than they were in the early part of this century. Congress is virtually in session from January through November, with the exception of their "at home work recesses," as they label them. But they are in place, more or less, in Washington, so there has to be more rapport, more accommodation, more contact today than in the older days.

QUESTION: Since I have interrupted you, I will do so one more time, and then take a vow of silence. You refer to the leaderless Congress the inability of the Speaker and the majority leader of getting anything done. Do you attribute this primarily to the deterioration of parties generally, and more especially, to the lack of party discipline in the two houses of Congress? If Rayburn made an arrangement with the president, the president could be confident that he would carry it through, or almost through. That is not true today. Could Rayburn now, for example, control this Congress?

PRESIDENT FORD: I don't know about the validity of the last statement, but I know that Sam Rayburn, because I was there, could deliver 99 times out of 100 when he promised President Eisenhower, or any other president, that he would get a necessary majority in the House for whatever his commitment was.

I made precisely the point you raised this morning: Is the current leadership unable to achieve success in organizing the majority party, or the House, or the Senate to get something done because of the lack of the political allegiance and because of political structure? The answer is absolutely yes. Sam Rayburn particularly, Joe Martin to some extent, did not have any Democratic or Republican policy committee in the House of Representatives. Sam Rayburn carried Democratic policy in his pocket. Joe Martin did more or less the same. But they ran their respective parties to a very high degree. Great reforms came along and now both parties in the House, and the Senate to some extent, have a whole organizational chart set up, a policy committee or research committee and all this and that, so the leader is no longer the sole person that runs the party. That splintering of responsibilities hurts.

Second, members of Congress on both sides of the aisle are more often than not today elected, or they think they are elected, not because they are Democrats or Republicans, but because they think their talents elected them. Television contributes to that egotism, if that is the right word. So they have no allegiance when Tip O'Neill goes to a Democrat and says, "The party needs you because the President's policy is at stake." There isn't that party allegiance. Or when John Rhoads goes to a Republican he has the same problem, or Bob Byrd or Howard Baker in the Senate. There is no close identity with or allegiance toward parties like there was.

When I first came to Congress, when I was a very junior member, I resented that, that Joe Martin made the decisions. I am sure my good Democratic friends resented the fact that Sam Rayburn made the decisions. But Congress got things done and in a much quicker fashion, and I think with better legislation.

COMMENT: And the leadership worked well with the presidents of both parties.

PRESIDENT FORD: That is right, I agree.

QUESTION: When you were president, you complained of the role of Congress, especially in foreign affairs. In particular, the pressure to keep the United States in a strong position in the world. Now, since you left office, it seems as if Congress has been pressuring the President to play a more vigorous role in world affairs, and it is the President who is resisting. My question is, on reflection, would you say that the problem is one that is institutional, or is it rather a question of who is president and what is the mood of Congress?

THE PRESIDENT AND CONGRESS

PRESIDENT FORD: Well, I did strongly object to certain actions taken by the Congress that in my judgment hamstrung my efforts to do certain things in foreign policy. Let me give you several examples. I strongly opposed the Turkish arms sale embargo that Congress imposed. I never admitted that the War Powers Resolution, for example, was applicable to six instances where I committed U.S. military personnel: the evacuation of Da Nang, Saigon, Phnom Penh, the *Mayaguez*, and two evacuations from Lebanon in 1976. I strongly felt the enactment of that War Powers Resolution was an encroachment by the legislative branch on the prerogatives of the president.

I also objected to certain actions of the Congress in the domestic field, with their one house vetoes and other parliamentary gimmicks that give Congress a second go around in policy implementation. I am trying to recollect now what experiences President Carter has had. He was plagued with the continuation of the Turkish arms sales embargo. I know that because he called me and asked me to try and contact a few of my friends in the Congress to get them to change their votes, or to vote right, as both President Carter and I thought, and we were successful. There were efforts under President Carter by the Congress to impose what I think were unnecessary limitations on the transfer of the Panama Canal from the United States to the Panamanian government. As I recollect they were successful, in the main, in getting those limitations stripped from the transfer legislation. I think that is right. At least it was acceptable to them. Whether they got them all out or not, I cannot be precise.

President Carter still has many of the same problems that I had with the Congress, either doing it or wanting to do it, to play a marginally unconstitutional role, if not unconstitutional, in foreign policy.

QUESTION: My question may be a little bit off the main theme, but I will ask it. It is appreciated that a president has so many decisions to make that it may be difficult to identify any one as being more difficult than another. During your incumbency, what decision in your opinion was the most difficult single decision for you to make? And related to that, in making that decision, who did you call upon to solicit advice, if anyone?

PRESIDENT FORD: I had my share of difficult decisions. There were two that you could isolate: one domestically and one in foreign policy. They did not have many peripheral ramifications, but they were very tough. Maybe I should take both of them, because one involved foreign policy and one domestic policy.

Probably the most difficult domestically was whether I should or should not pardon President Nixon. I can tell you how my thinking developed on it. I am not propagandizing the book, but if you want to get the details in writing, you can read the book, *A Time to Heal*. A whole chapter is devoted to it. But to summarize, when I became president in August of 1974, we had a multitude of domestic problems—inflation at 12 percent, high interest rates, a recession that was just around the corner. We had, on the other hand, serious apprehension among our allies as to the reliability of the United States to function, bearing in mind our problems in Vietnam and elsewhere. There was certainly a feeling that we sensed, and I think was there, that our adversaries were looking a little longingly at taking advantage of our problems. So we had a full platter of difficulties to deal with that obviously a president ought to concentrate on. But the first month that I was in office I spent 25 percent of my daily time listening to my counsel and other lawyers argue about what I should do with President Nixon's tapes, his papers, and so forth. They were in the executive branch's jurisdiction. The Court was involved, private parties were involved. Not only Mr. Nixon, but others were suing. I was spending 25 percent of my daily time listening to the lawyers argue pro and con on a one-man problem. After a period this got a little frustrating and very time-consuming.

Second, the first press conference I had, I was well prepared—this was a week or ten days after I became president. I had a long list of things that I had studied and had questions given to me by my staff as to what the press would ask me. Seventy-five percent of the questions from the press were, "What are you going to do about Mr. Nixon?" I walked back from the East Wing of the White House where we had had this press conference. I felt very depressed. I thought that there were more important things with our domestic and international problems that they ought to ask questions about. But no. And I could just foresee the same thing going on press conference after press conference. If he were indicted, if he were tried, if he appealed, that would be the headline for the next two to four years instead of the public concentrating their attention on our nation's problems. So over a period of a week or two, all by myself, I said, isn't there some way we can clear the decks and get down to the problems of 220 million people instead of one person's problems? So with a group of three in my office on a pledge of absolute secrecy—I was never tougher with staff and said if this leaks I know all three are going to go—I said all I want to know is what the process is. I have not made up my mind, but I want to know whether I have authority and what the process is. I want a report in x number of days. The final decision was made after reviewing it with about five or six people. It was not unanimous but, as Harry Truman said, the buck stops here. I made the decision, and of course, it was not a very popular decision, but I trust it will become better understood and I hope given more approval in the pages of history.

One point that I would like to make relates to what I have just recited and not to the relationship between the Congress and the White House. Many people have said to me, why didn't you wait to see whether there was a conviction if he had been indicted? There is a very interesting Supreme Court decision called the Burdick case. It was approved by the Court in 1915. It is an involved case, but the crucial point from my point of view, and I think it makes the point in answer to those critics, the Court's words, and I quote virtually precisely, were, "The granting of a pardon is an imputation of guilt. The acceptance, a confession of it," period! I think that answers most critics.

The *Mayaguez* was another issue in which I was pretty isolated. I woke up, I think it was a Monday morning, at the usual time of 5:30-5:45 a.m., and I no sooner got up than I received a warning from General Scowcroft, then the number-two man in the National Security Council, who said, we have fragmentary reports that an American merchant vessel has been seized on the high seas, and I just wanted to notify you, and when you come to the office I will get all the details we have, but right now this is just a vague report. So when I got to the office, there was more information, but not detailed information. It took us until about 11 o'clock that morning to have a sufficient amount of information to call a National Security Council meeting that afternoon. In the next two days, we had at least two more National Security Council meetings in which we had to make the decision of how we would go about it diplomatically, notifying the People's Republic of China because that was the only known channel to the Cambodian government. We had not recognized them, and they had not recognized us. We decided to go diplomatically to the United Nations. We took other initiatives through the Foreign Service. In addition, we demanded from the Pentagon their assessment and contingency plans. We had several meetings where we had decisions to make as to what kind of strikes and forces we would use.

There was one decision that was quite interesting, aside from the major decision. We were sitting in the National Security Council and we had overflights being made by Air Force and Navy aircraft to keep track of what the Cambodians had done with the *Mayaguez* and what the movement was from Koh-Tang Island to the mainland. Those U.S. aircraft were keeping the surveillance, and they had orders to preclude any boat to go from Koh-Tang Island to the mainland because we were fearful they would taken the crew off the ship, put them in a boat, and take them to the mainland. While we were sitting in a National Security Council meeting, a Navy commander or a lieutenant commander came rushing in. As I recall, Admiral Holloway was sitting in as the chairman of the Joint Chiefs of Staff because General George Brown was out of the country, and the naval officer whispered something in his ear.

Admiral Holloway said, "Mr. President, we have a message we have just gotten in the situation room. A pilot in the surveillance group, as he was trying to prevent a boat from going to the mainland, said he saw faces that he thought were caucasian on the boat. He wants to know whether you want him to destroy that boat." The means of communication are maybe a couple of minutes, halfway around the world. I ordered Admiral Holloway to tell the naval officer to tell the pilot that they should not interfere with that boat going ashore. It turned out that this boat had our crew on it, the *Mayaguez* crew, so that is a pretty specific question as to how I decided.

QUESTION: Did you consult with the congressional leadership at any time, or was this strictly executive branch?

PRESIDENT FORD: We did consult with the Congress. We had the Democratic and Republican leadership from both the House and the Senate down. We kept them constantly up-to-date. We followed to the letter the mandates in the War Powers Resolution, even though we denied its applicability to our actions. But for good future relationships with the Congress, we did exactly what the law said but denied its applicability.

We did find some practical problems, which I set forth in a speech given at the University of Kentucky on the War Powers Resolution. I gave the speech in April 1977, inaugurating a series of lectures in honor of John Sherman Cooper. We kept a very careful scorecard with my legislative liaison people on who in the Congress we contacted, what they told us, where they were, and what we told them. We had written instructions that all the legislative liaison people ought to read to every senator and every House member as to what was happening and when we wanted them down, and so forth. It is a very interesting recitation of where we found members of Congress, not only in this case, but for other cases. I won't bore you with where we found them at the time when they were in recess, but we found that better than 50 percent of them were overseas, and here while we were trying to conduct evacuations of Lebanon, the War Powers Act said we had to consult, report, and all this, and they were not around; and they wouldn't be most of the times.

QUESTION: Mr. President, to continue one subject of the morning, your staff and some of us have talked about the fact that there is a certain mystery to your leadership, and at the expense of modesty, maybe you would explicate this a little more. One of the arguments against a congressman or a senator assuming the chief executive office is that he has a tendency always to negotiate every issue, to bargain, to trim, to moderate; and yet, you not only had to

President Gerald R. Ford

face the decisions you mention, but you had to decide between members of your own Cabinet, and some of them, as you went along, dropped by the wayside. The other mystery you have not mentioned, but the literature on foreign policy, as you well know, emphasizes, is that the period of national consensus on foreign policy was as strong in foreign policy as it was because there was an unambiguous enemy. Monolithic communism was the threat, and we were able to respond to it without any pause or hesitation. You and your vice president and others had to deal with a mixed picture. You dealt face-to-face with Communist countries as well as free world countries. But in all this, you played a different role than someone might have predicted you might have played, given your background. Would you care to say anything about the mystery of your own leadership in this area?

PRESIDENT FORD: I'm not sure it was a mystery. Very few people would have expected me, as a product of the Congress, to have vetoed 66 bills in two-and-a-half years. Everyone would have expected that coming from the Congress, there would not be these confrontations. The truth is, I did it deliberately because I knew the Congress and it was the way to deal effectively with them. Any president who expects to gain success or to be effective with the Congress who thinks by patting them all on the back and giving them every project or program they want in their own district is dead wrong. Members of Congress can be very provincial and very parochial. I am not saying they don't have the national interest in mind. I say this even though I was one and I was probably no different than the rest of them. They can be avaricious. They want all they can get, and if you give them a little, they will take a lot and want more the next day. So the only way to gain respect with them is to say no, to exercise the constitutional right of the veto, and say, this is it fellows; you can override me, but I'm going to deal with you exactly the same way in the future. We developed, as a consequence of that tactic, a far better understanding.

People are always alleging that a veto by a president is a negative act. That is totally inaccurate. A veto is a constitutionally granted power of the president to make the Congress think. Congress can pass a piece of legislation by one vote in the House and one vote in the Senate. The president can veto it with a single veto and send it back up there. Then on their rethinking, if it is desirable legislation, they can pass it over his veto with a two-thirds vote. A two-thirds vote clearly indicates that it is legislation that's in the national interest, not in some parochial interest.

Some presidents come to Washington with the idea that the way to develop a good relationship with the Congress is to love them. I think it is totally wrong. I know a president who, in his first nine or 12 months, vetoed only one bill. That has not produced much result in the relationship between the Congress and the White House. I'm glad to see that there is a stronger, more affirmative action by having more vetoes. That will develop a better rapport between the White House and the Congress. I'm a strong believer that the president ought to use his veto, not indiscriminately, but as a scalpel, not as a sledgehammer. If he does, his relations will improve with the Congress. That is one thing that ought to be studied by a president if he wants to develop the right kind of leadership with the Congress. They should know that he means business, and he has that veto power.

QUESTION: Foreign policy is the same thing?

PRESIDENT FORD: Yes. I vetoed the Turkish arms embargo legislation twice.

QUESTION: You expressed the hope earlier that the pendulum would swing away from congressional dominance. What forces, if any, do you see capable of bringing about that kind of swing? How might it happen?

PRESIDENT FORD: The press has a big responsibility here. The press has to pinpoint the disorganization of the Congress today to a greater degree than I think the press has. It is a complicated body. You are not talking about one person, the president; and in the mass up there of 435 members of the House and 100 members of the Senate, the impression gets diluted. But one thing I noticed the other day was the poll, or the survey, the one that reported not very good poll data for the president—19 percent; but Congress was

President Gerald R. Ford

13 percent. I could not believe it. But the Congress ought to take a look at that. That doesn't put them very high on the priority of public support.

QUESTION: You mentioned the problems caused by the decentralization of Congress and its fragmented state. You suggest that the press, by highlighting it, could perhaps shame members of Congress into cleaning up their own house. Do you think that the problem might be more deep-seated than that? While the Congress as an institution is very low in the polls, individual members of Congress, when polls are taken in their districts, turn out to be well loved and respected by large majorities. It would seem that the decentralization of Congress might reflect the accelerating of the fragmentation of American society into special interest groups, even single interest groups, each of which are now able to get their own thing from the Congress, from their member of Congress. If this is the more deep-seated problem, press coverage and shaming members about their disorganization will not work. What role, if any, can leadership, presidential or presidential-candidate leadership, play in slowing down the momentum of this fragmentation of American society? Or is that a circumstance that we are stuck with because of the nature of our time?

PRESIDENT FORD: It is somewhat paradoxical. While the public image of Congress has plummeted to an all-time low, you are correct when you say individual members of Congress show up very well. That is a serious development. It shows that a member of Congress may be too oriented to his district, or the parochial and provincial problems of that area, and is not broadly based and is not giving his district the kind of leadership necessary for the country as a whole. He is identified as the fifth district congressman—not as a congressman who represents the state of Michigan or the United States.

They do have broadly based responsibilities. I firmly believe that a congressman has an obligation, not just to represent that district and get all kinds of accolades or get reelected, and so forth. He has a broader responsibility. He has to look at the problems from the point of view of the state, but more important, from the point of view of his country. I happen to be idealistic enough to believe that a person who takes that broad view and runs against an incumbent who has this high identification in this survey that shows he is locally popular could beat him. The American people, when you put the chips on the line, are more interested in the country than some dam or some flood control project or some other totally local project. I believe it. That is what we have to find in the public and in the candidates.

QUESTION: Can I get back to your opening statement about the advantage of having strong feelings and having friendships and knowing how to work with the Congress? Usually the long experience and friendships are the results of mutual service and mutual commitment. Usually the parties assume that for friendship on one side there would be friendship on the other; and usually, when a president is trying to get political issues resolved and tries to win over members of Congress there is another understanding that in return for service rendered, there will be another service rendered; and in the nature of things, these services are not always the sort that the president would be happy to discuss freely and openly. So doesn't the record of work with Congress, like the effectiveness of the president once he is in office, depend on certain kinds of relations that themselves produce difficulties?

PRESIDENT FORD: The times that I could call this congressman or that senator and ask for support were on the kind of issues where it would be an insult for that person to ask for a *quid pro quo*. I was asking it from the point of view of the national interest, not on what I could do tomorrow for him in his district or his state. That is a special relationship where I could be frank and put it on that basis. I know there are other illustrations that people can make, but I think they are minimal. The ones that were important were the ones where I could call and not expect a *quid pro quo*, or where they would not expect a *quid pro quo*. It was a relationship that was far deeper, where they understood that what I was asking was for the national interest and not for what I could give them tomorrow in return for their help.

II.

ADVISERS EXTRAORDINAIRE TO PRESIDENTS

~ *Three* ~

PERSPECTIVES FROM THE WHITE HOUSE ON LEADERSHIP*

James H. Rowe, Jr.

NARRATOR: We are pleased to welcome you to the Miller Center. The vital statistics on Jim Rowe's qualifications should be obvious. He is a graduate of the Harvard Law School and was secretary to associate justice of the Supreme Court, Oliver Wendell Holmes. From 1939 to 1941, he was administrative assistant to Mr. Roosevelt. He was a member of the staff of the Democratic National Committee, an assistant attorney general, and a member of the first Hoover Commission. He was also chairman of the Commission to Reorganize the Government of Puerto Rico in 1949, chairman of the Advisory Committee on Personnel to the Secretary of State, and was counsel to the Senate Majority Policy Committee in 1946. He served as a naval officer in World War II and was decorated with two presidential citations, eight battle stars, and a navy commendation ribbon. He has been the friend and confidant of five presidents.

He was a member of the Presidential Press Conference Commission that reviewed the organization of press conferences held during the previous six months. No one approaches the problems and the achievement of "Presidents I Have Known" with greater authority and competency. We have been pleased whenever he has graced these tables to benefit from the verve and the flair

---

*Presented in a Forum at the Miller Center of Public Affairs on 24 February 1981. Reprinted from *The Johnson Presidency: Twenty Intimate Perspectives of Lyndon B. Johnson* (Lanham, Maryland: University Press of America, Inc., 1986).

and the enthusiasm that he brings to every subject he addresses. It is a great honor for us to welcome Mr. James Rowe.

MR. ROWE: Thank you, Ken. I should say something about presidential leadership. I do not know how to define it or describe it, but I do know it when I see it. I know, for instance, that Franklin Roosevelt had presidential leadership. There was never any question about it. I know that Hoover and Carter did not, maybe because they were engineers. They did not have it. Roosevelt had it all the time. I think what we should look for, or what I look for, in a president or a candidate for president is intelligence. He should, I think, be a professional politician, spend his life in it. I'm convinced of that. Maybe after our last president, I think he should have flair for what is going on in the world. I think he should not be ideological; the best ones were not. And that, I think, is almost all I can say about presidential leadership until we get to the questions.

Mr. Reagan is not on my list to talk about. He is, I suppose, a professional politician. He has been campaigning for a long time. He was governor of our largest state, as was Franklin Roosevelt. The thing we probably ignore about Roosevelt is that he spent eight years in Washington as assistant secretary in the Navy, including the war years, and if you look at his appointments, the New Dealers were young, but the older men had all been young men of the Wilson camp—Joe Davies, and 10 or 20 others I could name. Louis Brownlow was commissioner of the District of Columbia in World War I.

I am not going to talk about the presidents I have known chronologically but sort of peripherally because I knew them in many different ways. I knew FDR very well because I spent four years in the White House as an administrative assistant. I finally went to him and told him I thought it was a great job, but it seemed to be qualifying me only to be president, which I did not think I would ever be. For that reason, I asked to go over to the Department of Justice, and he did send me there. The other good friend I had was Lyndon Johnson because I got to the White House just as he got to Congress, and we were friends in our youth and friends ever since, all the way through until he died.

James H. Rowe, Jr.

Someone once said that every man has his heroes before he is 30. Well, I was in the White House when I was 28, and FDR is still my hero. He is still the standard to which we should all return, in my view, as president. He was all charm. You have all heard about his charm, and if you had met him, you would know firsthand. His staff adored him. In the back room when we were working, his charm would sort of disappear.

He was all business. It is hard to tell stories because I have so many about Roosevelt. I do remember two which I will tell you quickly. He used to say, "You're a bird dog and I'm going to send you out to do various jobs." He sent me out once, and I can't remember what the job was, but I came back and reported: "This is what it is, Mr. President." He had a habit of looking at the ceiling, and he said, "You know, there was some fellow in here the other day. I can't remember who he was, but he told me such and such. Did you run into that?" Then I realized I had not turned all those stones over; I missed. After you got caught that way a couple of times, you would do your homework very carefully.

In the other story I remember, we wanted to move Leon Henderson from one place to another, and he said, "I want to do this, but you go out and talk to some people and tell me how it should be done." After doing so, I came back and said: "Leon should be moved, Mr. President, and this is the way it should be done." "Well," he said, "I think you're right, I have to move him, but I'm going to do it this way." I think I had reached age 29 by that point, so I said, "Mr. President, I don't think you should do it that way, I think you should do it the way I suggested. It saves you a lot of trouble." He replied, "Well, no, I think I'll do it the way I suggested." Still, since I was 29, I came back the third time and said, "Now, Mr. President, if you don't do it my way, I think you're going to have a little trouble." He smiled and said, "Jim, we're going to do it my way, and I'll tell you why. The American people may have made a mistake, but they elected me President, not you!" I said, "Yes Sir!" In other words, when he made up his mind, that was it. You shouldn't fool around any longer.

He didn't like public controversy, but I think he used it as a tool. He liked to have Harry Ickes and Harry Hopkins out there fighting in public, or Jesse Jones and Henry Wallace, because he could make a pretty good judgment on the reaction of the people or the newspapers or the politicians. So he encouraged it. He just let everyone fight longer than we would have thought he should.

His other quality, I think, as a politician was that he never tried to get too far ahead of the American people in his judgment. In 1943, he went to Chicago and made the quarantine speech about possibly using the Navy to quarantine the Nazis' and the fascists' shipping, and the reaction was so strong against it that he pulled back for a while. He was always trying to help the Allies, but he did not know how far he could go. I can remember, I think it was late 1941, that I went to talk to him about some minor point, and he looked rather crestfallen. He said, "The Japanese are moving their troops south; they're moving them into Indonesia, maybe Singapore, certainly more into Manchuria, and there's nothing I can do about it. The American people will not let me use the Navy to stop them." He looked very discouraged. Of course, Pearl Harbor came along and solved the problem. He was always watching the American people and keeping track of what Congress was doing, however, to determine how far he could go. He once said that someone whom he owed a lot wanted to be solicitor general, and he should have made him solicitor general, but then he said, "You know, we're getting into trouble in the world. I've got to deal with the Senate and the Senate has to confirm, and I was here in the Wilson days and remember all the trouble Wilson had. I'm not going to get crossed up with the Senate." These are the touchstones. He was essentially a politician, practically all the time. I use that in the good sense. A lot of people use it in a different sense.

Now we get down to Jack Kennedy. I used to say that Roosevelt was a man of style and substance, Kennedy had style, and Lyndon Johnson had substance. I really knew Jack Kennedy best in the 1960 campaign. I was supporting Hubert Humphrey and then Lyndon Johnson. I was always against Kennedy. As I watched him around the country, however—I was out battling for delegates and Kennedy was out trying to get his own delegates—I found him, I think, the best national politician since Roosevelt. He understood where the strength was in each state far better than Johnson or Humphrey or, I think, anyone that I had run into except Roosevelt.

James H. Rowe, Jr.

There are two reasons for that. The first is rather mundane. He ran for the vice presidential nomination in 1956. Adlai Stevenson threw the convention open at that time, and Kennedy made a great run for it on television. Because of that, after the convention, all the politicians wanted him to come and speak in their states, and he got around the country speaking at their dinners. That way he learned a great deal about the United States, far more than Johnson and Humphrey or anyone else. The other reason is that I think he was about the most detached man I have every encountered. We would go somewhere, and Kennedy would see me moving around and say, "Where have you been, Jim?" I would tell him what state, let's say Oregon, and then he would say, "Well, how do I look?" "Well," I would say, "you've got strength here, you've got strength over there. Hubert or Lyndon—whichever one it was—is ahead of you there." He would say, "Well, I think you're right about this, and you're right about that, but I'm not so sure about over there." He was as hard-boiled talking about himself as I was talking about him. I thought it was a remarkable quality.

In the convention, of course, he ran over Johnson, whom I was supporting at the time. Then he picked Lyndon Johnson for vice president. I don't think he wanted him, but I think he knew he needed him for Texas and the South. He just felt he did not have enough electoral votes unless he got Johnson to pull him through. All of Kennedy's staff were against Johnson, labor and the liberals were against Johnson, and so was everyone else except Jack Kennedy. He picked Johnson and he won.

In the group of presidents that includes Franklin Roosevelt, Herbert Hoover, Harry Truman, John Kennedy, and Lyndon Johnson, Johnson was the brightest. He was just as bright as anyone you have ever seen. He was certainly the most complicated man, and I think the most insecure man. I don't know why he was insecure—I'm not a psychiatrist—but it always kept cropping up. He did more for education and civil rights than any other president. Education was important to him because he used to teach young Mexicans, and he saw how little they had. This is really why we have been pouring so much money into education—because Johnson did it. I don't know if we will get results from it. As for civil rights, I don't think these bills would have passed without Johnson. I think only a southerner could have done it, and I used to tell him so. I said, "You've got to run for president because I don't see any solution for this country unless you do it." A southerner had to do it, and he did. I do not know where the end of that road is yet, but Johnson is the fellow who started it. I think he was the best parliamentarian. He is certainly the greatest Senate majority leader we have ever had. I think as a parliamentarian maybe Winston Churchill was better, but Churchill had an easier job.

Vietnam did bring Johnson down. He finally cut his losses when the Army wanted 206,000 more troops. Purely by luck, I happened to see him that day. Dean Acheson, Mac Bundy, and all the "wise men," the generals, and the older men whom he talked to switched on him that day. They had always been for Vietnam, but then they turned against it. I was going in to see him with Teddy White, author of the biographical series, *The Making of the President*. Johnson never would see Teddy because Teddy had written some mean things about him. Finally, he told me he would see Teddy because Teddy was a friend of mine. He said, "I'll do that for you." He was always "doing" something for someone else so he could get a favor out of it later. Teddy and I sat around and waited for hours. We finally got in, and Johnson was just exhausted. He sort of grumbled at Ted because he did not like him, and finally I said, "Look, Mr. President, this fellow is trying to write some history and maybe you ought to talk to him." What Johnson talked about was very interesting. He began comparing himself with Roosevelt, relating all the things Roosevelt had done and what he himself had done. He said, "Maybe I've done as much as Roosevelt." He was exhausted and tired, and it really sounded like a valedictory speech about how many things he had accomplished. When we left, I said, "Now Teddy, don't pay attention to that tone. He's always up and he's always down and don't pay any attention to the valedictory." One week later, he quit.

QUESTION: I was wondering if you might expand on your view of the role of the presidential staff. It is a huge staff now. What are your thoughts about its current position?

MR. ROWE: I still think the Roosevelt view is correct. We were just a handful. He had three secretaries and six administrative assistants until the war. Then the White House staff started building up, a little ahead of the war. Jimmy Byrnes left the Supreme Court and Judge Vinson left the Court of Appeals bench to work at the White House. Until then, we were a very small group. Of course Washington was small, and we knew everyone there—the senators, the congressmen, and the people in the executive branch. We did not think our function was to explain to the press what we were doing. That was for Cabinet members.

On one occasion, I got in trouble when a Cabinet member complained to the President that I was keeping him away from the President. It wasn't true, but the President called me on the carpet. I said, "This just doesn't happen to be true, Mr. President." "Well," he said, "If Cabinet members get the impression that you are blocking them from me, you're going to need another job." It was one of his favorite phrases. I sometimes wonder how I managed to keep my job. Roosevelt believed that the Cabinet should get in when they wanted to see him. Some Cabinet members were bores and he would not let them in on his own, but he did not want his staff coming between him and the Cabinet.

When I came back after the war and President Truman was in office, I asked a couple of my friends who were working for him about my old duties and who was carrying them out. It turns out that there were nine people doing what I did. It had just grown and grown. Every president has gone into office announcing that he is going to make cuts. Lyndon Johnson was thumping tables, saying he was going to make cuts. He ended up—each president ends up—with more than the other. I do not know why. Therefore, they are all over town and are leaking everything. Some things they should, I suppose, and some they should not. I personally think it is bad practice. But again, it is one of these things I that I don't know what can be done about it.

QUESTION: You mentioned ways in which Roosevelt had a sense of what the people would accept, or perhaps when he had gone a little further than what they would accept. How do they keep in touch with what people will accept?

MR. ROWE: Well, I'm not sure. You know, speaking of presidents making mistakes, the three great landslides in this country were Roosevelt in 1936, Johnson in 1964, and Nixon in 1972. Due to these landslides, at least in my view, all three of them were in trouble within two or three months: Roosevelt with the court packing plan, Johnson with Vietnam, and Nixon with Watergate. I think maybe if they do so well, they get a little arrogant.

There is another thing that seems to happen with presidents, and I think it happened with Roosevelt. It is a very natural thing. A president never really sees anyone unless that someone wants something from the president, whether it is a senator, congressman, Cabinet officer, businessman, or labor leader. It is a wearing business. Therefore, I think they have the tendency, the longer they are in office, to retreat and spend their time with their staff. Roosevelt, Truman, and Nixon all did this. With Carter, I think Camp David helped some. I think they get out of touch the longer they are in office. But I don't know of any way to get around it. I suppose if they had old friends who were senators and congressmen who could warn them when this started happening, maybe it would work. Usually it doesn't, in my view.

QUESTION: What was Johnson's relationship with FDR?

MR. ROWE: You have probably heard the story of Lyndon Johnson going to see FDR with the request for a dam in his district. You would not get much from an appointment with Roosevelt because he would "filibuster" you. I remember he did it to me. We would sit down to have lunch, and he would tell me all about Hyde Park. I once knew more about Hyde Park than any living person! In the case of young Congressman Johnson, he came in and was told by Watson, the appointment secretary, that he would have 15 minutes. Roosevelt started talking, however, and Johnson did not get a word in. Out the door he went, and he complained bitterly to the staff. It took us two weeks to get him back in. This time Johnson came in the door talking at top speed. He did get his dam.

You know, Roosevelt knew a great deal of what was going on, and I do not know where he got it. Johnson was a telephone president; he was never off the telephone. I don't think Roosevelt was on the phone that much, but he talked to many people and knew a great deal of what was going on.

QUESTION: Would you expand on your comment about the comparative lack of substance in Kennedy?

MR. ROWE: Well, that is an unfair comment, because he might have gotten a lot of that legislation through if he had lived another year or so. He made great speeches. I don't think he worked as hard at the job as maybe I thought he should. Again, that quality of detachment I talked about sort of bothers me. He did not twist people's arms and hit them over the head the way Johnson or Roosevelt did when they wanted something. He had been a playboy congressman, an indifferent senator, and a great campaigner. I may be unfair. It is not a matter of prejudice. I liked Jack Kennedy a great deal, but he did not work at it the way Johnson did, seeing people all the time. It was this quality of detachment.

QUESTION: Could you talk about the influence of Keynesian economics on Roosevelt, and then on Johnson in the period of the late 1960s when there were warnings about inflation and so on? To what extent were you worried about that?

MR. ROWE: We were all Keynesians, the New Dealers, including Roosevelt. Roosevelt saw Keynes several times. I never really understood Keynes. I don't know if we knew what we were supposed to think, but I believe we followed the Keynesian doctrine pretty much in those days.

I don't think any president really understood economics. In fact, I am not sure the economists understood it, looking at their record, but there were always a number of them around. I think the presidents try, but I don't think they are really capable of following theory very much. A good president, however, does get a feel for the direction in which he should go economically.

QUESTION: Why do presidents each have, in their own way, their mafias?

MR. ROWE: Even in foreign policy, most politicians rely on the men they knew in their youth. Roosevelt had his New Yorkers, Johnson had his Texans, Jimmy Carter had his Georgians—maybe presidents should not have had them, but they did. On foreign policy, Roosevelt relied mostly on Sumner Welles and Ambassador Philips. They had been young Foreign Service career fellows when he was assistant secretary of the Navy. He listened mostly to them, and he did it sort of surreptitiously because Cordell Hull was a great power with the Senate, and he did not want to get crossed with him. Some of his Cabinet members, such as Jesse Jones and Cordell Hull, were sort of independent barons.

NARRATOR: I'm sure I speak for all of you in thanking Mr. Rowe. He has not only illuminated our understanding, but through his wit and good spirit he has lit up this whole room as is rarely done. We appreciate it very much.

~ *Four* ~

POLITICAL LEADERSHIP: ROOSEVELT, JOHNSON, AND REAGAN*

Thomas G. Corcoran

NARRATOR: Thomas G. Corcoran is a graduate of Brown University and Harvard Law School with a Doctor of Law degree from Harvard University. He was clerk to Supreme Court Justice Oliver Wendell Holmes, counsel to the Reconstruction Finance Corporation (RFC), assistant secretary of the treasury, and special assistant to the attorney general. He was the major draftsman of some of the great historic legislation of modern times: the Security Act of 1933, the Federal Housing Act of 1933, the Federal Security Exchange Act of 1934, and a host of other vital and crucial legislation.

None of this, however, quite captures as vividly as does a passage concerning the role and the personality in government of Mr. Corcoran in the crucial days of the 1930s. The author of *The Second Hundred Days: Franklin Roosevelt and the New Deal* writes, "Corcoran was a new political type, an expert who not only drafted legislation but maneuvered it through the treacherous corridors of Capitol Hill. Two Washington reporters wrote of him, 'He could play the accordion, sing any song you cared to mention, read Aeschylus in the original, quote Dante and Montaigne by the yard, tell an excellent story, write a great bill like the Securities Exchange Act, prepare a presidential speech, tread the labrythian mass of palace politics, or chart the future course of a democracy with equal ease. He lived with Ben Cohen and five other New Dealers in a

---

*Presented in a Forum at the Miller Center of Public Affairs on 18 May 1981. Reprinted from *The Roosevelt Presidency: Four Intimate Perspectives of FDR* (Washington, D.C.: University Press of America, Inc., 1982).

POLITICAL LEADERSHIP: ROOSEVELT, JOHNSON, AND REAGAN

house on R Street. As early as the spring of 1934 GOP congressmen were learning to ignore the sponsors of New Deal legislation and level their attacks on the scarlet fever boys from the little red house in Georgetown.'"

Those of us who have listened, even for a few minutes, to the political insights of Mr. Corcoran know that his verve and the energy reflected in the historical accounts persist into the present. We find it a great privilege to have him discuss political leadership, Franklin D. Roosevelt, and Lyndon B. Johnson with some reference to President Ronald Reagan.

MR. CORCORAN: I was once a secretary to the Supreme Court and they used to say to the applicant before the Court, "Why are you here?" You are supposed to say, "I'm appealing from the Fifth Circuit." Why am I here? I'm here because my junior partner, Jim Rowe, of whom I am a protege, was here, and he asked me to come down and finish saying in my imprudent way what he did not say in his prudent way.

I would like to talk for just a few minutes before I answer questions. I know that Jim Rowe would say I am a hopeless romantic. But, I believe there is a connection between the administrations of FDR, Lyndon B. Johnson, and Mr. Reagan. My father used to say—my father was a Democrat and my mother was a Republican—that a child who doesn't take the politics of his father and the religion of his mother is either a victim of child abuse or a filial ingrate. So, I am a Democrat.

I am a Democrat for Reagan for one reason. There is one very essential reason why Roosevelt and Reagan are very alike. I think Mr. Reagan, whatever he says about what he is going to do about the Social Security Act, the tax bill, or anything else, has had the same effect that Franklin Roosevelt and Lyndon Johnson had. They unleashed the energies of the millions of Americans in this country who, by the very unleashing, will pull the country through, despite what a given piece of legislation is. Note the recent polls on the country's increasing optimism.

I was not a Roosevelt man when I first entered government. I had been legal secretary to Mr. Justice Holmes. As such I came to Washington in 1926 with Calvin Coolidge. I remember the

Teapot Dome scandal. I had been in the New York district attorney's office during the prosecution of Harry Dougherty. I had a very low opinion of what went on in government. But I was an employee of the Court; I was tied up with the Court.

The first president I ever met was Calvin Coolidge. I had to work my way through law school and spent the summers working on a fishing trawler out of Boston, fishing the Georges Banks. Consequently, I knew the waist, bust, and hips of every fish in the North Atlantic. I was taken by Mr. Holmes to the Judicial Reception at the White House to meet Mr. Coolidge.

Mr. Coolidge was a fellow who conserved energy. When he shook hands with you, he just held out his hand and your hand was supposed to slide off of it. By the time I got to the end of the line, his hand was rather sweaty. My first impression of a President of the United States was "haddock."

When people say to me, "Why are you for Mr. Reagan?" I say, "That's like the question, Do you love your wife? Compared to whom? He is here, isn't he? Who else is Commander in Chief?" In 1927, I went from Justice Holmes to Wall Street. Things were very prosperous at that time. But the old Justice, who was a very wise man who had watched the Harding administration and its trouble, said, "Son, we're only in the eye of a hurricane. There is another side coming."

I landed in Wall Street just in time to see the boom and the bust. But I was very fortunate. I went with a very small office, not one of these big ones that I don't believe in. My office was comprised of partners who had been in the Wilson administration during World War I, and they were followers either of Wilson or Teddy Roosevelt. All had been either in the Progressive Movement or with William McAdoo of the Treasury. All were very interested in what was going on in Washington.

So, although they taught me to be a good Wall Street lawyer, these men were always interested in how the government was working. I must say that I found out when I went back to Washington and was working for Roosevelt, there were more good Wall Street men and more good Republicans than one can believe who helped and were willing to help Roosevelt.

POLITICAL LEADERSHIP: ROOSEVELT, JOHNSON, AND REAGAN

Returning to Washington in March 1932, I spent one year with Hoover as a lawyer in his Reconstruction Finance Corporation (RFC) because my boss, who was Mr. Franklin of the Baltimore family and a former assistant secretary of the treasury, could not come down to help. My other boss, Joseph Cotton, had already come down as undersecretary of state for Hoover to try to pull us through the Manchurian crisis. So I was the only bachelor in the office; there was a call for someone to come down and help Mr. Eugene Meyer, then head of the Federal Reserve, later the head of the *Washington Post*. So I came down to help the bipartisan RFC in the banking crisis for a whole year with Hoover before Roosevelt came in. In those days a president was inaugurated in March, not in January. Because my bosses could not cope with the trouble on the Street, I came down in March 1932 to help all of the banks a full year before Franklin Roosevelt's actual inauguration.

In those days, maybe like you, I was a great Walter Lippmannite, and Walter Lippmann had a very poor opinion of Roosevelt as the governor of New York. He was then going through the Jimmy Walker problem with Betty Compton, and the Seabury Investigation. Lippmann, whom I then followed religiously as an intellectual out of Harvard Law School and a teaching fellow in the Harvard Law School, had a very low opinion of Roosevelt. "Remember," he said, "the only qualification Roosevelt has is he is a nice man and he wants to be elected." I left New York just as Roosevelt was in that trouble with Judge Samuel Seabury and Mayor James J. Walker.

In 1932 the RFC itself was in trouble because both the Democrats and the Republicans did their best to keep it in trouble. The Reconstruction Finance Corporation made loans on collateral to banks. The Democrats, in order to beat Hoover, insisted that every loan to the bank had to be publicly reported. If you were a depositor in a little bank down South and you read in your paper that the bank had to borrow and borrow from the government, what would you do? You would withdraw your money.

On the other hand, Hoover, for whom I had great personal respect, had a secretary of the treasury named Ogden Mills succeeding Andrew Mellon, who by this time had left to be ambassador to Great Britain. At that time, the Treasury under the

Thomas G. Corcoran

law as changed under Roosevelt had to put up the money for the RFC. Later the RFC, under Jesse Jones for whom I worked for eight years, had separate appropriations. Mills was against government spending, and he would not let the RFC spend too much money. Mills was a very strong and able man in his beliefs, belonging to the old Wall Street barons who in previous depressions used to wait until everything went to pot and then go and buy Wall Street out cheap. This time the country refused to let that happen, and by November 1933, Hoover was not reelected.

Throughout the summer of 1933, those in the RFC and the Treasury knew what had to be done to bail out the banks and keep them bailed out. Mr. Hoover tried to see Mr. Roosevelt to talk with him about it. But for complicated reasons I could not understand at that time, Mr. Roosevelt would not see Mr. Hoover. So for six months the RFC and the bank failures went along, and things got worse and worse until the big bank in Detroit blew up; Detroit is always the boom and bust point of the American economy. When Mr. Roosevelt was inaugurated, he had to close the banks the next day.

What did I think of Mr. Roosevelt then? Of course, at that time I had only a Wall Street lawyer and banker's mind, although I was later to be Mr. Roosevelt's assistant secretary of the treasury. Then I thought it was outrageous for Mr. Roosevelt to let the banks go under when we knew what to do (which we did do after the Hundred Days). I honestly suspected that he planned it that way for political reasons.

I always remember my problem of conflict of interest at that time. I had come from an old seafaring family. The rule of the old sailing ships was "When you go up in the rigging and it's bad, one hand for yourself, one hand for the ship." So, I went down to the only bank that was alive, withdrew only half of my money, and put it in my picket. "One hand for myself." I left the other half in for the ship. This strategy solved my conflict of interest in standing up before Mr. Roosevelt as he made that famous speech at the Inaugural, safe no matter which way it came out. But I honestly did not believe that Mr. Roosevelt would make it. Later that week when I could get an appointment, I went to see Justice Holmes to say, "Mr. Justice, I am going back to New York. Because I am only a junior member of that outfit in New York—it is a wonderful one—if I stay here much longer, I'll lose my place."

But my old friend, Felix Frankfurter said, "Did you know that I have seen Roosevelt?" Felix was a very clever fellow. He had known Roosevelt when they both were in the War Department in the old Theodore Roosevelt administration. Very cleverly, he outflanked Lippmann. There was a god higher than Lippmann to us liberals, and it was Justice Holmes. So about the third day of Roosevelt's incumbency, Felix managed to persuade Roosevelt to call on Holmes. That outflanked Mr. Lippmann completely.

When my farewell speech was delivered, Holmes said, "Well, you know more than most about this bank business and, son, we are in trouble. You know it didn't make any difference to me when I was a captain in the Civil War whether it was Burnside or Halleck or Mead who was commander in chief. Now Roosevelt is commander in chief." There is a story that as Roosevelt left the Holmes' library, Holmes saluted him as captain to commander in chief. That is the way I think about Reagan.

Holmes ended with, "Son, we are in trouble. You can make up your mind about your future, but I would think you would want to stay around to see if you can help. You know, he's Teddy Roosevelt again. *He may be a second-class intellect, boy, but he is a first-class temperament, and that's what counts in a president.* Because if he awakens the people, their own efforts as individuals will be enough to pull the country through no matter what he does." The justice's prophecy about FDR following TR was true.

So I went back to work for a new RFC and I have been doing something around Washington ever since.

We went through the Hundred Days. Much of its legislative approach never lasted. It was being changed and revised all of the time Roosevelt was in office. But what was important was that he did fire up the country. He got it off its despair. *And he adopted almost verbatim—because he had no platform of his own except to balance the budget—the old Progressive Party platform of Robert La Follette that was then represented by George Norris and Burt Wheeler who had come over to Roosevelt.* It was the old TR Progressive platform that brought in the Tennessee Valley Authority, the Housing Acts and the Securities Act, and the rest of what is called the New Deal. Franklin Roosevelt really adopted the whole Teddy Roosevelt program.

My first friend in Washington had been Dean Acheson. Dean had been the clerk to Brandeis before I was the clerk to Holmes, and Dean had another, a senior partner, who had been the Teddy Roosevelt organizer in Chicago named Edward Burling. Burling had a place on the Potomac River of about 400 acres where he hosted an unofficial seminar of all of the old Bull Moose crowd. There I first met Hiram Johnson and Harold Ickes. Another one who went into the RFC as general counsel and my boss, Stanley Reed, later became a justice of the Supreme Court. Reed was an important fellow in the Roosevelt administration. He came from a rich Kentucky agricultural family that had gone to Columbia Law School and the Sorbonne. He understood perfectly well that as Roosevelt poured in his progressive ideas, he had to have government servants who understood money. He asked me—I had been the New York recruiting agent for Harvard Law School—to find men for the RFC.

That's when there began to run into the Roosevelt administration the all-important first thousand men down. The number-one man of the Cabinet and the number-two man of the Cabinet are important. But without these thousand guys under numbers one and two, the nameless fellows in subordinate positions that provide the energy for the top men who had to go to political parties or home to their wives at night, one doesn't get driving power in any administration. Reed told me, "Find me men." Then, first with help from Franklin in New York and Felix, I began to find men.

Next take Jim Rowe. Jim was the last secretary to Justice Holmes. I had been in that position ten years earlier. Jim and I were with Justice Holmes when he died. I put Jim in the RFC as one of its lawyers. I met Harold Ickes at Burling's. I told Ickes about Jim. Jim transferred to the Interior where Ben Cohen was. After the Securities Act, Jim went to the SEC, then to the Labor Department. When the President's staff was regularized after the 1936 election, Jim became an administrative assistant to the President, then deputy attorney general until he went to war.

Jim Rowe was only a type. Others complained that an "underground railroad" that put Jim Rowe in the U.S. government completely revitalized the government. Imagine the *institutionalization of compassion*, as we used to call it. Think of what Harry Hopkins had to do all over this country finding someone in every county, in every city to do something that had never been done before. Remember there was no welfare abuse (or even welfare itself) in the Roosevelt administration, no government inflation, no government debt. Everyone who could work had to work for something called "jobs." At the beginning we had to find some lousy stuff to call work, but at the end, work was on bridges, tunnels, highways, and airports. For those who could not work, Roosevelt, with the energy of his young helpers, created Social Security.

All of this time, until he died, I was talking to Justice Holmes about government in the history of the United States. Holmes did not die for three years after Roosevelt had come into the presidency. Jim and I were always talking to him about what was happening to the administration. He backed Roosevelt, but he was always thinking. He told me something that in one way particularly found favor with Roosevelt. He said, "You know what really matters in the politics of this democratic country? Did you ever see a circus parade come down the streets of Salem, Massachusetts?"

"No."

"When the circus parade is formed where they get off the train, the elephants are in front of the parade. As the elephants move into the central part of the city, little boys come out from the side streets to strut in front of the elephants and pretend they are leading the parade. But if they should turn down a side street, the elephants will keep going where they intended to go in the first place."

"And what are the elephants?"

"Elephant number one is the resources of the country. Call it geography. What have you got? Oil, metal. Development of resources.

"Elephant number two is people. Call it demography. What kind and how many people—their living depends on its resources."

Think of the current U.S. demographic-resource problem now. The last census shows the United States is moving from the resource-emptied cities of the North—New York and Cleveland,

Thomas G. Corcoran

everything except my state of New Hampshire, which has no taxes, moving even out of the cities along the American Mediterranean, which is our Great Lakes—because everything really was based on a steel economy from the resources of coal, limestone, and iron.

But the present projected economy is from oil, sulphur, and water, and it is moving right down to the Southwest and the South. The Democratic party has got to understand that movement, no matter what my friend Teddy Kennedy says. The last census shows the movement of the country is out of the Northeast and the Midwest to the Southwest and the South, the places where the resources of energy and chemistry are running the economy and therefore the politics of the country.

That is what I think Reagan is about, and Wall Street knows it. I make no bones about it, and I have great respect for the fellows on Wall Street. I know someone can be a Wall Street lawyer Democrat. During the period when Roosevelt was trying to get his things through the Congress in the Hundred Days and the days thereafter when we had to redo what he wanted, there were more decent helpers out of Wall Street and the Republican party than are assumed. I remember particularly Robert Lovett, Paul Shields, James Forrestal, Stanley Reed, James Wadsworth, and Carl Mapes. The Roosevelt government was, in truth, a government of unity. For myself I have never cared much—and much less than Jim—what the politics of anyone was as long as he would work and deliver, with others going his way. That is where I hope the United States is now.

Back to Justice Holmes' elephants. The third elephant is technology. When my brother was with General Motors in Tokyo there was nothing but American cars on the road all the way to Bangkok. Now we are struggling to keep American cars on the roads of the United States. My brother went out with General Motors in the hopeful export era in the dream of Hoover, secretary of commerce. He came back in about eight years when he saw coming the invasion of Manchuria by Japan. He recently said to me, "You know what happened when I pulled out of GM? There was a fellow named Toyota working for me in the trucking department. I noticed how interested he was in the trucks. The minute the Japanese went into Manchuria, the first thing that happens is that Grandfather Toyota emerged in charge of the provision of trucks from the GM factory for the Japanese Army's invasion of Manchuria." America has given away its technology.

The United States was very generous to Europe in the Marshall Plan and to Japan. It put plants into places where there is a lower wage rate with U.S. technology and where there is a kind of society that more easily takes government's orders. U.S. research, even biological research, is in many fields perilously behind Japan, Germany, France, and the Middle East; and if the OPEC nations keep piling their money into technological education and production . . .

Getting for a moment into the Era and women's liberation, a very intelligent congresswoman who I think really saved Voyager and the Shuttle is Mrs. Hale Boggs. She once laughed at me, "Do you know where women's lib began? Not with male politicians. It began with the invention by man of the sewing machine so women didn't have to make the family clothes anymore. You know where it got its next push? With the telephone. The telephone girl was the first to get out in the commercial world. She had nice clothes and she was the first woman who ever made a wage. And after that you know what you made for us? The typewriter. It was just exactly the socio-political effect of the invention of the cotton gin and its relation to the War Between the States."

By accident, I was on the edges of the atom bomb. The United States was six months behind Hitler, but I remember a remark of chemist Harold Urey who died not so long ago—the fellow who brought the Danish physicist Niels Bohr to the United States: "You know, we are six months behind. There are only four men, probably, in England, and in Germany and the United States, who understand the theory of this fission. But we're going to get there first because we have so many thousand more steamfitters and electricians." The government locked them up in Hanford, Washington and produced it. Whether anyone has unforeseen consequences from that invention is beside the point here.

One thing that always interested me about the war was how much the United States won with brains and productivity and not with bayonets. How did we pull off the invasion of the Pacific?

With Kaiser's assembly line product of "tinships." The factories were turning them out at a rate of ten a day.

The war in the Atlantic? With a Polish person's help, the United States broke the German code as well as the Japanese. It was done with accelerated technology, and we can do it again. Maybe I am an enthusiastic romantic, but I honestly believe with this third elephant, technology, the United States can get ahead again. The boys at the Massachusetts Institute of Technology and the boys down in NASA, which Lyndon Johnson set up as the counterpart to MIT, tell me that if the United States would really want energy hard enough, as it wanted that atom bomb hard enough, we could have hydrogen fusion maybe in even three, but no more than five years, instead of twenty. That would end dependence on foreign energy that is causing inflation all over the world.

What interests me about what is going on now is that I think the point is that Mr. Reagan understands the elephants. I watched Mr. Reagan work once when he was to eliminate the Communists in the Hollywood unions. Not so long ago, after I had lost on another candidate, because I cannot keep my cotton-picking fingers out of this business, I talked with him.

"Do you remember when I worked on the Hollywood unions?"

"Yes."

"Just remember, Governor Reagan, that when you were getting that done you were both a Democrat and a union leader. There are not enough Republican registered voters. The old Roosevelt liberals that have become conservatives as we built up the middle class are the voters you have to reach. Don't say anything against Franklin Roosevelt."

Did you notice his speech accepting his nomination? At the Inaugural? He's just like Roosevelt. He's just like Teddy Roosevelt, as Holmes said. Justice Holmes had his differences with Teddy Roosevelt. Holmes voted against his president's wishes on the dissolution of the North Pacific Railroad, and Roosevelt said he could cut "a judge with more backbone out of a banana." They did not invite Holmes to the White House for a while. But, the President came around.

Again, about the manpower in government. What I am thinking about these days is that unfortunately, as a result of the abuses of the Nixon administration, the thing of reforming the relationship between the executive branch and the Congress was overdone. With the best intentions, Common Cause did it. For instance, Mr. Reagan is out there today trying to find people who will take Cabinet positions that require being picked over for peccadillos by senators seeking fame. Many people saw the other day the "revelation" of Justice Lewis Powell's worth that he had $5 million worth of real estate and Chief Justice Burger had a million dollars worth of real estate. I am even wondering about ABSCAM. I am saying that we went through all of this business with the best intentions. But I wonder whether it has gotten to the point where it has become almost dangerous for an able man, if he has a wife and children he cares about, to run for Congress or take a government job.

I was lucky enough, with Jim Rowe as an example and helper, to help energize Roosevelt's administration when it had to take on this enormous job of government helping on everything when there was no one else to help. But suppose you are now a young fellow at my age at that time—Jim was a little younger. You have a family and children, and you are asked to move to Washington. It would cost $3,000 or $4,000 in a private school to put a child in the third grade that you would feel you had to do because if you came to live in Washington you would find a particular public school system that you would hesitate to put your children in. You would also find costs sky-high and no place to rent. The reason isn't only inflation. It is because anyone who ever came to the lovely city of Washington never wants to leave it. No wife would let you, and I don't blame her. It is one of the most lovely towns for a woman to live in this world. Maybe Virginia is also nice, I don't know. So what are these young people going to do?

If you are a congressman, it is too dangerous to raise your salary. If a congressman raises his salary, he may get beaten for that move. So you cannot get people in Washington of the kind it was easy to get in Roosevelt's day. It is generally assumed that the Cabinet Mr. Reagan has now is not composed entirely of his first choices. He could not get a man, for instance, from Citibank because that bank has loans to the Third World guaranteed by the government. It is said he could not get his first choice for secretary of the interior because his choice had sons who ran cattle on government-owned land in what is called a conflict of interest. I think first that people have to stop being so antisystem or a government of such enormously complicated responsibilities cannot function. Second, the congressional salaries have to be raised to $80,000 so some young fellows can work all night to energize this government at a comparable lower salary.

Roosevelt was always interested in the Pacific. When the war came, few were interested in the Pacific among his crowd but me. Why? Because of my brother and my senior New York partner, Mr. Joseph Cotton, undersecretary of state, who had placed me in Hoover's administration. So, the White House asked me, eight months before Pearl Harbor, to help on the job of putting into the American Lend-Lease Plan—possibly in violation of the Neutrality Act—the U.S. aviation personnel of the Flying Tigers that went into China with General C. L. Chennault to help keep China from surrendering to Japan. I have watched that Pacific situation ever since.

Whatever happens in Europe, it is no use kidding yourself about China. I have maintained an interest with China for a long while, and I think Reagan sees it clearly, even though Alexander Haig (secretary of state) is going to go to Peking next month. The Chinese people hold the lever of my grandchildren's America, even maybe of my children's America of the future, and your children's and grandchildren's America too. If one studies what happened in China over the years when their once stabilized society was destroyed by European commercialization, one sees that they would have had a terrible hundred years of famine, warlords, foreign concessions, revolutions, and everything else. Too many people reside in their country, and they have not had enough to eat. They have famines and no medical facilities, and they have died like flies in infancy. What now remains is based on the Darwinian law of the survival of the fittest, the physically and mentally toughest people on earth.

When I quit at the end of the war, I was working at the time with the Chinese. We were all saying goodbye. A fellow who was number two to T. V. Soong, both foreign minister and ambassador to the United States, was my special friend. His name was Reichman. I had known him before the war as the head of the children's program of the League of Nations. "Tommy, are we always going to be friends?" I said, "Certainly." He said, "Are you sure? Do you know I'm number three in Polish Communist intelligence? Come on over to Warsaw with me and see the future." Well, of course I said, "No." He went on, "I will give you one piece of advice and I am not salting the mine. Have you watched the Chinese under a bombing?"

"Yes."

"No matter how little they have to eat and how badly they have been banged up they sit down at night and enjoy what little they have and make merry. The Chinese are a bright-minded people. But did you ever hear a joke in India?"

"No."

"The Indians are a dark-minded people. But you foolish Americans are going to take the dark-minded people for your choice and let us Communists take over the bright-minded people."

Which is exactly what we did.

Now what is the United States going to do? The Mainland Chinese are trying to turn around. There are currently five other Asian countries that got out all of the fellows who had any capacity of managing anything to keep their heads from being cut off in the Chinese revolution. They are in Singapore, Malaya, Indonesia, Hong Kong, Taiwan, and there is a China on the Mainland—and an American China.

I was with my old friend, Ben Cohen, last night. The difference between Ben and myself is that Ben remembers that his ancestors were the High Priests of Israel, and he continues to believe in the infinite perfectibility of man. As a Catholic, I believe in original sin! I think I don't fool myself about people. So watch this China situation as the most important factor in the future of everyone's children. And how should one handle it? Maybe even Chiang Kai-shek must have realized that it was impossible to have two Marshall Plans. To get the Japanese out of China, the Allies had to knock them out by bombing everything in sight. There was nothing left to live on, but the Chinese survived. They are Chinese, and they are patient.

One wonderful thing the United States did after the Boxer Rebellion was to take U.S. indemnity and put it into a fund for sending Chinese students to the United States. Those students are in the five Asian countries outside of China, particularly in Taiwan. The Taiwan standard of living is now the second highest to Japan in the world. That wise Chinese mind on the Continent just keeping alive is thinking, "Why can't we live at that standard of living? Why can't we go to school? Why can't we have an automobile instead of a bicycle?" If the U.S.-trained Chinese outside the Mainland are kept alive, there is a chance that the Continent will come out all right.

During the Supreme Court Packing Plan, which was a mess for everyone in it, for and against, the only candidate who spoke up for a congressional bi-election in Austin, Texas, was a young fellow named Lyndon Johnson. Of the nine candidates, everyone was against Roosevelt except Lyndon and split the anti-Roosevelt vote. Mrs. Johnson put up only $10,000 to finance his campaign to pull him through. After the election when Roosevelt went down to Galveston on a cruiser, he met Lyndon, who had stuck up for him, and he brought Lyndon back on his train to Washington. Then he sent Lyndon to me for advice.

What mistakes they say Roosevelt and Johnson made were compensated by the great things they did. Johnson faced up to the Vietnam problem. I was associated with an airline that did the only air support at Dien Bien Phu because the French politicians in Europe forced the United States into it. They said: "We don't give a damn about Vietnam; we do care about the oil in Algeria. If we lose Vietnam, we lose Algeria. We mustn't lose Vietnam, and you Americans must hold it for us." That is why I am worried about Mitterrand; the way the French play us, "If you don't play with us and take care of Vietnam, we won't play with you in Europe." Long before Kennedy and Johnson, under Eisenhower, we were in Vietnam up to our necks to keep the French playing with us on the other side in Europe. Now don't blame Lyndon for it. Don't even blame Kennedy. This thing started under Eisenhower because France made us do their work. Lincoln crossed a great river preventing economic sectionalism from breaking up the Union. Roosevelt crossed the next great river preventing economic disaster in a poverty-frightened people from breaking up the Union. Lyndon crossed the next great river, preventing it from being broken up under the strain of racial differences. Together they led a people always tempted to division to develop a tolerant huge middle class, the biggest national asset of ability and stability in history. No matter what else is said about Lyndon Johnson, maybe he created the beginning of the solution to the race problem; he crossed the widest river of all.

Back to our three elephants—the technology elephant. The United States has a real problem of technology; that is, whether it is going to supplement, in time, the resources upon which the U.S. population explosion is putting pressure. That requires inventing new resources, whether it is hydrogen fusion or something like it. The demographic problem is creating the pressure on resources.

My mother's father was a genuine Forty-Niner. Their motto was: "The cowards never started and the weak died by the way." My father, whose father was an immigrant, not a Forty-Niner, to get respite from my mother used to take me down to where the Fabre Line was bringing in Italian immigrants when I was a boy. He said, "Son, every infusion of immigration in this country has brought people who just as truly as your mother's Forty-Niners believe 'The cowards never started and the weak died by the way.' What keeps this country going is the constant refueling of ambition and the willingness to work of those people who are coming in." Now we are facing it. You have to either stretch your technology to have room to take new people in with their increased push on resources, or you have to face up to turning them away. It is not only the problem from Mexico; it is the problem for the so-called boat people who are fundamentally of Chinese stock.

What I like about Mr. Reagan is that I think he thinks about Justice Holmes' elephants. I think he is capable of giving the American people hope rather than depressing them about their morale. As with Franklin Roosevelt, within one month he had transformed the whole attitude of individuals of this country. Re-energization of the able is the only chance we have. I think if he plays it wisely, the Democrats should be smart enough to give him a break. I think he is transforming the country, and he is not a political possession of his right wing.

I don't care whether ideologues consider him a "first-class intellect." The important thing that counts is temperament and whether he gives the able middle class hope. I think he will face the Chinese situation, the technological situation, and the demographic situation. I think he will pull the United States up to number one in this resource war.

When Holmes talked about how Roosevelt was doing, he said, "You know, he first understood and acted accordingly that the biggest waste of assets of the country is unused labor." What was the first thing he did with the CCC (Civilian Conservation Corps) Camp? He developed resources and put the unemployed youth to work. If Americans wanted something hard enough, they could do it today. For three years I have been asking, "What is the easiest CCC equivalent of taking care of the forest now?" I think it is rebuilding the railroad roadbeds of our whole system on a freight basis no matter who owns the damned things. But the unions won't let it happen. The maintenance men say, "You mean you are going to put these kids in to redo these tracks? What's left for us?" My reply is, "I favor our laboring man. I worked on the Fair Labor Standards Act, but I say, Mr. Maintenance, if you don't let this rehabilitation of the railroads happen, there is not going to be anything for you to do ten years from now as we go ahead at building truck roads, barge lines, and air freight airports." On the other hand, there is no way in the world to move goods cheaper than a steel wheel on a steel rail.

I think Reagan knows as a politician that he has to try to keep promises, but he was a wise governor. Like Roosevelt, when he knows a first plan cannot make it, he is going to find a way to change his mind. The important thing to understand is that no one is ever sure of how anything will work out when one begins. I do not like to talk to these intellectuals who think politics can be dealt with as abstract ideology. Everything is the next untried cake of ice.

Roosevelt used to say, "Did you ever see a smart engineer start a long train of coal cars? Do you think he eases the throttle in? He jerks it to beat the inertia." Do you remember Eliza in *Uncle Tom's Cabin* trying to get across the frozen, iceloaded Ohio River to freedom? Certainly Eliza had in mind the freedom on the other side of the Ohio, a free state. But what she was thinking of immediately was the next cake of ice. What bothers me about intellectual critics is their disregard that the immediate problem is always the next cake of ice. Reagan must know that cutting back Social Security was a mistake. Did you ever think maybe as a politician, he had to let the Democrats win that so if he let them win on the Social Security business, he might do better on his tax bill?

Once in 1936 I traveled on campaign with Mr. Roosevelt to help cut down speeches. My only value was that I boiled 120 minutes down to 20. One day we were in southern Illinois. We were whistle-stopping, and at every whistle-stop, the President would reward the head of the delegation cheering at the stop with the courtesy of riding to the next whistle-stop, then similarly taking on the next head of delegation. When we finally sat down to work on the speech, he said, "Did you learn anything today?" I said, "I was puzzled, Mr. President. You know I am a lawyer, and I think in very accurate, specific terms. Now, Mr. President, you let me listen today while you were talking with those men." This was southern Illinois. "Everyone of them wanted to be assistant secretary of agriculture." He said, "Yes, that's right." I said, "But you talked to them in such a way that everyone of them went off the train thinking you had literally promised it." He said, "That's right."

"Well, who is going to get it?"

"The ambitious man that makes the most trouble if he doesn't get it."

That's politics.

QUESTION: I have a question about Social Security. In 1934 or 1935, Leon Keyserling, who then was Robert Wagner's secretary, asserts that the Social Security Bill could have been and should have been passed in 1934. Because FDR appointed a committee and because of Elizabeth Brandeis's sort of silly objection, it came in 1935. It was obviously going to come. Even *Fortune*, in February 1935, said, "The question is not whether there will be a Social Security Act; the only question is, when?" Why did FDR postpone it from 1934 until the next year?

Thomas G. Corcoran

MR. CORCORAN: I don't know what went into the calculations of that incredibly skillful political mind. As I remember, we were in a lot of trouble, a lot of money trouble. That was about the time the FDR administration was running into the NRA, wasn't it? And of course he took these things when he could. It took some time. Miss Perkins was always working on that and Ben and Leon were working on it. I was not working on it, but I remember at that time we were having a lot of trouble. We passed the Social Security Act because of the Townsend business. Huey Long was pushing us around at that time to share the wealth. Maybe at that time, the time of the congressional elections, we were surprised when the Democrats won more than we ever expected. Maybe we just had too much to worry about. A fellow who is sitting up there has to balance what can get done with what he has.

QUESTION: The next cake of ice?

MR. CORCORAN: The next cake of ice.

QUESTION: I was much taken with the phrase *the institutionalization of compassion* when you were discussing the recruiting of the thousand middle-level administrators who were needed. Many of us have the impression that the people recruited now are not to make the government work but to prevent it from functioning, particularly in terms of regulations. Would you comment on this?

MR. CORCORAN: Well, it is for a reason, as I told you. Consider Joe Califano, for example. Joe is now writing about his troubles in HEW (Department of Health, Education, and Welfare). He deliberately picked HEW because, being responsible for that incredible operation in Lyndon's time, he wanted to prove it could work. But it won't work for this reason. The minute someone gets into the situation where he is giving something away, he finds political pressures from the people who want something from him to take over the organization of the thing. There is a great difference between the kind of thing like the SEC where someone is stopping people from acting and the kind where one is giving something to people. They try to take over. Right now, you people are intellectuals. You deliberately organized the Department of Education to get a racket, didn't you? Why do you think all of the teachers were for Carter the last time? So they could organize the Department of Education that the National Association of Teachers could run. So what one has to do is to sit down and see whether enough people can be persuaded to take the rap and be sure to be fired in two years. I quit when I knew I was going to be fired.

QUESTION: As one of the very practical matters, what will Reagan do about the arms race?

MR. CORCORAN: Remember that I represent Newport News Shipbuilding Company, but I can say one thing very clearly. There is too much tempting fat in the defense procurement process. Now, I am going to talk from my own problem. Everyone saw this business over in General Dynamics on the submarines, didn't they? Everyone saw the accusations made. For an awful long time—because I was in that row with Admiral Rickover—my crowd down here in Newport News would not bid on an undesigned ship like the Trident. But General Dynamics and everyone else was deliberately bidding below what they knew it would cost to get the contract. Then halfway through they would say, "You have to do better by us or we aren't going to deliver."

The first thing my friend, Secretary of Defense Caspar Weinberger, has to do is take out the fat. Some contractors are milking the Defense Department. The second thing that he has to do is face the fact that there will be—I don't care whether academics like it—a draft in two years because the trouble is that weapons are being built beyond the capacity of the fellows the United States has to man them.

The other day, the former head of the Marines, General Lewis Walt, said to me, "You know, we have more computerized artillery. But I am telling you, if a shell should hit the computer, we could not lay in a gun." There is no use fooling yourself.

I am concerned when I see all of these children turning their backs on speeches about defense and the rest of it. It is the same old racket. The real trouble in the last war and the trouble with the whole Defense Department theory is that the country is letting the children who want to go to college be excused from services in the Army, and their girlfriends are raising holy hell about human rights; and all of it to keep them from going into the service.

Another thing the government would want to do is to pay enough money to keep the defense personnel that are good and leaving by the dozens. The rest of them are going off on the atomic submarines built at Newport News and having trouble with their wives because they are out for six months. The country will have to take care of them. I am telling you that you are going to have a draft in two years, and that is going to be a great deal of political fun.

QUESTION: I agree with your emphasis on temperament being important. That quality is why Lincoln and Roosevelt were great presidents, and Johnson said something about "we shall overcome." What is there in Reagan's temperament that suggests he could be a compassionate person? How would this compassion be institutionalized? How will he take the next step? Temperament determines the way people respond to the next problem. What is there about his temperament that would suggest a compassionate man?

MR. CORCORAN: In the first place, he did get elected. Sam Rayburn once told me that a person who is effective as a politician basically has to be analyzed by his followers as a warm lively man. It is the sense of that quality about him on the part of the public that makes his communication with them acceptable. Reagan is a great communicator, and he knows how to fudge, if you don't mind my saying so. In some ways he is an amazing man to me. I was Adlai Stevenson's classmate, and I was in Adlai's campaign. Compare Reagan's success with Stevenson's defeat. It is an amazing thing that a candidate who had a divorce, has a daughter marrying a guy ten years younger than herself, and a son who was sending out ads for his business, should get away with it. Someone could no more have gotten away with that ten years ago than the man in the moon. No one would have put up a divorced man. What I am saying is, I feel very much that he senses what needs to be done to stay in office, and that is to be felt as human by his followers.

Now one more thing. I do not think the fellow wants to stay in for more than four years. He knows how he wants to leave this thing. I think he believes in the simple things, the family, for instance, even though he has had a divorce and many problems. I think he understands compassion, and I think he understands spending money for which one gets value. But it means something else. It means getting the kind of men, even from Wall Street if one dares, who can run an organization. I know Joe Califano. I said to him, "Joe, what happened in HEW?" He replied, "You couldn't keep special interest politics out of it."

I think Reagan has strengths. He is 70 years old; I am 80 years old. Old age ain't for sissies, even if you are 70. I think the fact that this president is 70 years old means that he is going to try to get this thing cleaned up before he finishes, and he is not going to run for office again. I have seen more trouble with men wanting to run for office forever. I am not sure, having watched the operation of politicians for a long time, but that Social Security change is something he let them propose to be objected to and then he gave in.

At the same time, there is this business about the budget. Of course, everyone has to think about the budget, but with spending, we also created a middle class from a poverty-stricken nation. I think it is a good thing to put some pressure on the middle class because now it has cars and television. I remember when we were playing with garbage cans. The middle class has children in college. It still wants those things so badly that it will work to keep them, and it can take a little squeeze. I keep saying that the thing to do is to get the individual human animal in the United States to want it hard enough to work for it. I think Roosevelt did that, and I think Lyndon did it. I think Reagan is going to do it. Besides, I keep thinking so because there isn't anyone else to do it.

QUESTION: I have a most unintellectual question. I have been fascinated most about you talking about Mr. Ickes, whom I remember vaguely. I used to get a good chuckle out of reading him. In the 1940 presidential campaign—you were talking about the 1936 campaign—I seem to remember that the phrase you used was used very effectively with a little addition to it by Mr. Harold Ickes against Wendell Willkie. Wasn't Mr. Ickes the one who said: "That poor, barefoot Wall Street lawyer?"

MR. CORCORAN: That's right.

QUESTION: Was that saying spontaneous, or was it planned?

MR. CORCORAN: Ickes was one of the great underrated people of this country. Ben Cohen and I were his executors after his death. Don't fool yourself about Ickes. Old Ickes was the kind of guy that Roosevelt could always call on. Do you remember that old story about English tradition in old medieval England? When a King was elected, a challenger had to ride on his horse armed "cap-a-pie" right into Westminister Hall and offer to challenge and fight to the death anyone who said the choice of King was not the rightful King. Ickes was that challenger for Roosevelt. He loved to do it, except he used to talk too long. His speeches were an hour long.

Whenever there was trouble, old Ickes would ride in to be the attacker. Roosevelt would never say the sort of thing about Willkie that Ickes said. Remember, Ickes was also the fellow who talked about Dewey as "the little fellow on the wedding cake." He had genius for this role and he loved to do it.

QUESTION: Would he just snap them off, or did he think?

MR. CORCORAN: No, he thought that way. He was a strange fellow. Many people thought he was a cantankerous old guy, but remember that Ickes came in with the Richard Ballinger (secretary of interior under Taft) controversy hanging over the Department of Interior. Remember Teapot Dome? The Department of Interior was supposed to be a place where they stole money, and Ickes had to be a very cantankerous old guy who kicked people around to stop the stealing.

There was another side to Ickes. He was a great botanist, like Thomas Jefferson. In Washington, a park is located between the old Interior building and the new one. It is one of the most beautiful little parks in the world, and Ickes was the person who built it. One can stand in the back of the Capitol and look down the great sweep of "magnificent distance" down to the Lincoln Memorial and the Washington Monument. It was not there when I came here. There were railroad tracks that crossed between the Capitol. Ickes put the railroad tracks to Richmond underneath in a tunnel.

When the war was coming on and we had to have the Pentagon in a hurry, a fellow named Somervell was a brigadier general there who had a great reputation for getting things done. He was ordered to build the Pentagon where the airfield was. So we had to have another airfield. The other airfield is now National Airport, located on the Virginia side of the Potomac. They had to dig out the channel and make that airport with fill.

At that time, Burton Wheeler was watching like a hawk for some indication that Roosevelt really wanted to get into the war. They had a specific limited appropriation for that airport. It was originally thought to be enough, but Somervell spent so much money that in the middle of the summer of 1941, that money ran out. So Roosevelt called me and said, "I don't dare ask for more money to finish the airport, but we have to have that money. Go around and see what discretionary appropriations Cabinet members haven't expended yet that could be diverted into the airport. It might be a violation of the law, but let's see what's available." I had to be careful, but finally I saw Ickes and told him about Mr. Roosevelt's problem. Carefully, I didn't suggest what to do. All I am going to say now is that every time I land on Washington Airport and hear the reverse thrust and squeal of tires, I think I hear a protesting Navajo. That is the kind of guy he was.

QUESTION: How many times did Ickes resign?

MR. CORCORAN: Oh, about every two weeks, and he was right! Remember that bill about the reorganization of the government to turn Forestry over to the Department of Interior to become the Department of Natural Resources? Roosevelt promised Ickes four or five times that he would transfer that from Wallace's Department of Agriculture to Ickes. But he never carried it out because every time he tried, the bureaucracy of the Forest Service went to Wallace and whined about it, and Wallace did not want to take it on. So he went back to Roosevelt and somehow postponed it. This example shows, again, the operation of politics. Ickes had his mind on Forestry because Gifford Pinchot, who was Teddy Roosevelt's head of the Forest Service, had knocked Ickes over the way he ran the Department of Interior. When Ickes did not get what he was promised, he resigned, and then Roosevelt would send me around to talk sweet to Ickes—I'm all over Ickes' diary. I would talk to Ickes and say, "There are bigger things involved than this. Let's think about oil, and let's think about the other things."

He was the first to think about today's oil difficulties. During the war when he first went in (remember the Hundred Days), there was so much oil being produced in Texas that a limitation was actually put on the amount of oil that could move across the state boundary. Ickes was in charge of this. He called it "hot oil."

The United States has managed this oil problem very badly, I think. First, under the "hot oil" New Deal policy, U.S. production was discouraged. Then when the war was over, imports were discouraged. Ickes was the person who forced the Americans into the monopoly that the British had in the oil fields in the Middle East. He sent me down to Texas about imports right after the war. He said, "These Middle Eastern potentates haven't sold their full production of oil because they can't. You go down and talk to Charles Murchison (chairman of the Tax Amortization Board, War Department, 1941) and say, 'Listen, why don't you fellows keep your oil. You can buy for ten bucks a barrel and let them make some money. You pour the surplus into salt mines, and we will give you a tax rebate for the oil you keep in the ground." Maybe that is what should have been done. Of course, the U.S. producers were thinking about the bank loans they had to pay off. Since the banks would not give in on their loans, the U.S. producers could not go along with Ickes. Maybe that is why the country is in the mess it is in today.

Ickes was a great guy. He did more for this country than anyone can dream; and he was always in trouble. The reason he was always getting things done was he would fight for them. Naturally, Franklin Roosevelt, being at the top, hated trouble.

Rather than for him to make a decision, if you had to raise enough hell, you would get what you wanted. I know people think this is a whale of a way to run a railroad. Churchill once said that democratic government was the worst form of government except any other. It is a kind of government that is constantly meeting the next cake of ice. The ordinary citizen cannot completely understand, but a president has to think over the long-term sequences. He has to watch the elephants. In the meantime he has to make all kinds of compromises.

Do you remember the silver bloc? Senator Carl Hayden of Arizona was jamming up the price of silver through 12 senators lined up in Montana, Arizona, Colorado, Nevada, and New Mexico. As a New Englander I could talk to my fellow regionalists and say, "Why don't you gang up on these guys with your 12 senators? If they are getting all they are getting out of the 12 senators in the silver bloc, why don't we put 12 senators together?"

"Oh," they would say, "that wouldn't be honest." Well, the silver bloc got what they wanted, and we in New England didn't. I am sorry, but that is the kind of free government we have.

Look at it right now. Did you see what George Meany's successor in the labor union said the other day? He said, "I am not going to worry about the Northeast. I know where production is coming from. I know where the plants are going to be and where the synthetic fuel is going to be, and we're going to rape the natural resources of the west, and it's the finish of the West. We are going to put coal out there, and we are going to put oil out there, and we are going to put metal out there. That's where the laborers want to be."

Now that is the way one thinks in a special interest group. Did people understand why such an effort was made to break the nonlabor situation down here at the shipyard in Newport News? It was because it was the biggest single employer of nonunion labor in the South. Many nice people think that government is something that God told Moses to write on tablets of stone. Instead, the United States has a government that has to play the game of the next cake of ice—this cake of ice, that cake of ice—one off against the other. The wonderful thing that Roosevelt had was a sense of timing. He knew when to try and when to hold back.

Now, one asks, where are we? One thing anyone can say is that FDR remembered elephant number one and saved a lot of the resources of this country, including its labor. He made the country resource conscious. On the other hand, one can say that he brought out discouraged people from poverty into a confident middle-class status. That means they are now difficult to handle. It's not as easy as the old days when one said, "Follow me and I'll give you something to eat." Poor old Hoover, whom I really liked, tried with two chickens in every pot, but he could not deliver. He did not know how to play little by little.

Did Lyndon lose the Vietnam War? Did Roosevelt lose his war? We fought that war to save the British Empire, and it is in ruins because it now has neither the resources of raw materials nor the closed markets it had in the Commonwealth. The only thing it has is North Sea oil and the Hong Kong markets. We did not intend that. We did not intend to substitute Russian—something worse than German—totalitarianism. We might have done something about the Germans, but we can't do anything about the Russians except beat them, that's all.

On the other hand, one has to say that FDR tried, as no one else ever did, to make a better world. Holmes used to say about Wilson and the United Nations, the League of Nations: "The goddamn fool, didn't he understand that when he was on this side of the water, he was a remote power and they were afraid of him? When he went over to Paris, he was just a human being to be lied to."

I don't pretend to know where the country is coming out. I am only thinking about what the United States is going to do about defense. Only one thing is sure—we have to be strong.

What the Russians have is a society that does not represent their people any more than Mao represented the Chinese people, but they know how to organize force. The simplest thing to organize is not a productive economy, but military force. So they get by the way Genghis Khan used to get by, as they did in Finland. They just threatened a productive society with physical force and took over its production, just as they took the plants out of Germany and Manchuria.

Well, the country has to face up to it. I think Reagan will be hitting the United States right where it is needed when he gets us to face up to it. So at 80 years old, I think it is going to be a wonderful time!

I shall report to my boss, Mr. Rowe, that I said the things he did not dare say because he may still run for office. Thank you.

NARRATOR: You can also report that one man sitting at this table counseled me some months back, "Your Forums are fine, but if you want a Forum on politics, you had better invite Tommy the Cork." That man is probably as pleased today as all of the rest of us are. Thank you for an unforgettable hour-and-a-half of reflections on politics.

~ *Five* ~

THE "COMPLEAT" PRESIDENT: DWIGHT DAVID EISENHOWER[*]

Bryce Harlow

MR. THOMPSON: What we have been asking people to talk about is the political leadership of Dwight D. Eisenhower, how it took shape and where it received its impetus; what Eisenhower's concept of presidential leadership was; how it changed if it did change at all; what you think of revisionist thought as it has developed. Professor Fred Greenstein did part of his work at the Miller Center. It is quite a departure from the media view that President Eisenhower paid very little attention to the politics of issues that came along. That is one area we would like to explore.

Another area is how you became involved with President Eisenhower; what your perceptions were in the beginning; how they evolved and developed. Did you change your mind at all about him and about the problems of the office—anything that could be brought in, in that respect. In your case, of course, one of the things that would interest us a great deal is President Eisenhower's relations with the Congress and with the party as you saw it.

We have had people who have hit pretty hard on two or three points. We had Richard Strout visit us the other day for another purpose and he made some nice comments about President Eisenhower, but then he immediately reverted to the McCarthy thing in Wisconsin and the speech, and you undoubtedly have insights on that.

---

[*]Taken from an interview conducted by Kenneth W. Thompson with Bryce Harlow on 14 June 1983. Reprinted from *The Eisenhower Presidency: Eleven Intimate Perspectives of Dwight D. Eisenhower* (Lanham, Maryland: University Press of America, Inc., 1984).

THE "COMPLEAT" PRESIDENT: DWIGHT DAVID EISENHOWER

MR. HARLOW: I wasn't with him then.

MR. THOMPSON: Well, any thoughts, first of all, just on Eisenhower and your association with him—how that began, what you expected of him, and what he expected of you.

MR. HARLOW: Shall I just start talking free-style?

MR. THOMPSON: Surely, that will be perfect.

MR. HARLOW: You are going to regret it.
   I went grudgingly to the White House. I tried hard not to go there. It is hard to believe that in 1953 I had already been in Washington for 15 years. I had served in the Congress and I had served General Marshall during the war. I had had five additional years on Capitol Hill after the war with the Armed Services Committee of the House. I was already a burned-out bureaucrat by the time the President was elected. I had resigned from the Armed Services Committee and gone back to Oklahoma City, which was my home. I did *not* want to go back to Washington, D.C. But General Persons, for whom I had worked during the war (he and I had worked on Congress for General Marshall), wanted me to be one of his two major reliances in the White House for Eisenhower. He called me and talked about it, and I started sparring with him for six weeks, trying to stave him off. I figured that White House jobs are so precious, so eagerly sought after by people, that some campaign contributor's son or daughter would seize upon that slot, so if I just stalled long enough, Persons would be forced to take someone else. Well, six weeks later, he was still badgering me. I stalled through the trip to Korea, thinking that by the time he got back it would be over with. But the day he got back, he called me in Oklahoma City, and I was back to square one. My father was sitting there with me when the call came in, and he finally interrupted me and said, "Son, give up. You can't keep saying no to the White House; a good citizen just can't do that." So I gave up and returned.
   So you see, I went grudgingly, but not with any hostility, not angrily, not antagonistic to the President. I admired him

enormously and had strongly supported him for President in a region where it was somewhat costly to be a Republican, in Democratic Oklahoma. So it wasn't that. I just did not want to stay in the government. When I came back, I was used in the White House congressional section as a special assistant on the White House staff by General Persons, who was then deputy assistant to the President. I remained in that configuration for some nine months, then became Ike's speechwriter. I did that for a couple of years and then went back to congressional work and speech writing, which is what I did the rest of my time in the White House. Thereafter, I stayed with him as his Washington representative, you might say, throughout his retirement and was his Washington "commissar" until his death. I would say it was a very wonderful experience, that he was an extraordinary person, whom I came to regard as utterly admirable.

Early in Nixon's term, I was contacted when I was back in the White House by some reporter who was doing a special anniversary story on Eisenhower. He was going around the country asking people who knew the President best, most intimately, for one single word that would best characterize him. I never saw the article that he wrote. It was for the *Saturday Evening Post* or some such publication. I responded instantly—it came to me instantly what the answer should be, and I have never changed my mind. I said, "Oh, that's simple. It's the old English word 'compleat'—that's Eisenhower." He was the most completely rounded American I shall ever know. Not a perfect man. He is more like the Olympic all-around athlete, decathlon—not the best in everything but best in most things, and therefore the finest athlete of all. That's Eisenhower. Personality-wise, ability-wise, motivation-wise, he was about the finest leader we have ever had.

I put together a montage of pictures I had of him taken in Paris when he was commander of NATO. I escorted some 30 congressmen over there, and of course each of them had to have his picture taken with this hero. The man's face mirrored his feelings, you know. He had a majestic face that went from a five-star general's cragginess to the Kansas grin and to the captivating boy-like quality of the grin, almost a mischievous thing, and then that five-star look that was far from mischievous. I captured all of that in this wheel of snapshots showing his face breaking into this big grin, then sobering up into the five-star sternness, then coming back up to the grin. I had enough pictures to make it come alive. It shows the real Eisenhower in his various configurations pretty well.

He was a marvelous person. No hang-ups. He was at peace deep down inside, deep in the psyche. He never felt internally secure. He was not defensive in any aspect of his life that I know about, with the exception of certain isolated experiences. There was nothing personal in this, but he was very defensive about General George Marshall; he was ashamed of the McCarthy episode. He thought he blew that. There is no question that he thought he blew it. He felt he was put upon by aides who induced him to blow it. He gave in to them in a season when he was still getting his sea legs in politics. I think my beloved General Jerry Persons was one of those who made him blow it, probably. I cross-examined Jerry about that, and I doubt not that he had a big hand in it—he, Sherman Adams, James Hagerty, and so forth. I can understand their doing it, but I can also understand Eisenhower's hindsight that this was a terrible thing they had him do. He never quite said that to me, but he said its equivalent to me several times.

MR. THOMPSON: Did he ever feel he ought to take the advice of the political professionals, even though his own instincts pushed him in another direction?

MR. HARLOW: Sure he did. He knew he was not an expert in everything. He was a great commander; he would depend on the corps commander to tell him what was going on in the corps. That is the way he believed, the way he was trained in delegation. It was one of his great skills. That is one of the hardest skills to master—how to delegate.

He was not at all pleased with how the Marshall affair came out. Neither was he pleased with the stories about that English girl. I know that just bugged the daylights out of him. I never discussed it with him, believe me. I did not know anything about it other than the rumors I had heard, and I did not care to try to find out from him, so I cannot say anything about it. He and I became trusting friends and talked about everything, and he never mentioned this one thing, so I did not mention it.

He had a kind of interesting temper. You have talked about that to many people, I know. Of course there came a time when he put it under control, after his heart attack. It was marvelous the way he controlled his emotions after that. But he blew up at me once in 1954, and I relished it because I saw it close up and it was like looking into a Bessemer furnace. It was exciting to see it, and so dramatic, so spectacular a sight, that it did not affect me in the least. I was not bothered by his anger, I was simply fascinated by what I saw, and I leaned forward to see deeper into that furnace. It showed the enormous, vital force in him.

MR. THOMPSON: Was there any warning sign?

MR. HARLOW: Yes, he would look beet red. He would put out all kinds of signals. I might add that it was like an Oklahoma thunderstorm or tornado—whoosh, and it was gone.

MR. THOMPSON: No grudge.

MR. HARLOW: Just gone, amazing. He jumped on me because I had rewritten a speech that he did not want rewritten. He thought I had deliberately violated his instructions. He wanted to know in very explicit terms, very fast, why I had done that. I was busy looking into that flaming furnace. I almost did not hear him because I was so intent looking at that! Then I realized I had better answer because, after all, life is short at best. I said I had been up all night doing the speech over, I had not been to bed, and I had not had hardly any sleep for almost a year, and I was so tired I did not care if he fired me or not. I never wanted the job anyway, so it was to me a matter of relative indifference, which was the greatest strength I had with him. So I leaned forward in the Oval Office and I said, "Well, Mr. President," in almost inaudible terms because I was so exhausted, "goodness knows, I would not have spent all night doing this if I had thought you did not want me to." I just looked at him, and if he had said the wrong thing, I would have picked up my papers and walked out and quit. I think that was manifest. Then I saw the furnace door clank shut completely and totally, the fires all turned off, and he said, "Why, of course that's right. Let's get this all straightened out now." Just that and it was gone. But that was a manifestation of the man. He was capable of losing his temper on things important to him, which I think is an aspect of strength and not weakness.

MR. THOMPSON: Editing and writing were important to him?

MR. HARLOW: Oh, yes. As you know, he edited with great enthusiasm. It is well-nigh impossible to write effectively for someone who is a writer, and he was a writer. It was no picnic writing for Eisenhower, not if you have editorial pride. He edited, edited, edited at least half of what he saw. He edited everyone, and he was very good at it. He was a very good writer. Many people did not think so, but he was.

MR. THOMPSON: What about his press conferences? The people who say he is a good writer say that either of two things happened there: either that he confused the press deliberately and that is why the syntax was so bad; or the other view was that he was confused.

MR. HARLOW: Well, assuredly he was not a confused man. He was a man of great confidence and intelligence, and I note that Greenstein believes it was a calculated move to put off the press and keep them befogged. I don't believe that either. I think he openly groped for the right words in talking on complicated matters, protecting the presidency as he did that. You cannot do those broad and pearly expressions if you are conscientious about it. I believe you cannot, some think you can. At any rate, I think he was being careful, trying to be very careful, to protect the presidency. They knew what he was saying but wanted to pick at him anyway. If he had been glib, they would have said he did not mean what he said. That is what we would have had if it had been the other way around.

MR. THOMPSON: If he was protecting the presidency, one of the interesting things is that Truman got so much credit for his love of the office and respect of the office. Many journalists kept saying Eisenhower really was more proud of being commander in chief than he was of being president.

MR. HARLOW: Well, that could be. The last major job he had me do for him was to get that bill passed on the Hill restoring his generalship so that in retirement he would be called general instead of president. That was his object: He wanted to retire as a general not as a president. You may not like that answer, but that is the right answer.

Again, I remind you, this was an uncommon experience in the history of our country involving the presidency. We had a career public servant as president. You get those only rarely. To get a comparable generalship situation, you have to go back, I suspect, all the way to George Washington in order to discover this kind of selfless approach to the presidency. It was a matter of public service, period, that he was in there for. He did not want a damn thing personally. All he wanted was to get out with his reputation intact. He wanted to serve the country, to do a good job for America, and he wanted to do that the best he could. He had certain convictions about that. He was a deep-dyed, true-blue conservative, far more than people credited him or knew, including Bob Taft, who was dumbfounded when he sat down with him and saw what Ike really was. In some ways he was more conservative than Taft was, and to Taft's consternation, Ike lit into him about his housing bill. He said Taft was being socialistic.

He did not want anything for himself from the presidency. He was a career public servant, and he had a great sensitivity about the dignity of the presidency. He was extremely sensitive about it, so much so that it almost was a hang-up. As an amusing little aside, I can recall one incident: We were out at Frazer, Colorado, at a little retreat of Axel Nielsen's, a nice, secluded, rustic place in the mountains. I had to go up and work on some speeches with the President, so Howard Snyder, the President's physician, and I drove up in the White House car from Denver. This was in 1954. We were getting ready to go on a campaign swing that congressional election year, so this day I was to finish off his speeches for that trip. General Snyder and I got there at noontime. We were going

THE "COMPLEAT" PRESIDENT: DWIGHT DAVID EISENHOWER

to lunch with him, then go over his speeches. Then General Snyder wanted to check him out physically. We parked in a clearing between cabins, and there Ike was in front of a grill, cooking. He was having great fun, dressed up in a chef's hat and apron. He was cooking a huge rainbow trout on the grill, wrapped in tinfoil and over hickory chips. Oh, he was just having fun.

A group of men were standing around, friends and Secret Service and so on, while he fixed lunch. I don't remember who the people were specifically, but all of us noted a big herd of cattle sauntering down the mountainside, all of them registered Angus cattle. They were following an absolutely huge bull. There is nothing that looks erotically more puissant, as you know, than a bull, and down he came, and this bunch of lascivious men looked at him, and you know what happened—someone had to make some obscene remark about the animal. Well, a fellow did that, and this was intended to be heard by President Dwight David Eisenhower. The General did hear, and he looked up, his blue eyes turned crystal cold, off came the hat, off came the apron, down went the spatula, and without a word he wheeled and walked into his cabin. It was devastating. The man turned, left the group, and broke into tears before he got to his cabin.

Now this involved the dignity of the presidency, in Eisenhower's view. You did not talk smut in his presence while he was president. Not that he was a prude, but you just did not talk coarsely around him while he was President of the United States. This contrasts with Harry Truman, who loved barroom talk all the time, in such a measure that the press had been known to walk away. That happened at the Press Club one night. I remember the language got so bad even the press couldn't take it. So you see, two different guys, neither of them bad. But that dignity of the office was profound in Ike.

MR. THOMPSON: What about his dress? Would he have held a televised speech with a sweater on or would he have walked down Pennsylvania Avenue? Was there any of the populist at all in him?

MR. HARLOW: He wasn't much of a populist. He was a trained senior officer in the armed forces, and he had great poise and reserve. He was not nearly as reserved as George Marshall or Robert E. Lee or George Washington, but he was more reserved than Bryce Harlow, more reserved than you are, more reserved than most, and it was the reserve of a leader trained not to fraternize with the troops. He was an extremely popular leader during the war, as you know, and his relationship with the troops was very good. He would mix with them, and they would love it as he would go down the line with a friendly and happy face, yet with that gravel voice and obvious leadership force. They admired him, and they liked him. But he wasn't one of the boys; that would have eroded effective leadership. I do not recall that he used to run up and down airport fences shaking hands. Lyndon Johnson "pressed the flesh" and so forth, which is today par for the political course, but I don't believe Eisenhower ever did that.

Another vignette may give you a measure of the man: In 1958, I believe, there was a senatorial election in New Jersey, and Jim Mitchell was running. He had been a very popular and very good secretary of labor, widely respected in New Jersey. Well, his campaign was doing very poorly, so Eisenhower, Bob Shultz, and I went up there; I helped him with his speech, and he came out swinging for Jim Mitchell, rode in the parade with him, waved his arms, and all the rest, doing all he could to help Jim Mitchell. The night before the parade, Jim Mitchell, Eisenhower, and I and General Bob Shultz had dinner at the hotel and had a nice and enjoyable conversation. Then Ike pushed back from the table and said, "Jim, I want to tell you something. I've been watching you. You've got to change the way you're going after this thing—you're too wooden. Now, Jim, tomorrow in this parade, I want you to do something. I want you to move your lips, I want you to be talking to the crowd, wave your arms and talk to them, look at them and move your lips; you don't have to actually say anything, just look like you're talking, look like you are genuinely interested in them, Jim." Well, I sat there and almost went ahem-em-em. Here is this nonpolitical general who reputedly does not know a thing about politics, one who came up with the biggest landslide in American history just two years before, lecturing his Irish friend. Possibly that is an example of his political sensitivity—his populism, you might say. He was telling Jim how to relate to the public.

THE "COMPLEAT" PRESIDENT: DWIGHT DAVID EISENHOWER

Let me give case number two: In 1961, it must have been, Bill Miller was chairman of the Republican National Committee. He had me drive him to Gettysburg to entreat the President to entreat to go to Texas and campaign for the open House seat in the first special election since Miller had become chairman. Miller wanted badly to win that to get the Republican party going again after the Kennedy election disaster. So he talked the President into going; the President grumbled mightily about it, groused like he always did, but then did it, as I was sure he would. So we flew there, and our candidate was a Marine Corps hero, which had something to do with Ike accepting the assignment. The Democratic party's candidate did not serve in World War II and was left-wing politically in the Texas legislature. He is still in Congress. His district is in San Antonio. On top of all of that, thousands of the retired military of the United States live there, so it was a great place for Ike.

We went there to campaign, and Ike rode up and down the streets of San Antonio waving his arms for this candidate (I don't recall his name), a nice, handsome Marine who was inexperienced in politics but an attractive candidate. So the President sat down to reassess things after our first sally at campaigning, which was rather unsuccessful. This was about two o'clock in the afternoon and we had not produced the large crowds we had expected, or enthusiasm either. So he had a little emergency review in the hotel. Ike asked the campaign manager, the candidate, and the national committee woman to be there. Ike said, "I want to ask a question. I have been over this campaign plan. Where's the Catholic college? I don't see a Catholic college on this list anywhere. Why am I not going to a Catholic college?" Well, they just waffled—they didn't know what to say. Ike said, "Well, this is a Catholic place, isn't it? So let's get busy showing a concern for Catholics." This is our reputedly nonpolitical general telling the politicians what to do! So there was a rush, calls were made, and some poor college president was scared half to death as suddenly, Dwight David Eisenhower was thrust right down his throat. We went racing out to the campus with a presidential caravan. They let the classes out and put on a warm reception, so the President rubbed off on the Catholic university.

He had reserve, poise, and did not like ordinary politics much, but yes, he was very, very good at it himself. Once he got into it you had to head him off; he would get too excited about it. He loved it, once he got started. As a matter of fact, he had trouble at first relating to his new career. You see, in 1954 he was starting his first congressional campaign year. It was very important to him because he was trying to salvage a Republican Congress. But he began by refusing to make a political speech—this was in his pre-presidential configuration. He just would not make a political speech. I knew, I was then his speechwriter and I had replaced Emmett Hughes. Indeed, I was his one and only speechwriter at that point in time.

He called me in to say that they were to have a big speech in the Hollywood Bowl, very important. It was to be the theme-setting, take-off speech for the entire campaign. I wrote two speeches—one, the kind I wanted him to make, all fire and brimstone. The other one was what he ordered me to write, which was professional and deadly dull, on foreign policy. It was like a kimono—it did not touch anything. For him to get up before a fired up political audience and deliver that as his take-off speech for the campaign would be, in my view and the view of many others, an absolutely irretrievable disaster. Some 5,000 to 10,000 Republicans were to be there eager to scream, wave their arms, and stamp their feet, not sit there woodenly and be preached to about foreign policy.

Well, I must admit that I did what the President told me to do. I put my asbestos-fiery address in my desk drawer, and I proceeded to draw up a lilies-of-the-valley version. This I sent along with violins to the White House for Sherman Adams and his crew to go over and make all right for the President to give it and to make sure it was factually right and let the State Department pick at it. Then I received a call from Sherman Adams. "Bryce," he said, in his crisp way, "this is a conference call, just so you'll know." I said, "Bully for you, Governor—who is on the phone?" "Leonard Hall, Herb Brownell, Jerry Parsons, Jack Martin, Jerry Morgan, Gabriel Hauge." All were sitting there, all the White House staff brass, and I said, "Yes?" I knew, of course, what they were calling about. I knew perfectly well and was elated. I was in Denver all alone and could not do anything with this teeth-clenched leader who was dead set on being nonpolitical. I pretended that I didn't know what they were up to. "We have a copy of this address that you've written for the President," Sherm said. I said, "Yes, what do you think of it?" "Well, Bryce, it's awful." I said, "Yes, it is, isn't it?" And that disconcerted Sherman; he did not know quite what to do with it. He thought I was going to say, "Oh come now, you are hurting my feelings." Instead I said, "It sure is, isn't it?" "Well," said Sherm, "I didn't expect that answer. If it's so awful, why did you send it out here like this?" "Because I had to," I said. "Look, we can save lots of time, Governor. You and your buddies there—I know what you're talking about. You don't like that speech; I don't like that speech. You want him to make a hot political speech; I want him to make a hot political speech. I have written him a hot political speech; it is right here in my desk drawer. You would love it. You'd want to tone it down, it's so hot. I just haven't the guts to give it to the President. You give it to him. You come out here and give it to him if you want short service in the White House." He said, "Oh, you can make him believe it." "Oh, no," I said, "I've broken my pick; he will not let me do anything even a little like that. The speech you have is exactly what he has ordered. He has been over it; he thinks it's jim dandy. But it will be a political disaster, Governor. So you come and talk him out of it; I can't." He said, "That's exactly what we will do."

He hung up, and the next thing I knew an airplane arrived at the Air Force base and here were all those men, so we had what was tantamount to a summit conference with the President. It was even set up like one. To me, it was funny as hell. There was Ike, sitting at a desk in one of the briefing rooms for the Air Force, and in front of him we were all lined up, looking with great solemnity. Here was Sherman Adams and all of his staff making speeches to the President, and he was just sitting there looking grimly silent, motionless. They told him, "Mr. President, you have to make a political speech. You cannot make a boring foreign policy speech at the Hollywood Bowl. That's a group of our party members wanting to cheer and shout and roar and give the party a charge for this campaign. You can't go in there with that kind of an address. You'll ruin us, you'll just ruin us." The President just listened, obviously displeased. There were some 30 or 45 minutes of this.

We all took turns, and when one was done we would say, "It's your turn, boy," and up would get the next one to make a speech; and Sherman spoke, and Jerry Persons; they all spoke, and it was in sum a gutsy performance. When it ended, he said, "All right, Bryce, have a draft ready by seven o'clock tonight. We'll meet in the basement of my house. All of you are coming," and he turned around and strode out of the room, leaving a trail of smoke behind him. I turned and they said, "Can you do that?" and I said, "I've got it already done. It's in my desk drawer," and I said, "We just need to clean it up. Let's come to my office, clean it up, and there's no problem."

So we got to the President's house, Mamie's house in Denver, and to the gameroom downstairs and spread out around the table and started working on this speech until midnight or so. Eisenhower had a ball. As I said, at first he would resist getting into one of those political exercises, but then you would have to catch him by the coattails. He would start putting in things you wouldn't dare say, and it would be tougher and meaner and more bitterly partisan, because he did not know the metes and bounds of politics. So we created a torchy speech. He went out and delivered it at the Hollywood Bowl and was resoundingly cheered by Republicans nationwide.

But now, you see, politically we often had that experience of his initially resisting making a political speech and then making it with great gusto and enjoyment. He loved doing it but hated getting ready to do it, an odd behavior.

MR. THOMPSON: Did it hurt when it came from the other side? Frank Pace, I think, and someone else said that when Truman played the political game he had been playing all his life and made statements in the campaign against Ike in favor of Stevenson, Ike never forgave him. He could not forget that someone who had once admired him had said bad things in the campaign.

MR. HARLOW: I think his relationship with Truman went much deeper than that. Truman jumped him on the McCarthy thing. I think he never forgave Truman for his attacks about the George Marshall relationship; that's number one; number two, Truman tried to make him to run as a Democrat and he turned him down, and Truman never forgave him for that. Truman thought it was an act of apostasy, as did Sam Rayburn. To accuse Eisenhower of apostasy is unforgivable in Eisenhower's context, and the Marshall thing hurt very deeply too.

I might say something else about this Truman relationship. Late in the administration, 1958 it must have been, I went to Sherman Adams and said, "Governor, there is one thing about the President that has to be cleaned up. He has never invited the Trumans to come here. I understand why; it is because he despises them; I understand that. But that's going to plague him in later years because he should have invited them. He just shouldn't do that to a former president. There's no point in his going on in later life saying: 'Ah, that was a fool thing I did and unbecoming. I should have invited him over and maybe held my breath while he was around but, the heck with it, I should have done it.' Let's make him do it so it won't trouble him in later years. I know it will." The governor looked at me and said, "Are you kidding? Do you expect me to go in there and tell him to invite Harry Truman in here? You've got another thing coming!" I said, "All right." So I went to Jim Hagerty and made the same request. Jim said, "You think I'm going in there and tell him that? Great God, I'm not crazy." So I went to Tom Stevens, and I went to Jerry Persons—no takers. So I went to Ann Whitman and said, "Honey, let me in that side door now. Is the boss busy?" Ann said, "No one's there right now. I said, "I'm going in. You leave that door open so when I skid, I won't hit the wall. I'm going to do something that's going to infuriate him, and I just want not to hit the wall when I come out skidding." She said, "What are you going to do?" I said, "You wait and see."

So in I went, and the President looked up at me and said, "Hello, Bryce, sit down," and I sat down. It was late afternoon, he was putting on his golf shoes. He was ready to go out to hit some drives on the South Lawn. He said, "What's on your mind?" I said, "Mr. President, I want to make a comment to you that I think you will dislike. I am suggesting it, I think, in your own interest. I think you will see later that, if you will let me finish what I am trying to say, I am correct in making this proposal to you. So I want to ask you, before I tell you what I am going to say, please let me finish." He started to look at me with that five-star look. But then he said, "All right," and he looked at me hard and questioningly, and I went into my recital. I told him, "I think you ought to invite the Trumans to come here. I think you should clear this deck so you won't be harassed by this in later years. I think you should not have the country feeling that you never invited him here. It won't hurt you to do it; it will be unpleasant, but you have done other unpleasant things in your life that you've thought you had to do. Truman is going to Europe; we can intercept him and ask him to drop by here on the way and bring Bess with him and they can spend the night. Mr. President, I talked about this in confidence with one of Mr. Truman's closest associates in Washington. He is delighted; he feels the same way. He says Mr. Truman can't turn it down." Ike said, "How would you say this?" I said, "I just happen to have a telegram draft right here," so I handed it to him, he read it, and said, "He'll never do it." I said, "Let's try it, Mr. President. Mr. President, really, I hope he doesn't accept so you won't have the mess and the unpleasantness to go through. If he turns it down, that's fine. That's best. That's what I hope the answer is. Send it." He told me to go ahead. I walked out of there and thought, "I hope I did the right thing." In the end, Truman didn't accept the invitation. The trip to Europe was the excuse, saying this and that, a sloppy response. It was his way to get out of the obligation and he got out. The President never told me "I told you so" even though he had every right to, but that was all right. I felt very good about it.

As a matter of fact, I went back and did it all over once again on the day that the second unknown soldier–the Korean War one–was honored at Arlington Cemetery. I told the President, "That's Harry Truman's war. What's more proper than having him there, riding with you in the car to Arlington Cemetery? Perfect. And Bess and Mamie in the follow-up car–perfect–and you will be hailed from coast to coast for doing it." I thought, Truman couldn't turn that down, but he did. Later he was asked on the gangplank of a ship as he was boarding, "Why hasn't Eisenhower ever invited you to the White House, Mr. President?" He said, "I don't know; I guess he doesn't like me." He made that response even though this was the second invitation he had turned down. But the point it, Ike overcame his intense revulsion toward Truman to proffer those two invitations, and I can tell you that is factual because I was personally involved. I don't know why no one has probed into it, but there it is.

MR. THOMPSON: It will be there for the future in our little book. I think that is a terribly revealing story.

MR. HARLOW: Have you seen it written anywhere?

MR. THOMPSON: No.

MR. HARLOW: It is one honest, unwritten story of two presidents as far as I know.

MR. THOMPSON: Could I ask one more question on his political attitude? Greenstein advances the idea of the hidden hand. He states that Eisenhower was continuously involved politically, but he did not want anyone to know it and that he studiously avoided any public perception of him as being politically engaged.

MR. HARLOW: I disagree with that. I don't like to say it. I think the world of Fred Greenstein, but I will tell you why I disagree. There may be some truth in it, but the best way to answer that, I think, is to refer to a press conference answer he gave one time. He was asked why it was that he was not truly a Republican, apparently, as far as the American people were concerned. Was he trying not to be, or what? That was what they were implying—you really are not a Republican, are you, Mr. President? He answered somewhat testily. He said, "I don't know the answer myself. I'm a Republican president. I send Republican programs to the Congress of the United States. I request Republican support. I advertise for Republican support. I go across the country and speak for and demand Republican help. And still they say I'm not a Republican, that I don't try to be a Republican. You answer that, I can't." This is an approximation of his response, and it was true. In 1954 and 1958 he campaigned from the White House, on the road, and out in the country much harder for the congressional candidates of his party than any of the earlier "political" presidents. He never was so regarded, that is true. He participated very actively but nevertheless received little or no credit for it, one main reason being that the Republican party itself never quite felt he was one of them. That was a tough problem. He wanted to be an accepted Republican; he tried hard to be; he tried hard to rebuild the party that had been decimated by the New Deal years.

MR. THOMPSON: One of your predecessors in our Portrait series said that he was actually hurt that Dick Nixon did not call on him more often to speak on his behalf.

MR. HARLOW: Well, I know a good bit about that. I was jerked off Nixon's campaign. Eisenhower and Nixon threw me into Nixon's campaign where I did not want to be because I was burned out by eight White House years. I had tried to quit, but I was thrown into the campaign with Dick Nixon, to whom I was very close. I was made his speechwriter, and we careened around the country back in that campaigning business again. What a way to go! Then comes the time for Eisenhower to make his coming-out speech. It had been carefully timed by Leonard Hall and Dick Nixon and Bill Rogers and Fred Seaton, I believe, although I do not know for certain. They had timed it late in the campaign on purpose so Nixon would not appear as Eisenhower's little boy. Nixon was aware that he had a serious problem with that image, and he did not want to appear as Ike's lackey. Understandably, he wanted to be his own man, but that was a mistake, I believe, in hindsight. So when it came time, Ike was going to make his coming-out speech on a Friday in Philadelphia according to their plan. Ike called up and told me to get right back to the White House and write the speech for him. So he snatched me off the Nixon campaign, much to Nixon's distress. I told Nixon—he was upset over it and said I should not leave until midweek, or something like that. I said, "Dick, you know better than that. You don't write a speech for Ike in a day or two. He'll edit the thing ten times. I'll be working all night every night from the time I start doing it. If you think this is a trip I'll enjoy, you're mistaken; it's going to half kill me. You ought to be very glad I'm doing it, though, because he'll deliver the speech I write for him, so you'll get a good hot speech. This is worth far more to you than my wandering around the prairies with you. This will do you some real good."

So I went back and reported to the President at about 7:30 Monday morning. The President said, "We sure got to have a good speech; I don't like the way the campaign is going at all. Something isn't going right. We've got to get this going." He was so eager to get involved he could hardly stand it. He told me that he could not get in earlier because, "It is Dick's campaign, not mine. I'm very sensitive to that. I will not do anything he doesn't want me to do. He's going to have to tell me what he wants me to do, and I'll do that." He was almost pathetically eager to do it. So we wrote a hot speech that he gave in Philadelphia, and it went over very well with a stodgy audience in tuxes—a horrible political spectacle. Then Nixon used him more after that, used him in fact much more than he expected to as he realized his fortunes were endangered. By this time, though, he was running headlong against Mamie Eisenhower, who had turned into a tigress protecting Ike. She wasn't about to let politicians destroy her President, so she would scratch and scream every time they tried to put him back on the road. I agreed with her. It wasn't an easy time.

The story, you see, is correct. Eisenhower was desperately eager to get into the campaign and would have liked to have helped much more than he did. Dick Nixon wrote about that. He said he did not lean on Ike because he was asked not to do it by Ike's doctor and Mamie. I must accept that as true.

MR. THOMPSON: You used the phrase *rebuilding the party*. One of the things that has absolutely baffled me is that we have held numerous sessions with the people you know who have come in and who give us very perceptive accounts of Eisenhower. Our Forums are part university and part community leaders who have come together with our visitors. The only community people who have stayed away are the far, far right, and to them a discussion on Dwight Eisenhower is more repugnant than a discussion of Harry Truman, Franklin Roosevelt—you name the president. They quote *Human Events* and other papers carrying the John Birch line on

Dwight Eisenhower. Did he ever have any view of how you might deal with the far, far right?

MR. HARLOW: He thought they were kooks. That is why they don't like him. He said there were extremists in both parties that were necessary to make the parties find the middle.

MR. THOMPSON: So he let them alone.

MR. HARLOW: You have to have perimeters to find a center. He had little patience with political extremists. He thought they endangered our system. He had little patience with the left. He was surprisingly conservative. The only time he was relaxedly happy in the presidency was 1958 to 1960. He was never really happy before. He liked the last two years because he just threw bombs at will; he was himself. He was not going to run again, he was getting out of the troublesome business. He was Ike straight away, and he turned out to be a hard conservative. He said what he thought ought to be done in this country, to what and to whom. He stood for what he thought he should stand for; he didn't shade it. He whaled away. He had a bully time. He was his own man. He was still under the doctor's orders to keep Cabinet meetings absolutely quiet, so he would go to meetings with agendas so watered down it was ridiculous. You could not so much as hiccup because everyone said you should not upset the President. So what did he do? Leadership meetings with the Congress became his way out, first because the doctor had not thought about that, and second, because we could not control the agenda very well. We had to let the leaders participate in the agenda, and we would prepare a red hot agenda and sit down and fight it out, and Ike would love it. He would get in and throw his weight around and argue to beat the band, and Dirksen, Halleck, and everyone else would have a wonderful time.

He enjoyed those last two years, but he did not like the hard right. He thought they were counterproductive. He did not like the hard left, either, for the same reason. But I don't have to remind you that he never attacked anyone by name of the right or left because he had too much sense. President Truman did not appreciate that, and he created the ogre of Joe McCarthy out of a political nobody. Once I rode with Joe McCarthy to Quantico in a bus, side by side with him the whole distance, thinking he was a Senate staff member. Not until we got off the bus at Quantico did I realize he was McCarthy from Wisconsin. Even so, back then he did not amount to a hill of beans. I was the senior veteran in a bus-ride discussion; he was the junior. I had been around Washington endless years, and he did not know much. Truman attacked him personally, by name. Thereby he created a monster. Eisenhower killed him simply by ignoring him. The press almost went wild trying to force Eisenhower to attack him. There was White House staff friction over this, but Ike didn't bite. He would not attack McCarthy by name. The result proved him right.

MR. THOMPSON: That was his own idea and own style—no one had to tell him?

MR. HARLOW: That was his style. It was again this business of understanding the use of power. He had had a lesson in this when he was in command of NATO—he criticized the Belgian government once and it fell. He told me about that. It frightened him. It was the first time he realized what he had become. He was no longer Dwight D. Eisenhower—he was a figure of immense influence. He never did that again. So he learned that he had to be careful in using such power.

MR. THOMPSON: He got that from experience. He didn't read Acton about abuse of power?

MR. HARLOW: No. It wasn't that absolute power corrupts absolutely. Great power can be benign. Acton was too severe with that. Great power can do immense good. He said it corrupts absolutely; it can, but it doesn't have to.

There are three experiences I had with Eisenhower that I treasure, which I will give to you. It is a window into the soul of Eisenhower and to his motivation on things. They were all in 1954 when I was doing his writing.

Bryce Harlow

The first one was in respect to Dixon-Yates, the first "scandal" Ike had to deal with in his administration, and it involved, of all people, his own budget director, and it was a very embarrassing, troublesome thing. Everyone cried, "Let's not get Ike in the mess." So we went to him, Jim Hagerty and all of us, with a press release on Dixon-Yates. It was a mealy-mouthed thing, sort of lame, sheer bureaucratic blather. The President read it. Hagerty handed him this proposed release, and he threw it across the room. He said, "Now, listen boys. You go out now and sit down and write exactly what happened, whatever it was. You bring it in to me and I will issue that, whatever the facts are. The story will be dead and gone in three days. You issue this thing and it will destroy us all." Nonpolitical? An insensitive general?

Number two: I wrote a press release for him. It had to be issued quickly, and I wrote up a legal-size, double-space statement, and we came running to give it to him. I sat down beside him, and he then picked up his pen, struck out a word, handed the paper to me, and said, "Bryce, I want to explain what I did there. I struck out the word *deliberately*. Let me tell you something: Don't ever attack a man's motives because he will never forgive you for that. You can attack his judgment forever, you can argue with him forever, and he will respect you for that. Remember that in the future writing for me."

The final example is this: I came to him with a "last" draft of a speech, and we went through it for about the tenth time. I thought it was all wrapped up and ready to go, but suddenly he came to the end of it and said, "I can't say that, and I want to explain to you why so you won't have this problem in the future. You said that "with the help of God"—I never say that. I won't say that. I don't believe that. I believe that the Lord deals us a hand, that's right, but he expects *us* to play it." That is almost an exact quote; that is an insight.

Again, decentralization of power, under him a reflection of the fact that he was a public servant. His approach to this was very different from other presidents. He was selfless in the presidency and we only rarely see that. His White House staff was a reflection of it, too. Here was a man who had 45 years of experience in

THE "COMPLEAT" PRESIDENT: DWIGHT DAVID EISENHOWER

government before he became president. He brought in seasoned people to serve as aides.

You see, Carter could probably have been reelected. Reagan might have lost if Carter had done similarly, for two reasons: number one, his staff would have protected Carter from his difficulties—every president has them—if they had been seasoned by experience; number two, Carter could have done it if he had had enough sense to be presidential. I don't mean to kick him, but he manifested himself to be a small-bore politician, and he beat himself in 1980.

III.

VIEWS FROM THE CABINET

~ *Six* ~

THE PRESIDENT AND
THE SECRETARY OF STATE REVISITED*

Dean Rusk

NARRATOR: It is a great pleasure to welcome you to another Miller Center Forum. It is a matter of personal satisfaction that we are able to have with us this morning the Honorable Dean Rusk. One of the themes of the Miller Center has been the relation between theory and practice, a long-time interest of Mr. Rusk. Another theme that has been sounded again and again around this table is the question of overloading the executive and the need for devoting presidential time to the fundamental issues of the government. Mr. Rusk in his article, "The "President," in the April 1960 issue of *Foreign Affairs*, says much the same thing:

> The President must prepare himself for those solemn moments when after all of the advice is in from any quarter he must descend his lonely pinnacle and decide what we must do. It is in this realization, not in petty criticism, that we can be jealous of his time and energy and resistant to every influence which comes between the man and his burdens.

In one sense Dean Rusk needs no introduction. He certainly has been before you as a public figure for several decades. But, as I watched the public figure, I missed certain qualities that I knew were present in the man himself. One was his enormous generosity

---

*Presented in a Forum at the Miller Center of Public Affairs on 4 February 1980. Reprinted from *The Virginia Papers on the Presidency* (Washington, D.C.: University Press of America, Inc., 1980), Volume III.

and kindness to his colleagues; another was his abiding interest in younger people. In my opinion we have had few public servants who have devoted themselves so selflessly to the national interest and concerns of the public and asked so little in return by way of ongoing, continuous public flattery and attention.

It is a great pleasure to have as our topic this morning the subject of "The President and the Secretary of State," because this too is in keeping with our central concern at the Miller Center. It is a subject on which Mr. Rusk, perhaps before he knew that he would have any responsibility in this area, had addressed himself.

SECRETARY RUSK: Certainly before I knew!

NARRATOR: It is a great honor to have you with us.

SECRETARY RUSK: Thank you, Ken, and thank all of you for being here. I am delighted to have a chance to visit the Miller Center, both because of my long friendship with my former colleague, Ken Thompson, and because of the attention that you are giving to the study of the presidency. It is very important, timely, and will be very productive.

Just a footnote on the article that some of you have looked over again; this was the first of three lectures at the Council on Foreign Relations in New York. The first was on the presidency, the second on the Congress, and the third on the Department of State. This was the only one of the three that was published. These were given at a time when the last thing in the world that could have been in my mind was that I might be asked to serve as secretary of state. A kind Providence caused me to procrastinate so long that the articles on the Congress and the Department of State never appeared. I would have gotten some rather gruff questions in my confirmation hearing had the one on the Congress been out in print. I thought that at some point, I might want to revisit this particular article in the light of experience of eight years in the Cabinet. But if you define the major inadequacies of this article in its treatment of the Congress or the Department of State, this is because there were two other lectures that followed it.

Dean Rusk

When we think of a president, we think of a moving target. Let me just go back through my own memory and list some names that I can remember. As I do so, please reflect for a moment on the extraordinary differences among the people I will name: Woodrow Wilson, Warren Harding, Calvin Coolidge, Herbert Hoover, Franklin Roosevelt, Harry Truman, Dwight Eisenhower, John F. Kennedy, Lyndon Johnson, Richard Nixon, Gerald Ford, Jimmy Carter. What extraordinary diversity among those people! About the only thing they had in common was that they were white, male, American citizens over 35 years of age, and each became President of the United States. Generalizations about the president are pretty tricky. Franklin Roosevelt was not the president that Calvin Coolidge was, John F. Kennedy was not the president that Lyndon Johnson was—I'm not putting that in any particular order. We are talking about birds on the wing.

Then, circumstances play a major role, as with the Great Depression in Franklin Roosevelt's years. I was sitting with President Kennedy when he called in about 30 congressional leaders late one Monday afternoon to tell them about the Cuban Missile Crisis, what he proposed to do about it, and what he was going to say in two hours in a television speech to the nation. No senator or congressman present raised any question whatever about the President's authority to bring us to the brink of a possible nuclear war. At that moment, the prevailing feeling around the table was expressed to me by two or three of them on the way out: "Thank God, I'm not the President of the United States!" So, circumstance has a lot to do with the office and how it operates.

John F. Kennedy did not feel that he had a mandate in the election of 1960; he was elected by a few tens of thousands of votes. He used to say the votes of Cook County, Illinois. So he was very cautious about selecting the items on which he was prepared to do battle, particularly with the Congress. He was much more cautious than many people think, given his other attributes, whereas Lyndon Johnson, with his massive vote in 1964, put through the Congress a formidable legislative program because the circumstances of his office were different.

I would suggest that we often overlook the fact, or sometimes play down the fact, that the United States has the most complicated constitutional and political system of any nation in the world—at least since the Dalai Lama was driven out of Tibet by the Chinese. I think his was probably more complicated. The late Chief Justice Earl Warren visited the University of Georgia Law School shortly before his death, and on that occasion said that if each branch of the federal government were to pursue its own constitutional authority to the end of the trail, our system simply could not function. It would freeze up like an engine without oil. So when we think of anyone who is in our federal government, one thinks of this constitutional complexity that forces us to try to reach a consensus, with all of the adjustments, compromises, and effort that it takes. One must think of the extraordinary amount of time that is required just to make the system work. The president's secretary of state spends more than half of his time on the domestic arrangements that are required to have a policy before he talks to the foreigner at all. I don't know of any other foreign minister in the world of whom that is true.

Since we are talking about relations between the president and the secretary of state, we might note in passing that foreign policy is that part of our public business that we ourselves cannot control. Subject to certain self-imposed constitutional limitations, we can pretty much do what we want to do within our own borders. But when we go outside our national frontiers, we find almost 160 other nations out there, living in different parts of the world, to whom the very globe itself looks different. Each has its own history, aspirations, and problems. No one salutes when we speak. It is a world not of command but of adjustment, compromise, and negotiation, of differences of views, confrontation, and in tragic moments, of violence. So the secretary of state and the State Department will never be popular with the American people nor most of the time with an American president. Too often you are having to say to the president, "Sorry, Mr. President, you can't have it that way because these funny foreigners won't do it that way." Presidents don't like to hear that, and some of them don't like to hear it more than others (I'm thinking of LBJ, for example). There are elements of disappointment and frustration built into the very nature of our foreign policy, and that has some bearing on the relation between the president and the secretary of state.

Dean Rusk

Let's start at the beginning. One of the most neglected sentences in our society is the first sentence of Article II of the Constitution. "The executive power shall be vested in a President of the United States of America." Now, "a President of the United States," is singular. There is only one president. It is the president who is elected by all of the people to give direction to the executive branch of the government within the laws and the Constitution. On occasion I have heard senators and congressmen talk about the powers of Congress, because they are the representative branch. Surely that needs a small footnote because the Congress is a representative branch only for those matters entrusted to the Congress by our Constitution and in no other sense. Surely it is the president that is the representative branch for those matters that are entrusted to the president under our Constitution. The president is the only one elected by all of the people trying to give direction to the executive branch of government.

That means there should not be, constitutionally, something called democracy within the bureaucracy. If these people below the president in the executive branch who are not elected by the people to make policy decisions do not accept the direction of the president, then the fundamental democratic process, the election of the president, is frustrated. I, therefore, draw a very sharp distinction between what should happen before and what should happen after a decision is made. Before a decision is made, everyone in the executive branch who is involved owes the president a full and frank and candid exposition of the issues. Presidents are well advised to take special pains to be sure that they hear different points of views. No one serves the president well by screening from him points of view that he or she thinks the president would not wish to hear. But after all the information is in and after the president has finally come to his conclusion, then it seems to me that those in the executive branch have a constitutional duty to accept the guidance of the president, whether they are in uniform or whether they are in civilian clothes.

George Marshall had a very clear sense of these relationships. If I quote him two or three times today, it is not through pretentiousness or with the thought that I am another George Marshall, but because I was a student of his and I learned a good

THE PRESIDENT AND THE SECRETARY OF STATE REVISITED

many things from him. George Marshall was once asked by a friend, "Well, what is your personal opinion, Mr. Secretary, on this particular matter?" He said, "Personal opinion? While I'm secretary of state, I don't have any personal opinions. My opinions are the opinions of the United States government and I reach those through the constitutional process."

On another occasion President Truman pulled the rug out from under him pretty hard on a matter involving Palestine, and some of Marshall's friends told him they thought he ought to resign. He said, "No, gentlemen, you don't take a post of this sort and then resign when the man who has the constitutional responsibility for making a decision makes one. You can resign at any other time for any other reason or no reason at all, but not for that reason." My particular view is that within the executive branch, if someone is not prepared to accept the guidance of the president, they are in the wrong racket. They ought to get out of the government and do something else, oppose it, if they wish, from the outside. It is fundamental to our system that the president give that direction within the laws and the Constitution.

Today is a working day in the Department of State. Some 3,000 cables will go out of that department to our posts and to other governments all over the world. A considerable number of those cables will be based, not upon personal direction from the president and the secretary of state, but on law. A much larger percentage of those cables will have their content determined by law rather than by something called policy guidance emanating out of the White House or the seventh floor of the State Department. So, the law is very important. If there are times when a president asks you to do something that is contrary to the law, then he has a problem and you have a problem.

President Kennedy once asked me to spend some money on a particular matter. My lawyers and I concluded that there was no appropriation that would provide funds for any such purpose. It would be unlawful for us to spend for that purpose. So, I called the attorney general, whose name was Bobby Kennedy. I did not get much help from him because all he said was, "Well, if you go to prison your salary will continue while you are in prison." I reported back to the president that I simply could not make the expenditure because we had no appropriation to cover it, and he did not pursue the matter. That issue can arise on more important matters.

There is something that I think is anathema in our kind of governmental system, something called "New Deal resignations." Some of you will recall that during the FDR period it was more or less customary for various and sundry people to go in periodically and offer their resignation to Franklin Roosevelt, either to get a fresh vote of confidence or to bring some pressure to bear on the president to take their particular point of view in some dispute. I don't think that such resignations should be allowed to operate as leverage on a president or indeed on a secretary of state. George Marshall brought that to an end as far as the State Department was concerned. One of the senior officers of the Department, shortly after Marshall became secretary, a man who had been active in the New Deal, came in to see Secretary Marshall and said, "Now, Mr. Secretary, here is what I think we must do on this." Then he added, "If you don't think you would like to do it this way, I don't think that I could be of much use around this department and so I would have to resign." Secretary Marshall said, "Well, Mr. _____, whether you or I work for the government of the United States has no bearing whatever on the merits of this question. So let's remove this irrelevancy. I accept your resignation, effective now. Now that that is done, let's put it aside. If you are willing to spend a little time with me on the merits of this question, I will be grateful."

Since I was the senior officer in the Cabinet, Lyndon Johnson used to talk to me from time to time about some of my fellow Cabinet officers. On one occasion, one of my fellow Cabinet officers told the President that unless he did so and so that he would have to resign, and President Johnson said, "Well, be in my office this afternoon at 3:00 with your letter of resignation." At 3:00 that afternoon, the Cabinet officer came in with an apology rather than a letter of resignation.

The secretary of state serves at the pleasure of the president, and that is a very extensive word. Mr. Vance is our 57th secretary of state, Mr. Carter is our 39th president. A little arithmetic will show you that being secretary of state is a hazardous occupation. Mr. Truman had four. Woodrow Wilson had three primary ones. So, secretaries of state under our constitutional system are there at the behest of the president. The Senate, of course, has some control over the door marked "entrance," but it has no control over the door marked "exit." That relationship is fundamental.

Dean Acheson once remarked that in the relationship between the president and the secretary of state, it was of the greatest importance that both of them understood at all times that one is president. Sometimes that can be forgotten. Mr. James Byrnes, for example, forgot that about Harry Truman and Harry Truman was the wrong president to be forgetful about. Sometimes the secretary of state will have an independent political base: William Jennings Bryan, Cordell Hull, James Byrnes. That does not always work out very well because of the underlying and fundamental constitutional relationship.

Nevertheless, I think it is well for Cabinet officers to have a measure of independence in their relations with the president, at least enough to cause the president to have to think about what the Cabinet officers say to them. How do we achieve that? The Dutch have an interesting way of doing it. I have not checked lately to see whether it is still in effect, but in the Netherlands when someone joins the Cabinet, from that moment on they are guaranteed a full year's pay when they leave the Cabinet. This is sometimes referred to as the "go to hell fund." It seems to give a little measure of independence to the Cabinet officer under those circumstances. I think in our system the key thing would be that a president know that a secretary of state is not trying to hang on to the job, but that he is ready to go at a moment's notice. I tried to make it very clear to both President Kennedy and President Johnson that I would be happy to take my departure at any time they wanted me to do so; and that, I think, is the way the relationship ought to be.

In the old days the secretary of state was looked upon as someone who was on the way up the political ladder. Well, that little complication no longer exists. It has been almost 150 years since a secretary of state has become president. Over the Department of State is a sign with the famous words of Dante: "Abandon hope all ye who enter here." If anyone is interested in the political process, he is out of his mind to take on the job of secretary of state, particularly because elements of disappointment and frustration are built into the nature of our foreign policy. That

Dean Rusk

idea of political ambition is something that is pretty far behind us now.

Of course, a president and secretary of state should officially be very close. Should that extend to their personal relationships, to something called genuine personal friendship? Well, one has to be a little careful about that. Again, George Marshall felt very strongly that personal relations should never be allowed to intrude into public policy matters. You should never approve or disapprove a recommendation because Bill or Joe made it. He went to some pains to keep himself at arms length, for example, with Franklin Roosevelt. On one occasion at least, when Franklin Roosevelt called him "George," he said, "It's General Marshall, Mr. President." Secretary Marshall always called us by our last names, never by our first names. He very rarely complimented anyone who was still working under him, although he could be very generous when that relationship no longer existed. I suspect he had in his mind that he might at any time as a matter of public duty have to fire someone. He did not want personal relationships standing in the way.

I was very close to President Kennedy, for example, but I never played touch football; I never got pushed into Ethel's swimming pool. I laughed at Bobby Kennedy when he tried to get me to go on a 50-mile Cabinet hike. I reminded him that when I was a captain of infantry, if I had taken my company on a 50-mile hike without proper conditioning, I would have been courtmartialed. So, I was never a part of the Kennedy social circle, although the relationship officially was very close indeed.

There must be instant and ready access to the president on the part of the secretary of state. The president is free to seek and get advice from anyone in the wide world, from his chauffeur if he wants to, from senators, congressmen, people in the media, political leaders in the precincts, around the countryside. But he must always be available to, and hear the views of, the secretary of state. I personally think it would be intolerable if a Cabinet officer had to get the permission of a White House staff person to see the president. In my own case I had access to President Kennedy and President Johnson at any time, and that sometimes included 3:00 in the morning. The world is round, and at any given time only a third of the world is asleep and the other two-thirds are likely to be up to some mischief somewhere; you have to be able to be in touch with the president in the middle of the night.

Dean Acheson once was asked about the primary qualification for a secretary of state. He said, "a killer instinct." What he meant by that was that the secretary of state must never let anyone get between him and the president. President Eisenhower once named Harold Stassen to be a Special Assistant for Peace at the White House to work on disarmament. It took Foster Dulles about six months to get him out of there. Then President Eisenhower named Nelson Rockefeller to the White House staff so he could keep an eye on Latin American problems. It took six months to get him out. The secretary of state must be very jealous about access to the president and the right to be heard by the president.

This raises a question about White House staff, and I will just hit it quickly because I have a very deep bias on the subject. I think the president makes a great mistake if he fails to keep White House staff people in a *staff* relationship. It is a great mistake to inject White House staff people into the chain of command. A Cabinet officer, for example, has a five-foot shelf of law governing his department and his policies. He is the one who goes down to the Congress to meet with its committees and subcommittees. He spends an enormous amount of time there. He is the one who holds press conferences and the one who gets out in the country and makes speeches and answers questions. Those things are not true of White House staff. They do not go to the Congress and have themselves raked over the coals by senators and congressmen. They do not carry the same kind of responsibility. So I would be concerned about any development that would tend to inject White House staff into the chain of command.

I think Henry Kissinger would now agree with me on that. He demonstrated that he did not think the arrangement in the first part of the Nixon administration was very good because when he became secretary of state, he held on to the other job so there would not be another Kissinger in the White House. I have heard him say since he left office that the arrangement there in the early 1970s was not the right arrangement.

We should bear in mind that the conduct of foreign relations is a mass business. We sometimes hear about presidents being their own secretary of state. That is nonsense, partly because the secretary of state cannot be his own secretary of state. Look at those 3,000 cables going out of the Department of State today; they all bear the signature of the secretary. For those out on the receiving end of these cables, I am sure one of their favorite indoor games is to figure out which ones the secretary actually saw and who in the Department of State actually sent them out. The secretary of state may see six or seven before they go out. The president may see one or two. The rest of them go out on the basis of authority delegated to literally hundreds of officers in the Department of State who have the authority to send out cables with the signature of the secretary of state. The government must get on with the day's work.

Today the United States is attending somewhere between 12 and 20 multilateral, intergovernmental conferences somewhere in the world. I do not have to count today because this happens on every working day throughout the year. Anywhere from 700 to 900 of these conferences are held in the course of a year. Each one requires a delegation, sent out with position papers coordinated among the interested departments. Delegation of authority in such instances is not only good technique, it is sheer necessity.

Some people are more comfortable with delegation than are others. President Truman believed that George Marshall was the greatest living American and delegated very extensively to him. Marshall himself believed very strongly in delegation and so he would delegate downward into the Department to those in whom he had confidence. Marshall as secretary of state would do those things that only the secretary can do. If anyone else could do them, he would expect them to do it, and he would go home about 4:30 or 5:00 every afternoon. I suspect that was a better way to do it than the way I tended to do it when I got there.

Delegation is important, and therefore the secretary of state must give a great deal of thought to how the troops find out what is expected of them in matters of policy. Let me throw out a little figure that none of you will believe. Two million, one hundred thousand cables went out of the Department of State with my name signed to them. I had seen only a fraction of 1 percent of them before they were sent. I can remember, however, only about four or five of them that had to be called back and rewritten and turned around because those who sent them out had failed to get the point of policy that the president or I wished them to follow. To me that was an extraordinary professional performance by those in the Department of State.

How can that come about? There are a number of guidelines that everyone takes for granted that have not been very well articulated. Someday, someone might want to try an article—I might try one myself—on what these guidelines are. For example, junior officers in the Department of State do not have to go up to the seventh floor to find out that we prefer to see disputes settled by peaceful means rather than by violence or that we pay attention to domestic law and international law. As a matter of fact, no one in the executive branch below the president is likely to make a decision that would put us in violation of international law. If you go back over the postwar period and take note of situations where you think we were in violation of international law, my guess is you will be talking about presidential decisions. These officers know that we give effect to our treaties, 7,000 or more of them, in our relations with other countries. There are many such guidelines that one does not really have to ask about every day.

There are meetings, sometimes interminable meetings, in which matters are discussed, morning staff meetings in the State Department with the secretary of state, or particular meetings throughout the day with different officers from the Department. I think I managed my own time rather badly because my appointment books—which are now in the LBJ Library in Austin—showed that on average, I met with individuals or groups about 30 times a day on every working day. I am not sure that is the efficient way to use management time, but you did get to many people that way. (Incidentally in passing, there is a little problem that I will mention. If you meet 30 times a day on different subjects, this means that 29 times during the day you have to unload your mind of one whole set of data, criteria and thought processes, and reload it for the next meeting. I suspect that such change of subjects exacts a toll in nervous energy.)

There are also meetings, press conferences, speeches. Sometimes officers of the Department learn about policy by listening to a press conference. I remember coming back from a press conference once and one of my colleagues mentioned a response I had made to a particular question, and he said, "That's not our policy." I just smiled at him and said, "It is now." Presidents very frequently set a policy, set a policy framework or tone, for the government by what they say in press conferences.

Congressional testimony normally is worked out very carefully in advance because, among other things, they want advance copies. It is cleared around the government and checked out very often with the Bureau of the Budget and the president. There is a kind of process of osmosis that goes on by which these things get passed around. So I really don't think there is too much of a problem in getting the troops informed as to what is expected of them.

I was criticized after I left office by some colleagues who said that they found it difficult to know what I thought about particular problems. Well, this was a habitual procedure of mine that may or may not have been a good idea. I did not wish to give a premature indication of my own views because I did not want to distort the discussion that might go on over the merits of that issue. There is some tendency in the bureaucracy to favor what seems to be expected of them from on top. Secretary Marshall again would expect us to present his views before he would give his. He wanted to know what we thought.

Domestic politics—of course foreign and domestic policy is an unbroken skein, as one merges into the other—and foreign policy cannot be separated. Yet to what extent or at what stage should foreign policy matters be considered against the background of domestic politics? Mr. Truman once took the extreme view. He said to the State Department: "I don't want to get recommendations from the State Department based upon domestic political considerations. In the first place, good policy is good politics. I want to know what you think good policy would be. Second, you fellows in the State Department don't know a damn thing about domestic politics, and I don't want amateurs fooling around with important business." That was somewhat of an extreme view. My own personal hunch is that at the level of presidential appointees one must begin to try to put oneself in the shoes of the president and help him think about the totality of his job, about all of the hats that he wears simultaneously. Nevertheless, the secretary of state must try to concentrate on the foreign policy issues.

Normally, in this postwar period, foreign policy has not been partisan, as between the political parties. It has been my privilege to have attended literally hundreds of meetings of committees and subcommittees of Congress, and on no single occasion have I ever seen differences turn on party lines, Democrats versus Republicans. There were differences, because on many occasions, the issues are complicated and require on-balance, razor-edged judgments on which honest men and women can disagree. I have never seen those differences turn on party lines. I personally think there is a good deal of strength in that fact. Every four years the two political parties go through a considerable agony in drafting party platforms about foreign policy in which they do their best to say something: (a) that sounds good, and (b) that sounds a little different from the other party. I have sat in hundreds of meetings in the government where decisions were made in both Democratic and Republican administrations, and I have never heard anyone say, "Let's get out the party platform and see what it has to say about this." These are quadrennial wonders, and that is the end of it as far as policy is concerned. Platform generalities have little relation to the many-faceted problems of the real world.

Ensuring that the president is informed is a vitally important matter. The president must also spend an enormous amount of time keeping himself informed. I don't know anyone in the country who has a more diverse network of information coming into him than the President of the United States. It takes a great deal of time. Yet there isn't time for the president to take a look at 3,000 cables a day, either incoming or outgoing. A constant flow of information goes over to the president from the intelligence community, State Department, and Defense Department, including information that does not compel a decision on any particular day. Much of the flow is in the nature of preparing the president for things that might come later. Our practice during the 1960s was to send to the president a page or two every day that contained a series of short items, maybe two or three sentences long, telling him what we had done during the day and what we were proposing to do in the next day or two on various matters. This helped to keep the president from being surprised by what he read in the papers and to give him a chance to pull something onto his desk if he wanted to get into it.

This matter of which questions go to the secretary of state and which questions go to the president is part of the art of the business. I do not know of any criteria by which that can surely be determined. At the assistant-secretary level in the Department of State, that is one of the crucial questions. Can we go ahead and act upon this or does it have to go upstairs? The secretary is daily having to make judgments about whether or not he should be in touch with the president on a particular issue. It takes a good deal of working together over a period of time to resolve that question.

I personally believe that if there is going to be an effective relationship between the president and the secretary of state, there must be a high degree of confidentiality in their communication with each other. I believe the president is entitled to have no blue sky showing between him and his secretary of state on foreign policy questions. As President Kennedy once put it, domestic questions can only lose elections, but foreign policy questions can kill us all. The question of confidentiality is of considerable importance. When I first became secretary of state, I found, holding over from previous practice, that when I talked to the president over the phone, someone in the outer office would listen in and jot down a very short memo on the conversation that would then be circulated to anyone in the State Department who was supposed to be involved in that question. That went on for some time before I discovered that it was even happening. I stopped the practice and used a phone in my own office to talk with the president that could not be cut in on by anyone in the outer office. I never wrote memos of conversations between myself and President Kennedy or President Johnson. I did not come home at night and write diaries about the day. I thought if the presidents wanted their own record—and they usually had note-takers at these meetings—that was up to them. I had a certain aversion to the practice of some that I have seen in the past (for example, Mr. Forrestal) who seemed to be building up their own record over and against the president.

Similarly, we would have meetings, such as National Security Council and Cabinet meetings, with as many people as are sitting in this room. Everyone wants to be there; it is prestige, it is fun, and it is exciting to sit in on a National Security Council meeting or Cabinet meeting. Arthur Schlesinger wrote in his book, *A Thousand Days* that in those meetings, I used to sit like an old Buddha without saying anything. He was quite accurate in that statement because when people like Arthur Schlesinger were in the room, I kept my mouth shut. My arrangement would be that I would meet with the president either before or after such a meeting, often with Bob McNamara, just the three of us. We would discuss what had come up or what was coming up before any final decision was made. You will find, when someday you get access to the notes on the famous Tuesday luncheon sessions with President Johnson, that the conversation was very candid, the disputes were very sharp, and there was full and free discussion. We knew that the people sitting around that table were not going off and talking to the *Washington Post* and the *New York Times*. I am quite sure that being in the public glare inhibits the frankness and candor of discussion.

I have gone on much too long already, but I have not discussed the Congress. The secretary of state flies on four engines: his relations with the president, his relations with the Congress, his relations with the Department of State and other departments of government, and his relations with the press and public opinion. Of course, the most critical one in terms of whether he is secretary of state or not is his relations with the president. In the case of the other three, he is a delegate of the president. He has some very definite obligations to be sure that the president has a full look at all of the issues before he comes to a decision. Let me stop here so you can raise any questions about the president-secretary of state relationship or how it ramifies in other directions.

QUESTION: From the article, I got the impression that you did not want the President to ever go to a summit meeting, and then right away President Kennedy went to Vienna. I assume you tried to talk him out of it.

SECRETARY RUSK: I think every secretary of state is going to be dubious about negotiations at the summit, partly because there is not time at the summit for the kind of detailed, careful, precise discussion and formulation that good negotiations usually require. If there is not time at the summit, the American president is at a disadvantage, because when he goes to one of these meetings, expectations are built up that he is going to come back with a success, so he is under pressure to produce a result. The other side may not be under such pressure. Then there is the problem as to when you bring the court of last resort into session. It could well have been disastrous if Chairman Khrushchev and President Kennedy had met face-to-face during the Cuban Missile Crisis. The trouble is that presidents do not agree with secretaries of state on this. There is something about the chemistry of being president that causes many of them to think that if they just sit down with someone, they can straighten everything out. So we will have summit meetings. Now, let's exclude goodwill meetings; there is no problem there. I am talking about negotiations at the summit.

President Carter went to Camp David with President Sadat and Prime Minister Begin. He had run out of other options. Other procedures did not seem to be very promising, and the situation in the Middle East was becoming more and more dangerous. But, more important, he was willing to invest *time*. He spent over ten days there with them in what President Sadat, with a smile, called "house arrest." This was an exception that proves what was said in my article about some of the dangers of summitry.

I, personally, was not enthusiastic about the Vienna summit in June 1961, and I think the results were negative. I don't happen to agree with Mr. Kennan and one or two others who thought that President Kennedy should have responded to Mr. Khrushchev's long, ideological opening with a long, ideological reply. Instead, President Kennedy said, "Mr. Chairman, you're not going to make a communist out of me, and I'm not going to make a capitalist out of you, so why don't we talk about some of our real problems."

I think we should be very careful about attempted negotiations at the summit. They tend to lead, at best, to agreements in principle. George Marshall used to tell us, never agree in principle because all that means is, you haven't agreed yet; wait until you get the fine print spelled out before you know whether you have a meeting of the minds. The Vladivostok agreement between President Ford and Mr. Brezhnev on the 2,400 ceiling for missile

THE PRESIDENT AND THE SECRETARY OF STATE REVISITED

launchers took years to try to put arms and legs on that sort of agreement in principle. I am still dubious about negotiations at the summit.

QUESTION: You mentioned at the outset of your talk the matter if circumstance. Certainly, circumstance is important, but other things are too. Madison was confronted with circumstance but did not come through. What are some intangible factors in a president that enable him to seize circumstances and prove what Sir Robert Menzies used to say, that "every disaster is a compensation"?

SECRETARY RUSK: I can't answer that question. I think certainly there are elements of character that make a difference. It was a happenstance, but a very fortunate one, that Harry Truman had had a lifetime avocation of reading about American presidents. He knew more about earlier presidents and the precedents of the office than anyone I ever knew. It turned out that President Polk was his favorite president. These are almost fortuitous differences, and if we are lucky, we will have a person ready for the circumstances in which he finds himself.

Circumstances also help to produce the man, and train the man. The circumstances that Mr. Truman faced immediately after World War II helped to make Truman into a great president, but there were some qualities that Truman brought to it as well. For example, he had a special knack for oversimplification at the moment of decision. If you think of an important foreign policy question with its dozens and dozens of secondary and tertiary questions, think of it as a great leap of jackstraws all laced together and pointing in different directions. Harry Truman would listen to all of the briefing, and he would study that heap of jackstraws and then decide which one was to him the decisive element. He would pull that jackstraw out of the heap, make his decision, and go home and never look back. Oversimplification at the moment of decision may be a very important factor.

Another matter of circumstance is that at the present time, we make it very difficult indeed for anyone to be president. He is the only one elected by all of the people to try to think and act for the country as a whole. When he tries to do so he finds that he cannot give any group all that it is asking for: the poor, the sick, the aged, big business, small business, the unemployed, organized labor, the cities, the farmers, the military, the blacks, the Spanish-speaking, the Indians; fill out your own list. All of these groups turn to Washington, all of them. Those at the bottom want guaranteed annual income, but if a big bank, a big railway, a big airplane manufacturing company, or a big motor company get in trouble, off to Washington they go to be bailed out. Our appetites have become both insistent and insatiable. We have a $40 billion industry called advertising whose primary, unconfessed purpose is to cause us to be dissatisfied with whatever we have. Add to this inflation of appetite the concentration of demands upon Washington and a president who simply cannot meet all those demands, and you have the certainty of margins of discontent in almost every sector of our society. This involves every president, whoever he is, whatever his name, and whatever his party. We may come out of it under the pressure of circumstance as we begin to think like citizens about society as a whole rather than about our own particular part of it.

QUESTION: In discussions of the presidency, it comes through to me loud and clear that it is next to impossible to handle the job well. That seems to me to come through from your talk and particularly when you added your last remark. Do you think so?

SECRETARY RUSK: I think it is a miracle of our constitutional system that anyone steps forward to want to be president, and I am almost of the conclusion that anyone who steps forward to seek the office is automatically disqualified because it proves that he does not understand the job. Fortunately, there are those who try. For example, the president, more than anyone else in the country, is subject to the *post hoc, propter hoc* fallacy. I can say to you that it is a matter of public record that when I left office, the Dow Jones average dropped 300 points. There is a poll taken every few weeks asking: How do you rate the president in managing the economy? The president doesn't manage the economy; he doesn't have the constitutional power to manage the economy. Asking the question is a fraud on the public, but the First Amendment guarantees the right to perpetrate such nonsense.

THE PRESIDENT AND THE SECRETARY OF STATE REVISITED

So whatever happens in the world, whether a president is a Republican or a Democrat, we tend to hold him responsible, whether or not he has the power to do anything about it or had anything to do with its development. In the early 1950s, we had a national debate on who lost China, as though anyone in this country had China to lose. So this *post hoc, propter hoc* fallacy is something for which presidents have to pay when they take the job.

QUESTION: Would you go so far as to say those who want it should not have it, and those who should have it do not want it?

SECRETARY RUSK: No, not really. We are now in the 18th presidential campaign that I can remember. In one sense it is the most olympian part of our constitutional system, but it also is our quadrennial silly season during which we say some very foolish things to each other to the confusion of our friends and adversaries abroad. I have considerable sympathy for Mr. Khrushchev's complaint that "it's very difficult to deal with you people in the West because someone is always having one of those damn elections." But we will come through it, and next January someone will take the oath of office and the Washington Monument will still be standing.

QUESTION: Following up on the last question, one of your former Cabinet colleagues gave a speech in which, having outlined the difficulties of the presidency and the country, he said:

> In such a world can we long continue to afford the luxury of the division of power and responsibility between our executive and legislative branches of government? I have no pat answer, but I do know that until we are prepared to examine and reexamine the basic structure of our federal system and its functioning rather than indulging ourselves in continuous personal and political recriminations, our problems will remain with us, and in all probability, increase in severity.

Dean Rusk

SECRETARY RUSK: I personally would not want to trade our constitutional system for any other with which I am familiar, and I have seen a good many of them in different parts of the world. It is complicated, but it also has great strength and resilience. I think one of the reasons is that our constitutional system forces us always to be seeking a consensus, at least among those who are carrying responsibility. That is tough at times and sometimes it is disagreeable and irritating, but that necessity of trying to find a consensus I think is an element of strength. People forget, for example, that it was Everett Dirksen, a conservative Republican senator from Illinois, who turned the key that unlocked civil rights legislation in the 1960s.

It is a difficult system. I understand that the Senate Foreign Relations Committee is just now embarking upon a long-term study of American foreign policy. I wish they would start with a long-term study of the foreign policies of the United States Congress and address themselves to the question: What do the American people, and what does the executive branch of the government, at any given time, have a right to believe is the foreign policy of the Congress? This would produce some extraordinarily interesting things. For example, some of you might want to take a look at something called the "Captive Nations Resolution." When I first became secretary of state in the spring of that year, my associates came in and put on my desk a proclamation that I was supposed to send over to the White House. This proclamation would break the Soviet Union into about 11 component parts, including one area that you could not even find in the *Encyclopedia Britannica*. So I asked, "What in the world is this?" My colleagues explained this Captive Nations Resolution to me. Utter nonsense, but it is there.

When Senator Fulbright discussed with the Senate Foreign Relations Committee, just before he left the chairmanship, that they should clean that sort of thing off the books, the reply was: Well, there are senators running for office, and they prefer not to have to vote on that bill. In the Congress you get the most direct representation of what might be called ethnic politics in this country, and there is a great deal of ethnic politics here. That is one further complication in our system.

THE PRESIDENT AND THE SECRETARY OF STATE REVISITED

QUESTION: In your remarks you emphasized at some length the importance of the secretary of state, and the administration generally, supporting a policy decision once it is made. It seems to me that no policy is absolutely perfect. Most of them, even the best, will begin to run into trouble. In the course of time you begin to pick up a certain amount of public criticism; there are always pressures for modification and change. I am wondering how you feel about the role that, say, Dean Acheson, John Foster Dulles, you, or Henry Kissinger played in this important task of not defending policy, but seeking the modifications that seem to be demanded by changing times.

SECRETARY RUSK: I think that within the structure of the executive branch, one should always feel free to propose and recommend a change in policy, provided it takes that form. But it is out of bounds, in my opinion, to go off and leak information to the news media for the purpose of undermining the policy or simply to refuse to obey instructions with respect to the implementation of policy. One should always be free to recommend changing the policy. Sometimes changes in policy can occur without going all the way to the President. Many policy decisions are made every day in the Department of State without going to the secretary of state or the president; the secretary makes a lot of changes without going to the president. So that is fair and free, and colleagues should be free to do it.

There is one very intriguing question, however, that is worth some thinking about in terms of a study of the presidency. Each person more or less thinks of himself as playing his particular role. The business of being limited to one's own role can be a very good way to serve a president badly. For example, in connection with the disaster of the Bay of Pigs, I had been a colonel of infantry, and chief of war plans for the CBI theater during World War II. As a colonel of infantry, I knew that this brigade did not have the chance of a "snowball in hell," but I wasn't a colonel of infantry, I was sitting there in a very special cubicle. I failed President Kennedy by not insisting that he ask a question that he did not ask. He should have turned to our Joint Chiefs of Staff and said to them: "Gentlemen, I may want to do this with U.S. forces, so you tell me what you would need in terms of U.S. forces if I ask you to do it yourself rather than with this Cuban brigade. I want that by noon tomorrow." By the time the Joint Chiefs had come in with their sustained and prolonged bombing, their several divisions, a massive fleet, and their big air force, it would have been obvious to the President that this little brigade did not have any chance at all. We were playing our roles too closely in the opening stages of a new administration. One thing that I think I learned was that a Cabinet officer should not limit himself just to his own role. He should feel free to move beyond it and talk things over with the president across the board.

QUESTION: My question has to do with the role of the legal adviser of the State Department at a level more than merely telling you that you cannot do something, because law is not simply a bundle of restraints. As someone said during the Cuban Missile Crisis, "It helps to have law on your side." In your experience as secretary of state, did you often call on the legal adviser, not merely to tell you what you could not do but to suggest how law could operate effectively in support of a policy? For example, you mentioned the approximately 3,000 cables that went out every day from the State Department.

SECRETARY RUSK: A considerable number of those would require clearance by the legal advisers office because matters of law are involved. The legal adviser during the 1960s was always present in the morning meetings. Even when we had smaller morning meetings in advance of the larger morning meetings, with these six or seven people, the legal adviser would be there in that smaller group. I myself have been criticized by people like Dean Acheson, George Kennan, and Hans Morgenthau for giving too much weight to law. When I came to Georgia Law School, I put two quotations on my first exam. One was from Dean Acheson: "The survival of nations is not a matter of law," and one from myself: "In a nuclear world, the survival of nations may depend upon law." I let my students sweat those two statements out.

What I tried to do with Abraham Chayes and his successor, Leonard Meeker, was to give them carte blanche to intrude themselves into any question in the Department without being invited. I remember calling them "the conscience of the Department." This will vary greatly with presidents and secretaries of state and the temper of the times. I think law is a very important factor, however, not for sentimental reasons but for hardheaded realistic reasons.

QUESTION: You have said that one of the glories of our system is that ultimately it produces a consensus. What happened to the consensus in the 1960s? Then, I think, we did not produce one.

SECRETARY RUSK: There was strong support for Vietnam through 1966 around the country. Almost literally every day we would have on our desk a 24-hour summation of evidences of public opinion. This would include resolutions of national organizations, important editorials and speeches, and excerpts from the *Congressional Record*, all sorts of things. But the American people are impatient about war, thank heaven, and the change came not because of what was happening on college campuses or in the streets; it came when people at the grass roots, like my cousins in Cherokee County, Georgia, came to the conclusion in 1968 that if the government could not give them some idea as to when the war was going to be over, we might as well chuck it. We became aware of that change at the grass roots during the first half of 1968, and I, myself, assumed that whoever took office as president in January 1969 would have to bring that war to a conclusion rapidly. It is quite right that the consensus disintegrated in the last two years of the 1960s.

QUESTION: I would like, if I may, to return to the question about meeting foreign heads of government. I want to talk about the value to the United States of the president meeting with allied heads of government, especially as the relative importance of allies is increasing in the world. I know from my own experience in the British Foreign Office how much every British prime minister has valued a personal relationship with the American president. I'm not talking about negotiation carefully prepared, but about the personal relationship.

Dean Rusk

Recently, an eminent man in the French Foreign Office said to me that one of the things that distinguished de Gaulle is that he was the only head of government in France that this senior official could remember who did not want to establish that kind of personal relationship with an American president as the head of our alliance. The secretary of state has a great responsibility, to be sure, that this finds a place in the president's timetable, in the president's mind. I wonder if you would comment on this?

SECRETARY RUSK: The general practice is that once a year, the State Department will recommend to the president a program for such meetings in the course of the coming year. Usually there are many more applicants than one can find room for, but usually one does find room for visits between ourselves and our key allies. Britain was always on the list if the British prime minister so wished. Even that gets complicated. There is great pulling and hauling among countries to get on the list; and for many countries—this is not true of Britain—they have the view that somehow if they come to Washington on an official visit, they will go back with a big bag of goodies. When you tell them that this is not the purpose of such a visit, that it will not happen, they say, "Oh well, we won't ask for anything." Then the visit is laid on and they say, "I can't go back empty-handed." So these things are a little more complicated than they appear at first.

I think we have a problem in the alliance. For instance, in the first paragraph of a recent lead article in the *Economist* not long ago, the writer said in effect that the movement of Russian troops into Afghanistan was the fault of Mr. Carter and the United States, as though somehow the United States, the American people are mercenaries sitting over here available to go and tidy up things in various parts of the world if they go wrong while Europe enjoys business as usual and the comforts of life. I am concerned that there are no British, French, Italian, Japanese, or German ships in the Indian Ocean these days. It would mean a lot to the American people if some of those other flags were flying there. That, however, is beside the point. Still, these personal relationships can be very important where the leaders are after the same purposes.

THE PRESIDENT AND THE SECRETARY OF STATE REVISITED

President de Gaulle is a special case, a very special case. Talking to de Gaulle was like climbing a mountain on your knees and opening a little door at the top to listen to the oracle. There was never any exchange. When I was in Paris, I would go in and make a courtesy call on him. He would ask me to be seated, then he would say, "Well, Mr. Secretary, I'm listening." He would never raise questions on his own initiative. He never got over the fact that you (the British) and we refused to accept his proposal for a tripartite committee to govern the free world. Eisenhower rejected it, Kennedy rejected it, and he never forgave us for it. It is ironic that the tactics he used to achieve his purpose of restoring the position of France had exactly the opposite effect. In NATO we got to the point where we just went ahead with our business without regard to France.

QUESTION: Should the role of the alliance be increasing in importance? The allies have considerably improved their condition economically. What role should the alliance play? This summer I saw in a German paper a criticism that when Carter retreated to Camp David, no foreign leaders were consulted and no allies were brought in on the series of consultations he had. What is the role of the NATO alliance?

SECRETARY RUSK: Well, one had to take account of the fact that when an alliance succeeds—and no member of NATO has been attacked since the alliance was formed—public interest in it and support for it tend to diminish.

This matter of consultation is a curious one. The way to consult is to consult. But should the President of the United States be the one that always has to take the initiative? If someone could check the records of NATO to see how often questions have come up on the initiative of the United States for consideration in NATO compared to how often this has been done at the initiative of any other member of NATO, you would be shocked at the result.

The same thing happens with Congress. They talk about consulting. Do you know that in eight years not more than six times did any senator pick up the phone, call me, and say, "Next time you're down this way, drop by; I'd like to talk to you about something," or, "Let me drop by your office on the way home; I want to talk to you about something." Let's give them full credit for being considerate of the time of the secretary of state. But they sit there expecting to be convinced, and very little initiative is taken from the Capitol Hill side of it to consult, except through formal hearings.

Even in the meetings of the Senate Foreign Relations Committee, Chairman Fulbright and I spent a good deal of time trying to get a quorum. Often I would go down there and the meeting would begin with two senators present, and in the course of the morning maybe three of four senators would come in to check their names on the list and stay for a few minutes and then go out. I wasn't there to do a "Flip Wilson Show." I did not expect to be the most entertaining fellow in the world. But when we had television, they all turned up, half of them with makeup on, all ready for the show. We have to work harder on this process of consultation between the executive and legislative branches. The most difficult thing, however, will be to get senatorial and congressional time.

There is something that has happened for years that I think the public does not know much about. In the mid-1960s we started having meetings at 9:00 on Wednesday mornings in the House of Representatives to which every member of the House of Representatives was invited. At each meeting there would be a senior officer of the State Department to talk about some important sector of foreign policy. They would spend at least an hour there taking questions and comments from any member of the House who wanted to comment. The attendance would vary from maybe 60 to 300, depending upon who was coming and what the subject was. Any member of the House of Representatives who did attend those meetings regularly would go away at the end of the year with a far broader and deeper understanding of what was going on in the world than any member of Parliament would through question in the House of Commons. In my time as secretary of state we never had an embarrassing leak out of those meetings. It was taken for granted that these would be private meetings and it was a great instrument for exchanging views back and forth.

Every committee of the Congress now becomes involved in foreign policy. I would like to see the Senate Foreign Relations Committee and the House Foreign Affairs Committee given overriding responsibility for looking at foreign policy as a whole and free to call in bills pending in any other committee for the purpose of putting in their own reports on how the proposed action fits into foreign policy as a whole.

There is another thing that makes a difference here and affects the president and the secretary of state in their relations with Congress. In the early 1960s we could talk to four senators: Russell of Georgia, Humphrey of Minnesota, Dirksen of Illinois, and Kerr of Oklahoma. We could go to the House side and talk to Speaker Sam Rayburn, and we knew what the Congress would and would not do. They could tell us, partly because they could tell the Congress. LBJ used to refer to these people as the "whales" of the Congress. I can make a pretty strong case against the whale system, but what do you say for 535 minnows swimming around in a bucket? There is no one today, no reasonably small group of people, who can speak for the Congress in the absence of a formal vote. This complicates our system to an extraordinary degree.

QUESTION: This question is a variation on those comments you have been making. I wonder if you would indicate in general terms how important you think good organization is to good policy formation and what changes might have helped you as secretary of state in effective policy formation within the Department of State and in the Department's relationship to other Cabinet departments?

SECRETARY RUSK: First, I would suggest that the real organization of the executive branch is not to be found in organizational charts, but in the way in which competence and responsibility are delegated downward by the president through individuals. Very often this network is not the same as the organizational charts. Your more sophisticated embassies in Washington, for example, the British Embassy, will be aware of this distinction and they will spend a good deal of time in finding out what the real chain of command might be inside the government.

Dean Rusk

I don't want to take anything away from people who work on such matters, but I am a little bit numb about reorganization as such. I have lived through so many of them in government, *plus ca change plus c'est la meme chose* (the more things change, the more they stay the same). There are some things that can be done. For example, I think the organization of the Operations Center in the Department of State, the so-called "Flap House," was a very useful thing to do. There are things that can be done.

The one thing that I am appalled by is the constant inflation of titles. It goes on and on. When I became assistant secretary of state, there were three. Now there are at least 20 in the Department who are either called assistant secretary or hold the rank of assistant secretary. Then there are those who want their particular assistant secretary to become an undersecretary, and on and on it goes. I don't think that sort of thing has much to do with how you get the job done. But I'm willing to look at organization.

When any indivisible whole is divided, there is always a certain illogic in the way it is divided. Therefore, at any given time some other organization tends to look better. We have that in business, on university campuses, and everywhere else. I don't worry too much about organization as such. The question is, who are the people who have responsibility and what is their relationship with the sources of constitutional authority? I think the actual structure is less important than the competence of the people.

QUESTION: Your word about the importance of a close relationship between the president and secretary of state prompts me to wonder what your view is of the office of the national security adviser. One hears a good deal these days about how troublesome the present secretary finds the national security adviser. Mr. Rogers certainly found his adviser troublesome. Those of us living at a distance from Washington often get the impression that today we have in point of fact two secretaries of state. Is there anything in the logic of the conduct of White House business that makes it necessary now for a president to have not only a secretary, but this additional figure who presides over the National Security Council and who seems to be a second secretary?

THE PRESIDENT AND THE SECRETARY OF STATE REVISITED

SECRETARY RUSK: Again, I am biased, but I was not aware of any problem during the 1960s with Mr. McGeorge Bundy and then Mr. Walt Rostow in that job. I think they had about a dozen officers on their staff. If McGeorge Bundy made a recommendation to President Kennedy on foreign policy, he would make it to me at the same time. We had complete confidence that no one was going to go around cutting someone's throat. During the early years of the Nixon administration the NSC staff went up to about a hundred officers—a little State Department across the road, away from the troops, away from the flow of responsibility and the flow of information. The number is now back to about 50, but that is still too many in my judgment.

When people are given these assignments they become promoters of their own pad, protectors of their own situation, and the possibility for tensions will be present. Mr. Brzezinski has his own press secretary; that's ridiculous. It is hard enough keeping the White House press secretary and the State Department press secretary on the same wavelength without having another person in there. It does not make sense. So I think this is something presidents have to watch very carefully.

QUESTION: Do you see an efficient and effective relationship between the secretary of state and the president and an efficient and effective national policy? Does the one in any way imply the other?

SECRETARY RUSK: During the Eisenhower period, they prepared a thick manual for President Eisenhower on U.S. national security policy. When President Kennedy took office some of the planners, including some of my friends, decided that they had to bring it up to date and to convert it to a Kennedy policy, and they worked on it prodigiously. When they finished, however, neither President Kennedy nor I would approve it as a matter of official policy because we could not tell what we were approving. If you talk about policies too generally, it does not give you any guidance as to what you have to do tomorrow morning at 9:00. By approving general statements, you may trick yourself into thinking you have a policy when you don't.

So I'm a little skeptical about the attempts to reduce policies for a world community of 160 nations and a throbbing, boisterous American people of 220 million into a few general statements. If people want to generalize about the way policy is hammered out over a period of time by what one does in a given situation, that is all right; I don't object to that, but some of these generalizations simply are not guidelines of policy.

NARRATOR: How do these issues appear from Mr. Jefferson's vantage point?

DUMAS MALONE: I wish I had heard this discussion with Mr. Rusk before I wrote my books on Jefferson the president. I was very interested in what you said about General Marshall. After all, he is going back to first principles because when the departments were established, the various secretaries were regarded as assistants of the president. They were so regarded.

When you were talking about the relationships between the president and the secretary of state, my mind reverted to the relationship between Jefferson and James Madison, which was certainly a very special case because it is almost impossible to know when one left off and the other began. It was almost impossible to make any distinction whatever. I have never tried to make any distinction between Madison's policy and Jefferson's policy because they saw eye to eye.

Another very interesting thing is that Jefferson would have all his public papers and he would submit them to Madison and Gallatin. We have their comments on his message to Congress and other such things. Gallatin used to pass little notes back and forth to Jefferson all of the time, but Madison did not do that. So I am at something of a loss to determine the relations of the two men during the time they were together. When they were separated, for example, when Madison was in Congress and Jefferson was not there, he would write in detail and we know about the relation then because it would be expressed in writing. As a matter of act, Jefferson makes very few comments on his policies in his papers.

One other thing I thought about summitry. I was thinking to myself that suppose Jefferson and Napoleon had met. I do not think the Louisiana Purchase would have resulted.

SECRETARY RUSK: I hope you will confirm one of my favorite quotations from Jefferson. Maybe it is spurious, but I will always live with the thought that he said on one occasion, "I have not heard from our minister in Spain this year. If I don't hear from him next year I shall write him a letter."

MR. MALONE: Speaking of that, poor old Monroe was in great difficulty because he could not communicate with his government at home and he made an ill-fated trip to Spain that he might have been talked out of if he had had a transatlantic telephone. This is the one case where he did not carry out his instructions, and I was quite mystified that the minimum for which he should have been willing to settle for was stated in his instructions and that he apparently disregarded them. I was talking with a biographer of Monroe and found out that Monroe never received the letter of instructions. In other words, you cannot go by the letters written, you have to go by the letters received.

SECRETARY RUSK: Quite right.

NARRATOR: We are all deeply indebted to Secretary Rusk for visiting the Miller Center and revisiting his important *Foreign Affairs* article, "The President."

~ *Seven* ~

CABINET GOVERNMENT: AN ALTERNATIVE
FOR ORGANIZING POLICY-MAKING*

Griffin Bell

NARRATOR: I would like to welcome you to a Forum with Griffin Bell this morning on a subject that is of continuing interest to the Miller Center, the question of Cabinet government. It is a subject to which, in one sense, we were introduced a couple of years ago when Judge Bell took part in a conference of former attorneys general at the Miller Center. It is an issue that has recurred in many discussions since that time. It is a subject that almost every text writer comments on, including a recent one saying, "Of all the advisory bodies to which the President can turn for advice, the Cabinet consisting of the government's ten department heads is the oldest and most prestigious."

Many presidents have also regarded it as of the least useful. Mentioned nowhere in the Constitution, the Cabinet was invented by George Washington who noted that Article II, Section 2 of the Constitution provided that "the President may require the opinion in writing of the principal officer in each of the executive departments upon any subject relating to the duties of their respective office." When Washington first met with these principal officers in 1789 there were only three departments of government: State, War and Treasury. By the end of his first term these department heads were known as his "Cabinet" and the term has stuck as more than seven other government offices have been

---

*Presented in a Forum at the Miller Center of Public Affairs on 23 March 1988. Reprinted from *The Carter Presidency: Fourteen Intimate Perspectives of Jimmy Carter* (Lanham, Maryland: University Press of America, Inc., 1990).

133

CABINET GOVERNMENT: ALTERNATIVE FOR ORGANIZING POLICY-MAKING

elevated to departmental status. Nothing in the law requires the president to meet with his Cabinet or listen to its members' advice, nor is Cabinet approval required for any action he may take. And then there is a long discussion of the different uses that have been made of the Cabinet by different presidents.

All of you know of Judge Bell's achievements and record. He was attorney general from 1977 and 1979; active in Atlanta affairs; a graduate of Mercer; he has an ongoing concern in questions of civil rights as well as questions of maintenance of order within society. We are fortunate that in a busy schedule at the University of Virginia he would take time to meet with us and discuss this subject. I think he may want to kick it off briefly but I know he hopes very much that you will raise questions following his presentation.

ATTORNEY GENERAL BELL: I was testifying in the House Judiciary Committee on Tuesday morning on an aspect of the antitrust laws. It had to do with a law that was passed in 1944 and the chairman of the committee read some letters that President Roosevelt wrote about this law urging that it not be passed. He commented that probably no president would ever write a letter now to the chairman of the House Judiciary Committee about a law. He would send some fourth-level aide over to speak to someone, maybe the committee staff. He remarked on what a change had come over the government just in those years since 1944.

I begin by using that as something of a text because it may be that it was certainly no later than the Johnson administration that the White House staff has become so large that it has really subsumed the Cabinet. There is some doubt that Cabinets are any more useful, although George Washington set the system up and it has served us well over the years. There is hardly any Cabinet post now that does not have a parallel over in the bowels of the White House somewhere, some person who has never been confirmed and whose name might not even be known to the public. So let's go back to the beginning when Washington didn't have a Cabinet. There were those three departments that you mentioned, State, Treasury and War, and then there was the attorney general and the

134

attorney general was a part-time post. But under the Constitution the president is charged with faithfully executing the laws and he can hardly do that without having some agent. So the attorney general was the president's agent.

Washington started out by letting the Cabinet vote on policy issues. Jefferson and Randolph and Couzens would usually take the same side and take issue with Hamilton and Jay and that is generally the way it started. I was surprised in doing some studying on the Civil War to know that President Lincoln let his Cabinet vote, particularly after Alexander Stevens, once president of the Confederacy, met with President Lincoln at Fort Monroe in February of 1865 to negotiate an end to the war. That was several months before the war ended. Lincoln and Stevens had served in the Congress together. They were Whigs. They sat beside each other so they knew each other. They could have ended the war after the conference, but Lincoln got back to Washington and let his Cabinet vote on it and did not get a single vote in favor of ending the war on the basis under discussions.

Stevens reported to Jefferson Davis and his ego was so great that he was not able to bring himself to end it unless he was made commander of all of the armed forces of both sides on the pretext that they were having trouble with the French in Mexico. That was the end of that.

But the Cabinet has played a big role. President Franklin Roosevelt used his Cabinet greatly, some members more so than others, but they were big men in the government during the Roosevelt years. When World War II started Roosevelt changed some of his Cabinet members to put some Republicans in because he wanted to have the Cabinet more bipartisan.

In those days the White House staff was always very small. We didn't have a National Security Council director then, and when you think about it, perhaps we don't need one or maybe we don't need a secretary of state. If we have a president who is not capable of being his own secretary of state we are in bad shape. We are in trouble to begin with. We had a governor who set out to reform the prisons of Georgia. He announced one day that he had done the best that he could do until we were able to get a better class of prisoners. It may be that we are going to have to get a better class of presidents, surely someone that knows enough about foreign affairs to be his own secretary of state. The same would have to be true about the Defense Department given the change in defense, and the sophisticated no-miss weapons that are being developed. The president has to know something about all of this or he has to have an aide who knows something about it and an aide who is someone that the American people would have confidence in. I don't know that the secretary of the treasury is needed anymore other than as a part of the State Department foreign policy—world currency problems and those sort of things. There are others who are duplicating the functions of the secretary of the treasury. The secretary may be more like a corporate comptroller, certainly given the fact that the president has an economic adviser over at the White House who does all of the things the secretary used to do. I don't think you can get by without an attorney general. After that I am not saying that there is any post in the Cabinet that is any more than an agency head.

I don't know how we could have Cabinet government now. I used to sit in the Cabinet and President Carter would ask every member of the Cabinet their views about something when many of the members of the Cabinet had only the foggiest notion about the questioning. But somehow most would give their views. Finally, after about a year-and-a-half, two different members of the Cabinet said to the President that the "show and tell" style meetings were no longer fruitful. That is how Cabinet government ended up.

Now it is worse than ever because as I understand the Reagan system, they have truly done away with Cabinet government. They have groups that study various things and reach a composite view, not necessarily in a Cabinet. On antitrust questions I notice that the secretary of commerce is the dominant person involved although the attorney general and others are in that group. There are groups to study everything, so I don't know that Cabinet officers are playing much of a role. At least that is the system that is public, the structure that the American people know about through the media.

In the Carter administration we did not have that. We had a counterpart for everyone. I do not think I had a counterpart, although the White House counsel was to some extent. I know that Brzezinski was Secretary Vance's counterpart and was often in command. He had a very narrow area as compared to the wide ranging duties of the secretary of state. He saw the President every morning and usually Secretary Vance was in the air somewhere, going to conferences or to funerals and those sort of things.

Mr. Brzezinski never appeared a single time in the Senate or before a committee of the Congress. He never had to appear—no one at the White House, think of this, ever appears in the Congress. They don't have to appear. They have never been confirmed and they tend to or at least try to dominate the Cabinet out of the White House but they do not have any responsibility to the Congress.

This has a lot to do, I think, with the breakdown—and that is all you can call it—between particularly the House and the President right now in the area of foreign affairs. Never in the history of our nation have we had committees of the Congress who wanted to have authority to decide whether we will have an intelligence operation, for example. The House Select Committee on Foreign Intelligence says now that President Reagan cannot carry on any kind of foreign intelligence operation without their concurrence in advance. This is a breakdown because it is contrary to the Constitution, the express terms of the Constitution, and the decisions of the Supreme Court that the president can make foreign policy subject to the power of the Congress of oversight to see if new legislation is needed or to control the appropriations.

As I now see it, we have co-Cabinet people in the White House and we have a committee of the House trying to be the co-equal to the president in foreign affairs. I do not believe we can get our government in much worse shape than it is in now, structurally. We will have to come out of this. I think this Center can render a signal service by getting into this area and letting the American people know what has happened to their government and how different it is now from what the Founding Fathers and the early Congresses had in mind, particularly the first Congress in 1791, and how they structured the government at that time.

I do not think the world is any more complex now other than scientifically. Political science has not changed that much but we do need to insist that the White House staff be greatly reduced. We will get a president eventually who will do that and who will go back to Cabinet government. When he goes back, however, he is going to have to eliminate almost half the Cabinet posts. They are just not needed. They are really agency heads. Some of the positions should be combined. I have never understood why we had a secretary of commerce and a secretary of labor. That creates a tension to begin with. You ought to have the same person worrying about that.

DUMAS MALONE: They did originally, you know.

ATTORNEY GENERAL BELL: They did?

MR. MALONE: Yes, commerce and labor were together.

ATTORNEY GENERAL BELL: Well, they ought to go back to that. That is my general approach to the matter. I will be glad to answer questions. I told Ken about how the Carter administration was set up. You can hardly speak on this subject generally because you would have to know the inside of the operation of every administration, just how they are doing it. All I know about the Reagan administration is what I read in the newspapers of how it is set up. I am in antitrust law so I am interested in that and I was struck by the idea that Secretary of Commerce Baldridge was very outspoken about the antitrust ruling in the recent steel merger questions and finally backed the Justice Department off. He started out criticizing the assistant attorney general, something I would not ever have condoned. You would have to take me on rather than one of my people. And finally William French Smith, the attorney general, did rise to the occasion in answer to Secretary Baldridge but the opinion was changed. Having said that, I don't mean the opinions should not have been changed. I think it was a bad opinion in the beginning. Sometimes the antitrust division seems to operate separate and apart from the government in policy matters.

NARRATOR: We are also privileged today to have our greatest historian with us, Dumas Malone. Do you want to ask the first or the last question?

MR. MALONE: All I know about what is going on now is what I read in the papers and see on TV. When did this business of having the National Security Council in the White House start?

ATTORNEY GENERAL BELL: In the Truman administration. We were doing many things after the war. That is a bad time, I guess, in a country. After the war you tend to be reformers and most reforms are bad. You have to beware of the reformers.

MR. MALONE: I don't know. I just wish you would tell us what we ought to do.

ATTORNEY GENERAL BELL: I once told President Carter what to do about the National Security Council. Just transfer the post to the State Department and leave everyone in place, right where they are, but have on the table of organization that the chairman of the NSC reports to the secretary of state, and just put it on his chart and leave everything else alone. And then Brzezinski would know that he was reporting to Secretary Vance. That would have ended it. Kissinger would have known that he was reporting to Bill Rogers. In Washington, status is status and that's it. Now he might never have reported, in which event he would have to go.

MR. MALONE: Would it do to require the confirmation of these people who surround the president?

ATTORNEY GENERAL BELL: That would be the second thing I would do. I would say if you are going to have these people over there who are exercising the authority of the Cabinet, let's have a list of them and they are going to have to be confirmed. The Senate is going to have to go into their attitudes and backgrounds. And it is a dangerous thing, actually, not to do that. Can you imagine what disaster may loom over our country when you have these people there who are not accountable to anyone except the resident and he hardly knows most of them? They are put in there on the recommendation of someone usually. I know that in the Carter White House, many people were Mondale people, who in turn were McGovern people. And they were not the people that

President Carter knew. He knew Brzezinski in advance, I don't mean that, but he probably did not know David Aaron, Brzezinski's deputy. He knew Stuart Eizenstat, who was head of the Domestic Council, but he would not have known Mr. Karp, his deputy, and so forth.

People have a right to have the Congress see these people. They have a right to see them and know who they are, what sort of people we have working at the White House, doing all of these things. They are exercising great power.

QUESTION: How do you think historians will evaluate the profile of the Carter administration's personnel and staff compared with Reagan's personnel or that of other postwar administrations?

ATTORNEY GENERAL BELL: I don't know how they will go about it, whether they will just evaluate President Carter or go off into different areas. I think many parts of President Carter's government were excellent; some were not that good. The perception of President Carter as a weak man has been wrong all along. I introduced him to the Atlanta Rotary Club about two years ago and made the startling announcement that when he was President, he had increased spending for defense more than anyone had done in many years. In real dollars Carter increased the allocation for defense spending more than Reagan has, but people did not believe that.

COMMENT: He did so mostly in the last two years.

ATTORNEY GENERAL BELL: But no one believed that; they thought he wanted to surrender everything. He is not like that at all. He is very strong in his views, and sometimes you can have a hard time convincing him of something. He is almost too rough with personnel. I was in the room when he fired Andy Young, and it was terrible to have him talk to Andy the way he did about meeting with the PLO. President Carter was big on using the word "disgrace," and he accused Andy Young of bringing disgrace on him when he met with the PLO.

Griffin Bell

Andy responded, "Well, Mr. President, you are right to fire me. You have to do what you have to do; I had to do what I had to do." That is the way they left the matter, but within 30 days Andy was out campaigning for President Carter. That is one thing that caused me to have admiration for Andy Young. He didn't carry any bitterness or rancor about his dismissal.

QUESTION: Why would he have been so sensitive to the press criticism of that, yet seemingly absolutely convinced in all of the interviews we have had with him that there was no political problem with the Vance-Brzezinski rivalry? To this day when you raise that question, he will say that the problem was greatly exaggerated.

ATTORNEY GENERAL BELL: I know. That is why he was upset with me about a chapter in my book called, *What Went Wrong?* He does not agree that Mondale was ever anything but a paragon of perfection. You are never going to convince him otherwise. He made his mind up about that and that's it. He will never admit that there was any problem between Vance and Brzezinski. Of course, everyone around them knew there was a problem, but he is not going to admit that. I do not know if President Carter ever sat down to rethink all of these things in his administration. Maybe a president ought to wait about ten years and then write what he thinks about his administration.

NARRATOR: Carter had a rationale for keeping Vance and Brzezinski. The rationale was that Vance, who was not good at public presentation, needed to be complemented by Brzezinski, who was. Carter felt that he needed to have both sides of every argument. He just did not seem conscious of the effect that would have on public perception.

ATTORNEY GENERAL BELL: Well, it didn't add up either. When I was getting ready to leave, I recommended two people to succeed me as attorney general. One was Warren Christopher, and the other was Ben Civiletti. I had told President Carter that I wanted to leave within a few months. I asked him what he was going to do about my successor, and he said, "Well, I've been thinking about it. I like Warren very much, he is a very fine man, but I can't spare him. I need him as deputy in the State Department." I told him that I thought it was a shame for Warren to lose out on being attorney general because he was needed at state as a deputy. It seemed to me that either Vance or Brzezinski could do Warren's job, but President Carter insisted that he couldn't spare him, so Warren missed out on being attorney general. Of course he did a great job at the State Department. He did all of the negotiating toward the end of the Iranian crisis. The President may have been right and I am probably wrong. He knew a great deal more about them than I did since he worked with them every day. Maybe he had it figured out that Brzezinski had strength of one kind and Vance of another. Yet the fact remained that they did not get along. There was tension between them or it seemed so to me.

QUESTION: You outlined the history of the establishment of the first Cabinet under Washington. What are the historical precedents of the constitutional guidelines about confirmation?

ATTORNEY GENERAL BELL: It is statutory for most offices. It began with the first Congress because you confirm judges, ambassadors, Cabinet officers, and I think it has been expanded over the years. There is no constitutional precedent for it except for those officers who must be appointed with the advice and consent of the Senate.

QUESTION: You suggested in a way that a president should at least be knowledgeable enough to be his own secretary of state. You are not suggesting that he be his own secretary of state in practice, are you? It troubles me a great deal that you could have a president who is commander and chief of the Armed Forces and virtually secretary of state who could become a rogue elephant.

ATTORNEY GENERAL BELL: No, he couldn't. It would be impossible. He would not have any money. President Ford had to withdraw from Angola. Congress has absolutely shut the government down, many presidents down, by no funds. They are getting ready to do it now in Nicaragua. There may not be funds there for the CIA. We may leave the ammunition and guns on the ground for the Sandinistas. That is the way we came out of Vietnam. No money. We left two billion dollars or more worth of weapons and equipment there that are being used all over the world now when we came out of there in such disorder.

There are so many checks and balances in the Constitution that this would not be a problem. I think we have had presidents who were their own secretary of state. Can you imagine anything more dangerous than having General Marshall and Truman running the foreign affairs of the nation? But we did well.

QUESTION: Franklin Roosevelt was his own secretary of state.

ATTORNEY GENERAL BELL: Yes and John Kennedy aspired to be his own secretary of state. He said he was. Most people now would think Dean Rusk was a pretty good secretary of state, keeping a balance. But Kennedy had a someone over there as head of the National Security Council who was doing a lot, but he was really doing it in Kennedy's name. I think Kissinger was the first time we saw the dual secretary of state system. That was solved by making him secretary of state. He finally got the best of Secretary Rogers and took over. I have forgotten, but I think he was very careful about who followed him as head of National Security Council. No one probably can remember who that was. It was General Scowcroft, a very respected person.

QUESTION: Isn't there a way that from the president down they could accomplish the simplification of government back to where it was?

ATTORNEY GENERAL BELL: If you have a president who has an innovative mind like that, he would start doing it and then he would drive the Congress into doing it. It has now infected the courts. You may have seen that Justice John Paul Stevens let two of his law clerks go, two of them out of four, year before last and said he just could not manage that many law clerks. The Justices ought to be doing their own work. He quoted Justice Brandeis who said the reason the public had confidence in the Court was, as he said, "We do our own." When I was a judge I had to start out with one law clerk, then I had two and then three. When I got to two I would not take the third law clerk. At that point I became a manager. It was hard to keep up with everything they could write. Could you imagine what a judge would be doing with four law clerks? Can you imagine having four assistants writing things for you? And every sentence may be something that is very important. And stuck in there somewhere is something that ought not to be there, not dishonestly but through lack of experience. This is not good. It is in all three branches of the government. You would have to have a leader who wanted to cut back and that leader would have to be the president.

QUESTION: For a good many years there was a tradition of appointing one Cabinet member who had been the campaign manager for the president. If this is going to be continued which one of the Cabinet posts would be the least detrimental to the country to follow this practice?

ATTORNEY GENERAL BELL: I would not favor doing that. You know the Republican party and the Democratic party headquarters are both in Washington and if you want to have your campaign manager around so you can have dinner with him every night, put him over there at one of the political parties, because that is what his business is, or he wouldn't be campaign manager. We no longer have a Post Office spot and I don't know just where you would put him, certainly not at the CIA. There are too many political decisions made in all of these departments and everyone who was helping in the campaign knows the campaign manager and they are calling on him for something and it is bad.

We have an ambivalent system. You want everyone to help you while you are running; then you don't want to see them anymore once you get in office. If you do see them too often, you will get into trouble. They will be calling up about some friend that is being investigated or they will be wanting to get a defense contract and so forth. There is no end to it. I am not certain that there is any place left for a campaign manager.

Griffin Bell

COMMENT: I think there are powerful reasons for wishing staff away, but I don't really think it is going to go away. I think we have full employment programs for young professionals everywhere. You see it in the courts. You see it in the White House and executive offices. You see it in Congress and for all I know, you see the same phenomenon in corporate life. I do not think we have really decided how this affects our accountability and responsibility for decisions.

ATTORNEY GENERAL BELL: It will go away. You can depend on that. We may not be living when it goes away, but it will go away when we get the deficit so large that we are bankrupt and we have changed the form of government. It will then go away. It seems to me we ought to be intelligent enough or have managerial ability enough to let it go away before that. But it will go away. We will get to where we are ungovernable at the rate we are going. This is quite a serious matter in the long range. We don't have to worry about it now. But look how it has changed just in 30 or 40 years.

I don't know what you are doing in your studies, but you should check one fact. President Carter never got a piece of major legislation through the House under normal procedures. It was always necessary to set up an ad hoc procedure to get something through. That tells me the House is unworkable, and if you were just keeping up with legislation a little bit you would know that. The Senate is not unworkable but the House at the present time is unworkable.

QUESTION: I was a great admirer of President Carter's and was state campaign chairman in 1980, so all of my comments and reflections are made with affection but also with disturbance. We have seen Meese recently and the sleeze factor and the teflon coating around Reagan and so on. I felt the pendulum swing against Carter with the Bert Lance affair because he appeared to vacillate when it appeared to be a question of morality and integrity and the things that he had talked about so much during his campaign. He was just unable to come to grips with the case in a decisive sort of way and I don't think he ever really recovered as

President from the way that situation was handled. Could you give us your reflections, both factual and your own personal views, on the way that situation was handled and how it was permitted to do as much damage to the President as it was?

ATTORNEY GENERAL BELL: The President and I are friends. They had dinner with us last Friday night. The President is very high on Lance, they are close friends. And besides the emotional attachment there was poor staff work. It was allowed to go on too long. Lance, after he was asked to leave, didn't leave for more than a month. Several people had to ask him and urge him to leave. At one point the President came back from Camp David and embraced him, if you remember. That was after a member of his staff told him he had read the comptroller's report and there was nothing in there bad about Lance. The next day when others read it, it was terrible. The President had already come back and embraced him. After that, it became obvious that he had to leave and it was a month before he left. You are right, that damaged the President greatly. That was the beginning of what you would call a "sleeze factor." A president has to demand that his people leave immediately, before the office of the presidency is damaged. You ought to think enough of your president, if you are there serving him, to leave your own image out of it. You naturally want to protect your good name but you cannot do that. That is one of the things you give up when you decide you're going to work for a president.

We seem to have lost sight of that kind of obligation in this country. We have to get back to those days. You ought to leave immediately if something is wrong. You have to protect the president.

QUESTION: Why are we tolerating things that way? Repeatedly in case after case after case.

ATTORNEY GENERAL BELL: I do not understand it. I would not have let anyone stay at the Justice Department an hour if something like that came up. If they didn't leave I would say, you just have to leave. Every president is being brought down by the same thing.

Griffin Bell

It is difficult to stay longer than four years anymore. President Reagan may get reelected but it will be almost an accident of history, an accident of politics because they are not getting a strong person to run against him. These staff problems keep happening over and over. No one can say how much harm it's doing President Reagan. He has had a way of being detached from his own problems. The public sees him as not being connected to these people, which is remarkable in itself but that seems to be the way it's going.

President Carter was never able to do that. We were talking last Friday night, not about any particular person but about his trouble with the press. The reason we were having dinner was that Jody Powell's book came out and there was a book party for Jody. He and his wife in Atlanta and several of us had dinner together. We were talking about the trouble. President Carter said that he had gone back and studied the presidencies of eight or ten presidents. He said the press was very kind to Roosevelt. I have not studied that. I was just a small boy then. I'm not saying that this was altogether true. I think there was not anything like the present White House press corps which is post-Watergate and just operates with a vengeance, although they do not seem to do so against President Reagan.

President Carter says they were easy on President Kennedy but Kennedy was not president long enough for us to know if that would have lasted. They never told anything about any of the outside activities of Kennedy. And they were hard on Nixon, hard on Ford, hard on Carter, hard on Johnson, hard on Truman, but they skipped Roosevelt and Kennedy and Reagan. He was just giving the facts, not giving an answer to it but that is essentially so. They (the media) drove President Johnson into not running for reelection, although the basis was of course the Vietnam War and the fact that he was thought to be sleazy. They made Ford out to be a stumblebum. He would fall out of the airplane, that is, off the stairway coming down. He would hit someone with a golf ball. Yet he was probably the finest athlete we have had in the White House. They made him out to be a person who could not walk. They can do you in like that. That is all the more reason, though, why your people have to be prepared to leave.

I didn't buy a house in Washington. I figured my job was one day long. I rented an apartment. I told the press I had to be prepared to leave on just an hour's notice. That's the attitude you ought to have when you are working for a president.

QUESTION: I wonder if President Carter is right in his generalization about those three presidents. It seems plausible that he is. I wonder if that is an indication of the press's real preference for entertainment. It does seem to me that those three presidents were more entertaining as interlocutors in press conferences than the others mentioned. Certainly President Carter had every bit as much if not more intellectual skill and acquaintance with issues than the other people we are talking about. If the press wanted an interlocutor who really knew his stuff it seems to me they would have done much better by Carter and much less well than they do by Reagan. But Reagan surely is more entertaining than Carter was. Kennedy was much more entertaining than Reagan. Roosevelt was very entertaining as a press conference man.

ATTORNEY GENERAL BELL: I will answer the question, not to make a statement, but did it ever occur to you that the press may be anti-intellectual?

QUESTION: Oh, many times.

MR. MALONE: I think there is too much of it. It is too open. You can't live life in quite such an open way and how any president can stand the sort of exposure, the degree of exposure that they now get—I don't think Reagan will do it for four more years. I think sooner or later that they will get him. It is just too much, and I don't know what the answer could possibly be. But now this present campaign for the Democratic nomination is overcovered, it's overreported, it's terribly overdone, and one result of it is that these men are so exposed that they are all going to say things they really should not have said and that they really did not mean to say about how they come out, and everyone knows about it. That is the trouble with our age. I sometimes think that this is the *de trop* age. There is just too much of everything. Too many people, too much publicity. Too much money, not well distributed, but too much. Just too much of everything. How Reagan has gotten away with it so far is amazing.

ATTORNEY GENERAL BELL: I have attended public functions two or three times where President Reagan was, and I will give you my view of how he gets by with it.

He is a person that people like. He is a person you enjoy being around and the press looks at it in that way. They genuinely like him. He is a hail-fellow-well-met type and he is not getting into details about anything. He's just sort of enjoying his job. I think they rather like that. You know they looked down on President Carter because he understood how the MX operated and all of these different weapon systems and he studied the B1 bomber and studied the Stealth bomber and decided we didn't need both and he cut out the B1. He knew about all of those things and had people briefing him on them. Well, that's too much for the press. You cannot write all of that. How would it sound? That's sort of the way it is. Reagan is very much like the prototype of the American male right now. He was a good athlete, he is a nice looking fellow and has been a performer. He is a good speaker. He has a laid-back style about him and that appeals to people and it seems to appeal to the press. They don't blame him much for anything that these people do. That will not last. You are right.

MR. MALONE: I don't see how it could for eight years. If it had not been for the war, Franklin Roosevelt couldn't have done it. Generally a president lasts about six years, and the last two are always bad.

ATTORNEY GENERAL BELL: That's the reason I favor a single six-year term.

QUESTION: Regardless of the press's attitude toward him, it seems to me that the picture of Reagan that comes across is that he is not too bright. I agree with everything you say but at the same time I think there is this impression that the job is just a little beyond him.

CABINET GOVERNMENT: ALTERNATIVE FOR ORGANIZING POLICY-MAKING

ATTORNEY GENERAL BELL: You know what people think about him? I have talked to many people about this. They think he is like Truman. He's not that bright, but he is tough. They want a tough man, someone who will make a decision. Many people equate him with Truman. Of course Truman had training as a senator, a lot of training during World War II as a senator during what they called the Truman Commission where they were studying defense contracts and that sort of thing. Now, as we look back we think of Truman as a person who was always direct and could make a decision no matter how tough it was. People think of Reagan the same way. We were embarrassed greatly as a nation by Iran, by the hostage situation. I don't know what any other president would do if he had the same crisis.

MR. MALONE: Oh, that would ruin anyone.

ATTORNEY GENERAL BELL: It made President Carter appear to be a weak person. His image became one of weakness. I had some lawyer friends out in Texas I happened to see the next year after the election of 1980 and they asked me how President Carter was. I told them and they asked, is he still wringing his hands and it turned out they voted for Reagan. They were Democrats who voted for Reagan and they had voted for Carter in 1976 and they called him a hand-wringer. I said, "Why would you say that about him?" They said, "Well, he never did anything about the hostages in Iran." I said, "Well, he tried, and it happened to be a failure and if it had not been a failure he would have been a great hero." But it was a difficult problem. It would have been for any president and would probably have brought any president down.

The other thing President Carter did that Reagan would not have done is he let those Cubans from Mariel in on the boats. Reagan has since turned the boats back. People really became upset with President Carter about that. What he did, he let the South Indo-Chinese people in, the legacy of the Vietnam War, because we owed them something. Then Castro wanted to get rid of the undesirables and saw us let those people in on boats. He put his undesirables on boats. We only had one choice, to turn them back, and President Carter did not turn them back.

I know a great deal about that because Castro had 25,000 people he wanted to release. He said they were political prisoners. The attorney general was then in charge of immigration, not the president. Congress has plenary power over immigration and they gave the power to the attorney general to let people in on an emergency basis. Secretary Vance wanted to let those people in. I said we would let them in if we screened them. He said in what way? I said we would send the FBI to Havana. If Castro would agree to that, then I would agree to it. He would not agree at first but finally did agree, and we sent the FBI to Havana and screened out about a third of them. His argument was and the State Department's was that they ought to be screened in Florida and I asked how we would get them back? Castro became very upset about that because we beat him at his own game. Then when he saw the boat people coming out of South Indochina he put his people on boats and we didn't turn them back.

Those two things hurt President Carter as much as anything I can imagine. One of them he could control and one he could not. He could not do anything about Iran.

NARRATOR: Do you think that people have already begun a revisionist view of Carter?

ATTORNEY GENERAL BELL: I don't see any signs of it, and the reason for it is his continuing political activity. He is always taking a position. During the first three or four years Reagan was in office President Carter kept fairly quiet. But since then he has been speaking out, taking a position on most everything, and it is hard for the revision to set in as long as he is as active as he is. I have heard people that are dissatisfied with President Reagan make statements like, "Carter sure is looking better how," and that sort of thing. But I have never heard anyone quantify it.

But, then, I never thought that he would be treated that badly by historians. I thought he had a good chance of being reelected, had it not been for the hostage situation. The fact that he could not do anything about it was frustrating to the American people, and that convinced them that what had been said about him was true, that he couldn't manage anything and he wasn't a good executive.

No one recognized that at a certain point, and perhaps down to the present, there was little anyone could do about the hostages.

NARRATOR: I think as much as we would like to continue, Judge Bell has a busy schedule. The last time he was here, Mr. Bell gave us ideas that we are still talking about and today he has repeated that performance. Thank you so much.

~ *Eight* ~

WHAT DOES AN ATTORNEY GENERAL DO?*

Herbert Brownell

MR. THOMPSON: Welcome to our award session for the 12th Burkett Miller Prize and Award. Long before his relationship with the Miller Center as a council member and commission co-chairman, Herbert Brownell contributed to the understanding of the American presidency. He served as campaign manager of twice successful and twice unsuccessful presidential candidates—Dwight Eisenhower and Thomas Dewey. He had a hand in persuading Eisenhower to run for the highest office. The President appointed him attorney general but then inquired about his interest in a Supreme Court appointment. Some columnists and historians rank him as the most outstanding attorney general of the 20th century. His book with John P. Burke, *Advising Ike: The Memoirs of Attorney General Herbert Brownell*, has been well received. His most enduring legacy is a love of politics. He brought dignity and resolve to politics. When confronted by harsh political choices, he never blinked. If the present tide of contempt and disdain for politics and politicians is to change, Americans need to learn what Herbert Brownell has taught us about the responsibilities and the rewards of politics.

In a countervailing view to the general mood of 1994, one political scientist writes: "There is no end to the praises that can be sung of politics. In politics, not in economics, is found the creative dialectic of offices. The true politician is a reforming conserver, a skeptical believer and a pluralistic moralist. Politics is lively

---

*Presented in a Forum at the Miller Center of Public Affairs on 11 November 1994. Reprinted from the *Miller Center Journal*, Volume II, Spring 1995.

sobriety, a complex simplicity, an untidy elegance, a rough civility and an everlasting immediacy. It is conflict become discussion."

Herbert Brownell has lived these truths and in honoring him, we also sing praises to the ideas he embraces.

GOVERNOR HOLTON: I have coming to my mind as I hear Kenneth's reading of this citation, a recollection of a quotation from someone whom I expect was a friend of Herb, though he was in the other party and a part of another administration. But Jim Farley said at a banquet in Virginia a little bit later on that he commended young people to politics because above any other profession save perhaps the clergy, it gave a greater opportunity for service to mankind. Herb's life has been an exemplification of that statement. More than anything else, I think he understood the leadership opportunities in politics. For us in Virginia, though our reactions at the time were not unanimously favorable, we have come to recognize what a great favor you did for us when you helped develop in the Eisenhower administration consensus in favor of the first Civil Rights Bill. We are much indebted to you for many things, but that to me stands out. For many reasons, including that one, it is a great pleasure for me personally to make this presentation to you.

MR. BROWNELL: I deeply appreciate it and even though it's overblown, I enjoy the praise. Thank you from the bottom of my heart because I had such a good time being associated with the Miller Center and think it is one of the institutions that keeps the government on the right track, and I am very proud to have been active in its affairs for such a long time.

I never expected to be as active on the political scene as I turned out to be. I will have to tell you how it happened. I got a call from General Eisenhower on Election Day in 1952 and he asked if I would please come and see him. He was staying at the house of the president of Columbia University, where he had officially been an occupant. I went to see him while the voting was in process. He was on the top floor and had made the top floor into a studio. He was dressed in his smock and was all set to copy a landscape—a very unlikely picture for a candidate being voted on at the moment for President of the United States. So after a little while he said, "How is it going?" I said, "It is going to be a landslide. There is no question about it." He said, "If you are right, I guess we had better do a little thinking about what's going to happen after we get to Washington." I said that it was a good time to do that. He was painting away, put in a branch on a tree in the picture, and of course he had given a lot of thought to it.

He said, "I'm going to organize the White House the way I am used to running an organization in the military. I want to have a chief of staff who will relieve me of a lot of the day-to-day headaches and serve up the important questions to me. That is the way I'm used to operating and I plan to do that when I get to Washington." He added a cloud and said, "I want you to be chief of staff!" Well, I really wasn't prepared for it and was silent for a little while. Finally I said, "I'm not the one for that. I'm a lawyer and have been a lawyer for 25 years, and I want to be a lawyer for 25 years more. I love the law and that is all I'm fitted for. Thank you very much, but I can't do it."

So he started painting in a very dark cloud—a little bit of temporizing. Finally he said, "So you want to be a lawyer." I said, "Yes, that is really my first love." "Well", he said, "how about being attorney general?" It did not take me long to decide. The dark cloud disappeared and everything was fine. I claim to be the only attorney general who was tapped for the job in an artist's studio, and perhaps the background was appropriate for the job because you have to learn to paint many dark clouds and many white clouds in any landscape that appears in the Department of Justice.

Then the next step was to accept his invitation to accompany him to Korea—as he had promised to do during the campaign. It turned out to be a very eventful and important trip for me as the incoming attorney general because in the first place, he told me I could choose my own assistants. What an important factor it is for the attorney general or any Cabinet officers to be able to choose people who are professionally qualified and who will be congenial and competent. He gave me full leeway, and I had the great pleasure of selecting such assistants as Warren Burger, afterward the chief justice and now valued council member of the Miller Center, William Rogers, who later became secretary of state, and a number of others who were indispensable to me as I went along. So I learned one lesson that is tremendously important in Washington—if you can have a loyal staff of competent people who work enthusiastically with you, it means all the difference between success and failure.

The other thing that came up on that trip, which is equally important to the office of attorney general, was that on the way over to Korea the President-elect asked me if I would draw a new will and a blind trust for him and so forth. Of course that was a great honor. After we talked it over, we decided that this was the wrong thing to do and that there had to be an absolute understanding that the attorney general neither represents the president as an individual nor advises him on private affairs and restricts his advice to the presidency as distinguished from the president. I have often thought since then what an important decision that was and one which he accepted readily. Even my old partners who would have benefitted otherwise came to accept it as being an important element in the structuring of a government that serves the public need.

By the time I got back from that trip to Korea, I had had a good start in being able to work in the Department of Justice in a way that I thought would bring lasting results. It is a big administrative job, but far and above the day-to-day administrative details that go with that or any other Cabinet position are the things that are of lasting importance. I thought I might mention a couple of them here today because they distinguish the attorney general's office from any other office that I know of in or out of the government.

Constitutional Questions Which Arose

There are two things the attorney general does that are really important and last for a long time. One is the advice to the presidency on constitutional questions and the other is the selection of lifetime federal judges. Those two things were the joy of my life during the years I was in that office, where I served longer than anyone except for two others in the entire history of the office.

Herbert Brownell

The constitutional crises that came during that period—they come in every period, of course—where I had an opportunity to advise the President were many because of the way our Constitution is established. We should thank our Founding Fathers every day for the form of constitutional government that they gave us. It was even important last Tuesday [Election Day 1994] when the people had their say and were able to let it be known to all of the government servants that we, the people, are the boss in the final analysis under our United States constitutional system of government. The president has to recognize every day that he is a constitutional officer, and that means there are certain restraints along with the powers of the presidency. Conflicts are bound to occur with the other branches of the government because that is the way the Founding Fathers set it up. That gives the attorney general, of course, a great opportunity to advise the president along the way if you have a congenial relationship with him, as I had with Eisenhower.

There is a constant struggle between the executive branch and the congressional branch over the powers of the presidency. It came up in a couple of interesting ways while I was attorney general. One battle was over the Bricker amendment, where the Congress sought to pass it as a constitutional amendment that would have severely limited the powers of the presidency in the conduct of foreign affairs. The President was faced with the fact that a majority of the members of his own party in the Senate favored such a constitutional amendment, crimping his powers and the powers of his successors in the field of foreign affairs. A long and rather bitter fight was waged to avert the submission to the people of an amendment that would have substantially reduced the powers of the president to make treaties and executive agreements with foreign nations.

I had to play quite a part. Interestingly enough, it came about this way: Ordinarily the secretary of state would have been the one to represent the administration on the Hill in the Bricker amendment fight, but John Foster Dulles, the secretary of state, had made a speech during the political campaign leading up to the election that indicated he thought there should be some restrictions on the presidency in foreign affairs. Therefore, the President asked me to lead the fight for the administration in opposition to the Bricker amendment. As you will remember, that amendment finally failed in the Senate by one vote. It was an exciting period and it gave me an opportunity to learn a great deal about the origin of our Constitution and the views of the Founding Fathers that the president should have the power to lead the nation in foreign affairs, restricted by the Constitution in certain respects, so that he is not a king or czar.

The other important dispute with Congress involving constitutional questions during that era was equally important because it involved the fight with Senator McCarthy. McCarthy had been empowered, as we all know, by the Senate to conduct these investigations for which he became notorious. During the Truman administration, preceding the Eisenhower years, the fight had been very bitter between Truman and McCarthy—a battle of words which didn't phase McCarthy at all because as long as the Senate supported him in his investigations, there was nothing that a president could do to fire a senator. So it was a very inconclusive fight up to the time that Eisenhower came into the presidency. Finally, McCarthy was reckless enough to attack the Army and call a number of generals in the Army traitors and Communists, people that Eisenhower had worked personally with when he was supreme allied commander of the armies that defeated Hitler. He came to realize in a very personal way the outrage involved in McCarthy's methods. He asked me to give a ruling as to whether or not he had any authority to stop the Senate investigation. I advised him that he did have power under the Constitution when a senator or the Senate really crippled the proper functioning of the executive branch. He issued an executive order that said no member of the executive branch or employee in the executive branch could appear before the McCarthy committee thereafter. It was a drastic executive order but it did the job, and McCarthy had no further fodder for his day-to-day conduct of public investigations. Then the media, some courageous senators, and a very courageous lawyer from Boston named Joe Welch all were in on the kill, and the McCarthy era was definitely ended, thus vindicating the power of the presidency vis-à-vis the legislative branch of the government when the Constitution is violated.

Herbert Brownell

Civil Rights and Other Challenges

An interesting constitutional development occurred in the field of civil rights. The *Brown v. Board of Education* case was up before the Supreme Court at the time that Eisenhower was inaugurated. The Supreme Court asked the attorney general to intervene in that case, although technically speaking, the government was not a party to the case. It was a combination of five cases that had been brought by parents of black school children against their school boards to try to vindicate their rights as American citizens to have equal opportunity for an education in the public schools. Eisenhower first took the position that this was a job for the judicial branch of the government and that he should not intervene in any way, even though the Court requested that the attorney general appear and file a brief and historical background for the decision. We had quite a debate over that issue. I finally took the position that while it is true there is a distinct difference and division of powers between the three branches of our federal government, at the same time the Constitution really mandates that there be enough cooperation between the three branches to keep the show on the road, so to speak, and bring about important changes that are required by the Constitution. He was finally convinced, and we intervened in that case with the results that you all know. This brush with the judiciary was an interesting offshoot of the provisions of the Constitution.

Then there was the conflict with the states. After *Brown v. Board of Education* was decided in favor of the schoolchildren and their parents and the black children were given an opportunity to go to public schools, the great challenge became how the decision should be implemented. The Supreme Court in this decision said with "all deliberate speed" the change in the mores of the American people should be changed to recognize that this great social goal would be accomplished. In the Southern states, that was greeted with some pleasure because they thought all deliberate speed meant at their rate of speed. They thought it would be possible for them to delay the implementation of the Constitution in this area of their daily lives for such a long time that they might be able to succeed and repeat the experiences they had after the Civil War with Reconstruction and delay the application of these constitutional rights.

All came to a head when the governor of Arkansas—remember, there were governors from there before Clinton—the governor was named Faubus, and he decided to defy the Supreme Court's interpretation of the Constitution and defy the orders from President Eisenhower to enforce *Brown v. Board of Education*. He called out the National Guard to keep black children from attending the public high school in Little Rock. That did create a great constitutional crisis, and Eisenhower, after thorough research of his constitutional powers, decided to send in the federal troops to support the black children.

It was the most exciting time in my public career, and it established a precedent that will last for a long time. When it comes to a matter of this kind, the constitutional power of the federal government is strong enough to overcome any opposition or defiance by the state government. It was a drastic change in the way of life in many states in the Union. As I said, it was the most exciting part of my term of office in Washington. You can see why there is such great satisfaction in holding the job of attorney general. It gives you an opportunity perhaps to have lasting influence on the way the Constitution of the United States is enforced. I enjoyed that part of the job.

There were parts I did not enjoy. For example, when I went before the Senate Judiciary Committee to be confirmed in the first place, they turned the questioning over to a very colorful character from Nevada named Senator Patrick McCarran. He said to me, "Mr. Brownell, are you resigned from your old office?" I said, "Yes, Senator." He said, "Did you take your name off the door?" "Yes, Senator," I replied. "You took it out of the telephone book as a practicing lawyer?" he asked. "Yes, Senator," I answered. Senator McCarran said, "So from now on you'll have no direct or indirect interest in the profits of your old firm?" I said, "That's right, Senator." "Well, Mr. Brownell," he said, "what investments do you hold?" I answered, "Senator, such as I had, I disposed of before I came to Washington." He asked, "What did you do with the proceeds?" I replied, "I put them into government bonds." He crossed over to the television camera and said in a loud voice, "Say, Brownell, you're in one hell of a fix if we don't confirm it!" I realized that what he was trying to say was that you had to divest yourself of all private interests and conflicting interests when you go into this job. It makes you unpopular. I had to send President Truman's appointment secretary to jail and 18 collectors of internal revenue, as well as a couple of congressmen. One of the congressmen, after we sent him to jail for tax evasion, was reelected unanimously and sat on the Judiciary Committee all of the rest of the time I was there. I don't think he ever voted for anything I proposed.

I think there was an attorney general of Great Britain who said that if the attorney general is a popular figure while he is in office, that just shows that he is not doing his job. There is something to that because he has to, in a sense, be the conscience of the administration and see to it that private conflicts of interest do not interfere with official duties.

Appointing Federal Judges

The other thing that is most interesting and satisfying in holding the position of attorney general was the opportunity to advise the president on the appointment of federal judges, who hold their positions for life. As a result, they have a lasting influence of their own for long periods of time because of their proper interpretations of the Constitution and the rights of individuals thereunder. There were five vacancies during the Eisenhower years on the Supreme Court and the appointment of Earl Warren, Bill Brennan, John Harlan, Potter Stewart, and Charles E. Whittaker figured in an exciting period in the transformation of the trend in the Supreme Court.

To me the most interesting appointment, in retrospect, was the appointment of Bill Brennan to the Court. Before the vacancy arose for which he was finally appointed, President Eisenhower had said to me that he wanted to appoint a Democrat to the next vacancy because he felt that, the Supreme Court being an unelective office, it was important to maintain the confidence of the people in the proceedings of the Court. One way to do that, he felt, was to be sure that all points of view were represented on the Court, so that the average citizen would know that his point of view had been carefully considered by the Court before it rendered its verdicts and handed down its opinions. Therefore, he said he wanted to appoint a Democrat. He might not agree with his ideology and all, but he wanted to maintain the confidence of the American people in the operations of the Court, and this, he thought, was one effective way to do it.

When the vacancy arose, he said to me, "I have had two pressure groups that have been asking me for consideration in the appointment of the next judge on the Supreme Court." One was the chief justices of the state courts who felt that it was time to appoint someone who had had experience on the state courts to properly represent the states in interpreting the Constitution and federalism, which is provided for under the Constitution. The other was the Council of Catholic Bishops, who said that for a long time there had not been a Catholic on the Court, and they thought that Eisenhower should give consideration in his next appointment to a Catholic.

Bill Brennan was a highly regarded judge on the State Supreme Court in New Jersey and seemed to fit the bill. Eisenhower was seriously considering him and finally made up his mind to appoint him. I knew of one man in the country who would be delighted about this: Cardinal Spellman in New York, who had been very insistent that a Catholic be appointed to the Supreme Court. I called him the night before the announcement was going to be made. I said, "Your Eminence, you'll be happy to know that the President is appointing Judge Brennan to the Supreme Court," and I expected him to explode with pleasure. Instead, he said, "Who is his parish priest?" I said that I hadn't the slightest indication of who his parish priest was, let alone what he thought of him. Well, he was rather subdued in his comments at that point. Afterward, when Brennan had been on the Court for some time and handed down some pretty liberal opinions, I was walking up the street in New York and I met Cardinal Spellman. He did not even stop to say hello or anything else. He said, "You should have asked his parish priest!" So there was a light side to the appointment of federal judges.

The other significant contribution in that area was that after *Brown v. Board of Education*, we had a difficult time finding qualified people from the Southern states to go on the various federal district courts which would implement *Brown v. Board of Education*. Everyone that was recommended to the President by the senators had taken a strong position in favor of segregation in their public remarks. We had to make many recommendations to the President from the Justice Department of people who did not have the endorsement of the senators from their states, and that created some difficult political problems. Fortunately, I knew a group of people there who were qualified for the bench. There was Elbert Tuttle in Georgia, John Minor Wisdom in Louisiana, Frank Johnson in Alabama, and John Brown in Texas—people that I had known in the course of my private law practice who had not taken any stand publicly on *Brown v. Board of Education* and who were singularly qualified for the position. They were the people who made the day-to-day interpretations of the effects of *Brown v. Board of Education* and developed the enforcement policies of the federal government in that respect. I took some particular satisfaction of seeing to it that men of that calibre were appointed—it was before the days when we appointed women to the courts. Working with the President, the Senate, and the Bar in the appointment of judges generally turned out to be one of the highlights of my experience.

The Rewards of Public Service

You can see why I liked politics in the terms that have been referred to here today, and why I found public service so satisfying and so exciting. If I had to do it all over again, I would make the same choice because I think citizen participation in the operations of a government is of paramount importance. As Benjamin Franklin replied at the Constitutional Convention in Philadelphia when they asked him what had been done: "We have created a republic if we can keep it." It is true that there has to be intelligent

WHAT DOES AN ATTORNEY GENERAL DO?

citizen participation to make the Constitution work and to make our form of government work and to see to it that we enjoy the blessing of freedom and liberty that is the goal of our particular form of government.

I am happy to have had a part in it, and I must say that I am very happy to have had a part in the enterprise of the Miller Center, which devotes its best efforts to the study of the presidency and to the significance of the Constitution and the betterment of the average citizen that can come from strict participation by everyday citizens in the operations of our government.

I am proud to have been on the Council. I think the job that Ken Thompson and the board members do is really magnificent and has not only contributed to the life of this community in a most constructive way, but it has really had an influence in the policies in Washington. So I thank you from the bottom of my heart for this recognition today. I will always enjoy it regardless of how many years I have left. I have had 90 years, and that is a pretty good start. Thank you so much.

QUESTION: How much practical control does the attorney general really have over the FBI?

MR. BROWNELL: It depends basically on the president. He is the boss, after all, and to a certain extent of the attorney general, himself, because he is in charge of the whole department. While you do give autonomy to the big institutions in the Department of Justice like the FBI, the Immigration Service, and so forth, still there are certain things that the attorney general can do.

I had a couple of run-ins with J. Edgar Hoover. Although he ran a good law enforcement investigative agency while I was there, once I found that he was sending out raw FBI investigative files of teachers to local school boards all around the country. The average school board did not have any experience in studying legal evidence of that kind and could not judge between rumor, gossip, and fact. The result was that many public school teachers were being unnecessarily damaged by that type of information. I put a stop to that practice.

The other time was when I found that in the area of investigation of subversive activities, the FBI had on its payroll a number of so-called expert witnesses and were paying them not by the hour the way professional witnesses are usually paid in the court system, but really gave them a salary. They could not be, in my opinion, independent witnesses, so I had to put a stop to that. There are certain things the attorney general can do in supervision of the FBI that can turn out to be quite important, but basically, it depends on the president. If he wants to use them in ways that Nixon did, for example, he can really lead the activities of the Bureau in the wrong direction, which in itself operates unfortunately under an executive order that was established by FDR, and they never had a congressional charter that restricts their activities. That is one of the things that has to be eventually remedied in our government. I say this because it does give the president and the attorney general the control over the FBI they want.

QUESTION: Could you tell us what happened for you and Eisenhower when he had his coronary and underwent surgery? We did not have the 25th Amendment then. Were you called in to advise him on what to do? I think he had an agreement with Nixon, but I'm not sure.

MR. BROWNELL: The history on that is important. At the time of his heart attack, I was in Italy and I came back from a sheep meadow in a Navy plane. We had to chase the sheep off the runway in order to get in the air. When I landed in Washington, I found out that memos had been prepared that called for Nixon to take over the government. I was kind of shocked by it and asked if they could make thorough studies as quickly as possible to determine what the Constitution meant when it said in essence that in case of the inability of the president to exercise the powers and duties of his office, the vice president should assume those powers and duties. I checked around and found there were no crises in foreign affairs. The Congress was not in session and there was nothing pending in the administrative departments that called for immediate action on the part of the President. I then consulted with the heart specialist, Dudley White, as to the actual condition of the President. He told me that the President was going to recover and would need a little time to do it, but he was not out of his mind in any respect. Therefore I gave the opinion, which the Cabinet accepted, that the constitutional provision, even though it was fuzzy, did not call for the takeover by the vice president.

I reported this to the President in Denver. He was in bed in the hospital. He said, "What happens if the doctors are wrong and I'm laid up for a long time, perhaps seriously so?" I said that it was very unclear under the Constitution. He said, "Then if that's true, you'd better get busy and change it." That was the origin of the studies that we made under the direction of Dr. Ruth Silva of the Pennsylvania State University as to the history and meaning of the constitutional provision, and we proposed the 25th Amendment as a result of that.

QUESTION: Could you tell me on what issue you were able to defeat the Bricker amendment? I was there at the time. I wasn't clear as to how you beat them, but I was delighted!

MR. BROWNELL: What was the basis on which we opposed it? It looked tough for a lawyer because the American Bar Association had come to the conclusion that the Bricker amendment was properly drafted and would be an improvement in the Constitution. One of the most important members of the American Bar Association who favored the Bricker amendment was the President's brother, Edgar, so he and I had that situation to face when we made our study which was based mostly on the views of Erwin Griswold, who was then the dean of the Harvard Law School, Professor Corwin at Princeton, and John W. Davis, in whom the president had great confidence as a lawyer. The President said, "Why can't you lawyers get together and agree on this?" But he did listen very carefully to those voices that analyzed what they believed would be the effect of the Bricker amendment. They thought it would affect not only treaties but also executive agreements, giving the Senate veto power as a practical political matter over any wishes of the president in the development of treaties and executive agreements as well as ratification of them. They felt it would be a fundamental change in the balance of power between the two branches of the government. That was the line that we took.

QUESTION: You were a power in Republican politics the last time the Congress turned back to the Republican party in 1946. What do you think will be the practical impact of the dynamics between the chief executive and Congress over the next couple of years?

MR. BROWNELL: I don't agree with the pundits so much on that. I think there will be a period of conflict between the two branches that will dominate the political scene for the next two years leading up to the presidential election and that, while it is true that they can "cooperate" in certain areas, the basic thrust will be conflict between two points of view that are very far apart and that will be intertwined with the personal ambitions of many people who want to be president. That goes not only for the Republicans but also for the Democrats. I think there will be attempts from within the Democratic party to run primary campaigns against President Clinton and of course there will be bitter intraparty battles among the Republicans as to what point of view shall dominate the philosophy of the Republican party in the future. There are many battles to be settled there. It will be a lively two years on the political scene.

MR. THOMPSON: We have a successor commission to the one that you chaired on presidential disability. The subject is the selection of federal judges and nine out of the 11 districts are in a state of emergency, the commission was advised. Their main problem in a way is the same problem that confronted the transition commission that Bill Rogers and Cy Vance co-chaired, namely delay. There is a backlog of substantial proportions. In the discussions thus far there is concern about the fact that so many agencies are involved—the Justice Department, the White House, the Senate, the ABA, the FBI. I wondered whether you thought that whole process was one which could be simplified and made a little more coherent than it is.

WHAT DOES AN ATTORNEY GENERAL DO?

MR. BROWNELL: I do think it can be improved. I think it is a mistake to have the screening of candidates for judicial office made in the White House. I think the atmosphere is too political there and every day the president and the White House staff are faced with demands from senators, and especially House members to a certain extent, that he take a certain position on legislation. They are very often willing to bargain their position on legislation if they can get their own candidates for the federal courts approved by the president. Thus, the atmosphere in the White House, and I am not picking out any particular White House, is bound to be too political to have the screening work done there. I think the best thing would be to have it in the Department of Justice where there again, without regard to any particular administration, the atmosphere is much more professional and there is bound to be more attention given to the professional qualifications of the candidates in the first instance, and the weeding out process. While the president is the final person to decide who shall be appointed, it is a good idea to have the candidates thoroughly investigated from a professional rather than a political standpoint. I hope that this process could be returned to the Department of Justice.

QUESTION: One of the very few unhappy moments in your life, I suspect, was in 1948 with the Dewey campaign where Truman ran against a so-called good-for-nothing 80th Congress and won. Mr. Clinton presumably has the opportunity to run against the good-for-nothing 104th Congress. What advice would you give to a Republican candidate?

MR. BROWNELL: I would have a little advice based on that 1948 campaign, I must say, and I think the Republicans should keep in mind that they can also be thrown out by the people as well as the Democrats. They have to establish an affirmative record. The 80th Congress was not all bad, especially in the field of foreign affairs, where they passed some very constructive legislation. Truman was a very clever political leader, and he said that it was a do-nothing Congress and he said it to everyone on every railroad stop in the country. People loved his brusque, not to say crude manner of slamming the opposition and so forth. The Republicans will be up against that in my opinion unless they first establish a record of accomplishment. Even though their proposals might be vetoed in the White House, they have to show that they are capable of governing and they have to support and make their ideological viewpoints. I think they have to prevent a repetition of the last Republican Convention which was dominated by one of the extreme wings of the Republican party. I don't care what your ideology is, you cannot successfully run a national political campaign if you do not stick to the center of the philosophy of your own party. The present chairman of the Republican National Committee seems to favor gathering together all of the viewpoints in the Republican party and having it more or less a centrist provision which would be essential, I think, to the success of the Republicans in the next presidential campaign.

QUESTION: Isn't there a danger that the Republican Congress might do what a Democratic Congress did on the Republican presidents, namely enact popular but perhaps harmful legislation, hoping or expecting that the president will veto them?

MR. BROWNELL: I will tell the story about the 1948 campaign before I answer your question. After the campaign, I was attacked. I had been the campaign manager for the losing candidate, Dewey. I was attacked by all sides, but more by Republicans than by Democrats. The Brownells went to Arizona for a little vacation, and the Deweys went with them. We had a lovely time and a restful vacation there for a couple of weeks to get over the election. When I got back to the law office, my senior partner put his arm around me and said, "I'm so sorry to hear what happened to you and Dewey." I said, "What was that?" and he said, "Didn't you read Cholly Knickerbocker's column? He said Dewey was so mad at you on election night that he picked up a chair and hit you over the head with it!" A story of that nature got very wide acceptance, and people were so shocked to see Dewey and me walking down the street together after that. We continued as close friends to the end.

It had many repercussions for me. Professionally, people did not want to be my client. It was the beginning of the Reagan movement in California, where he was especially violent in attacking the wicked people who pushed Dewey in the Republican party. It had many repercussions.

Regarding your question, people are too smart for that. If they do it on any widespread basis, it will hurt them, in my opinion. Even though, as I say, if they will pass legislation that is coherent and in line with the general conservative Republican philosophy, I think they will get credit for it regardless of whether it is signed or not. But if it appears to be slickly designed to embarrass the president, I think it will boomerang on them. I think you have to make some distinctions there. I think there will be thorough Whitewater investigations as a result of this change and that will run through most of the preconvention period leading up to 1996, which will dominate the headlines for quite a while. The investigative powers of the Congress will be very prominently displayed during the next two years. It isn't entirely a matter of legislation. I think the investigative activities in Congress will be of almost as much political significance as the legislation that is passed.

QUESTION: If my recollection is correct, President Eisenhower considered his appointment of Earl Warren as his greatest mistake because of the subsequent rulings of the Warren Court.

MR. BROWNELL: No. I researched that rather thoroughly. I never could find the slightest indication in his *Memoirs* or the conversations that I had with him or with Earl Warren's *Memoirs* or conversations with him that he ever said that or ever believed that. There were disagreements between the two men over some of the Supreme Court decisions, notably in the field of criminal justice and in anti-Communist decisions of the Court so that the two men had differences of opinion as to some of the Supreme Court rulings. That was kept on a high level and was not a personal feud. The only thing that approached a personal feud was that after Eisenhower had his heart attack, there was great speculation in the press as to who would be the next Republican candidate because they assumed he would die and there would be an open convention. The polls that were taken show that if Eisenhower did not run for reelection that Earl Warren was the leading candidate. The media asked Earl Warren about that and he said, "No comment", and

Eisenhower interpreted that as saying, "Boy, would I like it!" He felt that not only from a personal standpoint, but from the standpoint of the Court, Warren should have said flatly, "No, I'm not interested. I'm chief justice, I'm not running for president, and I hope President Eisenhower gets well." That created a strained atmosphere between the two men which lasted right up to the end. But as far as that statement being made, I don't believe it ever was made. I noticed after Justice Brennan got off the Court, the media carried stories to the effect that Eisenhower said that Brennan was the worst one. It is too good a story not to write, even if it isn't true. It is certainly true that many appointees to the Supreme Court hand out opinions that are disapproved by the executive branch and by the particular presidents. That is good! I don't think there should be any different result. But neither Eisenhower nor Warren was the type of man who would have made such statements either privately or publicly, in my opinion.

MR. THOMPSON: We thank General Brownell for one of the most memorable statements on the government at work ever made in this building.

IV.

PRESIDENTS AND THE CONGRESS

~ *Nine* ~

PRESIDENTIAL LEADERSHIP: LYNDON B. JOHNSON AND THE CONGRESS[*]

Jack Valenti

NARRATOR: It is a great pleasure to welcome you to another Forum. Jack Valenti is a veteran so far as the Miller Center is concerned. Some years ago he gave a Forum on the presidency. He also participated a year-and-a-half ago in a celebrated Rotunda debate on the six-year term. So he is not only known to us but we hope that we are beginning to be known to him.

He is, as you know, president of the Motion Picture Association of America. In this favorable tenure situation, his post is surpassed only by that of a Supreme Court Justice or a university professor. Since 1922 there have been only three presidents—Will Hayes, the postmaster general under President Harding from 1922 to 1945; Eric Johnson, the president of the United States Chamber of Commerce; and now Jack Valenti. He is also the president of the Motion Picture Export Association of America, Inc. and chairman of the Alliance of Motion Picture and Television Producers, nine groups that are among the major producers and distributors of film throughout the world, including Warner Brothers, Disney, and Twentieth Century Fox.

He was born in Houston; he graduated at the ripe old age of 15 from Sam Houston High School, from the University of Houston and he holds an MBA degree from Harvard University. He was co-founder of Weekley and Valenti, a public relations, advertising and

---

[*]Presented in a Forum at the Miller Center of Public Affairs on 13 November 1984. Reprinted from *The Virginia Papers on the Presidency* (Lanham, Maryland: University Press of America, Inc., 1987), Volume XXIII.

political consulting firm. He has a distinguished war record flying some 51 combat missions as a B-25 attack bomber pilot and winning four major citations including the Distinguished Flying Cross and the Air Medal with four clusters.

He is the author of a number of books: *The Bitter Taste of Glory*, a volume of nine political portraits; a study of the Johnson White House, *A Very Human President*; and *Speak Up With Confidence*.

It is known to many of you that he was on Air Force One on its return from Dallas after the assassination of President Kennedy. He remained from November 1963 to June 1966 as a special assistant to President Johnson, working closely with him in the civil rights field in particular. It is a privilege for us to have Jack Valenti as our speaker this morning.

MR. VALENTI: I told Kenneth that I would be happy to talk today about Johnson as political leader. I will describe essentially how Johnson felt about managing the White House and some of his concepts as leader about where this country ought to go.

First, I think it is fair to say that Lyndon Johnson probably was the single most intelligent man that I had ever met. I have never in my life attended a mind as capacious, as all-embracing, as able to sort out problems, to move six moves down the chess board when everyone else was trying to figure the next move. I do not say that Johnson was an educated man in the sense the universities would define that term. I don't believe he would recall who came first, the Greeks or the Romans, because it was a matter of small consequence to him. I think that for him Herodotus and Immanuel Kant were obscure figures. If they weren't in politics then they obviously weren't important. But he was a man of great intellect. I consider intelligence to be something that allows you to address a problem, be able to see all sides of it, and come forward with conclusions as to how that problem ought to be solved, whether it is managing a university, or deciding the fiscal course that a giant corporation should take or how to govern the country.

It is very easy to put plans on paper because paper offers little resistance, but it is very, very difficult to govern men. The art of governance is still one of the most obscure art forms that we have.

It does not lend itself to Bernoulli's theorem or Boyle's law. There are no immutable formulas. So what you are dealing with is the one thing that a computer cannot decipher. A computer can do all sorts of magical things, but the one thing computers cannot do, and I daresay will never be able to do, is to chart human behavior. The reason why economists so often miss their mark is because their econometric models that come clickety-clack out of a computer are barren of that essential element. That is why it is difficult to raise a family. It is very difficult to do anything where the human being is the essential creature. That's why in my own business, motion pictures, it's crazy and risky. No one to this hour has ever been able to figure out what it is that you can put on film that will engage people. So each time a film is made it is as if a brand new business were being born, with no prior research.

If you go back into Johnson's early career everything about him was all there and visible, revealed, and ready to be appraised. At age 25 he was head of the National Youth Administration. If you want to look at how Johnson ran the presidency you merely go back and assemble all of the facts about how he ran the NYA. It was a 24-hour-a-day operation. He never slept when there was a job to be done and he would not let anyone else sleep either until that job was completed. When he became a congressman at age 28, he was the first congressman to run an office 24 hours a day. He had two shifts of people. You could call his office at four o'clock in the morning and someone would be on duty, and sometimes Johnson himself would be there. It is this relentless energy that pervaded his life and marked his presidency.

The other part of the Johnson background was that he always catalogued errors that others made and profited by them. He never thought he would be president. He intended to go back to Texas and retire to his ranch when the second term of the Kennedy presidency was completed in 1968. His political life, as he saw it, was over. But as a result of a senseless act of mindless malice in Dallas he was suddenly president. Almost immediately his mind began to retrieve from these nooks and crannies where he had stored all of this information, all that he had dreamed of if he were ever in ultimate command.

LYNDON B. JOHNSON AND THE CONGRESS

Bill Moyers, the late Cliff Carter, and I were in his bedroom the first night of his presidency at his home on 22 November. We were with him until about three or four or five in the morning on 23 November. He was lying in bed and he began to ruminate and to paint for us the canvas of the Great Society. Within four or five hours he had taken all of these tangled threads of governing America and had woven a tapestry. The first thing he said was, "I'm going to call Dick Russell." Richard Brevard Russell was the patriarch of the Senate, senior senator from Georgia, leader of the anti-civil rights forces, Johnson's closest friend in the Senate, and the man who had made him majority leader. "I'm going to tell Dick that we are going to pass a civil rights bill—no quarter given, no quarter asked." He thought Kennedy had compromised on this. He said, "I'm going to run him down if I have to. Then we are going to pass the Voting Rights Act, and an Equal Housing Act." Now mind you, this was on 22 November 1963, and before he left office all of that was done.

The first thing on his agenda was the redemption of the promise of human justice in this country which he thought had been ignored. He was determined to set right what he found to be so plainly wrong. And so he girded his loins for a battle which he thought would lose him the South.

The second thing on his agenda was to make education a big priority. He said that he wanted to make it possible for every boy and girl in America, no matter how poor, or what their color or where they lived, to be able, "to get all of the education they can take and to do it at the finest universities in America and to do it by loan, scholarship, or grant, paid for by the government." In 1963 that was a revolutionary concept. He ran smack into the protestant ministry of this country who were violently opposed to that. On the other hand, he knew that people like myself had been able to get a first-class education because of the GI Bill of Rights, which never existed before. I went to Harvard with all of my tuition paid and $65.00 a month in cash. I could never have gone to Harvard without that GI Bill of Rights.

Johnson recognized that probably the single most important asset in this country is education. Too often bright young children, because their families were poor, just could not go to school. Now that is not right, and he determined to set it right.

The third piece of legislation he was going to pass was Medicare, which had languished since Harry Truman's time. He was concerned that old people in this country were unable to get medical care because they could not pay for it. Johnson said, "That's not right and we are going to change it." So those were the three great wrongs that he was going to right.

At that time these were such radical revisions of the social mores and the economic forms of this country that it was a revolutionary cry. If only someone had looked into Johnson's background to see the tenacity with which he approached things, the resolve with which he embraced things, and the commitment which he attached to things, then no one would have doubted he would have done it. But at that time, I thought he had gone out of his mind, and that politically it was just impossible to do.

The point I'm making is that the concept of the Johnson presidency was formed in his mind long before he became president. The moment that he assumed command he was absolutely prepared, that hour, that day, to begin to bring his objectives to life. He prepared for it by first getting elected. He had to do that; he had to establish his primacy as a leader on his own. And all of 1964, and indeed in those early days of the presidency, he tried to demonstrate to the country that while the light in the White House may flicker, the light in the White House never goes out. There is a linear continuity in this country that binds it together. He demonstrated how very thick and strong are the strands of the Constitution. To do that he had to be calm and composed.

I think those hours after the assassination and the months after were his finest hours. He soothed the nation's fevered brow; he put to rest all of these anxieties in the world. He demonstrated that he was strong and wise, and that his would be a good hand on the tiller. That was how the Johnson presidency began. It was all of a piece; he never strayed from those objectives. He managed the White House in a way that made it very clear that he was not going to have anyone around him straying from the goals he wanted to accomplish.

LYNDON B. JOHNSON AND THE CONGRESS

I cannot emphasize this compass course too much. A leader without convictions is going to be right only by accident. Unless you really know where you want to go you cannot lead. You are doing it by hesitancy, you are doing it by chance. Only when a president has a clear-cut course, following that needle on the compass, can he really accomplish anything.

Although Reagan is remarkably detached from government he does have convictions about where he wants to take the country. Unlike Johnson he allows other people to move this elephantine apparatus called the federal establishment forward, while he stands back and observes. But he nonetheless has made it clear to the American people that he has a clear sense of where he wants to go. I think this landslide victory was in part due to the fact that people believed that.

So did Johnson have a clear-cut course. However, Johnson did not stay on the mountaintop observing. He was down at the very edge of the firing line, leading his troops, commanding them and leading the cavalry charge.

The second thing that he did was to make sure that the Congress worked. In our form of government, and thankfully so, unless you are able to persuade the Congress to your point of view, you are going to have problems. So he set out very early on to make sure that he had allies within the Congress. The Johnson method of doing that was very simple. He worked 24 hours a day making sure that Congress was courted, cosseted, taken care of. At the same time he instilled fear that if you really crossed him, he would cut your head off. Love and fear must go together if you are going to be a great leader.

He told all of his staff that they could not leave their office until they had called every senator and congressman who had called that day. "I don't care what time of night it is. I don't care if your wife and your children are screaming for you. You cannot leave until you make those calls. Then when you get the congressman or senator on the phone, you treat him with deference and respect because he was elected to office and you weren't." He ordered his staff to respond to whatever it is that he or she asked. "If you have to say 'no' you don't shove the dagger in, you do it gently."

Jack Valenti

And finally, "You treat them all alike whether they are rookie congressmen or a herd bull." That is what he called the chairman of a committee, a "herd bull." He didn't care whether they were a Republican or Democrat. You treat them all with the same kind of respect. When the time came for us to go to the Hill to get Southern congressmen in 1964 to vote for a civil rights bill, it was not easy. Some of them would rather be caught seducing the minister's wife on the courthouse steps at high noon than to vote for the civil rights bill. It helped if you had established a kind of rapport with Congress.

On many occasions I would approach a congressman, saying, "The President needs you. You recall, Senator, when you asked us about this dam, the President went along." The Congressman would say: "Yes, I remember." I would say, "Well, now next time you come around for that, Senator, the President says we might not hear. Somehow our hearing aid will have been turned off." He had to think whether he wanted to incur the wrath of Johnson after he had been treated so gloriously and so lovingly. You would be amazed at how many votes we got that way. Johnson believed that passing civil rights bills, passing Medicare, passing the elementary and secondary education act were so much in the public interest that if you had to kick a congressman a couple of times to get his attention, it was worth it. He did it, and we passed them all.

I remember calling congressmen at midnight and saying, "Senator, this is Jack Valenti. I know you called me. I have been awful busy today, but I didn't want this day to end without returning your call." Well, if there was any venom it drained away quickly. He would say, "Well, that's very nice of you, Jack. I have some things to talk about but it's midnight so can we talk at nine in the morning?" I said, "Where can I call you?" and I made sure that nine in the morning, right on the dot, I called that senator.

As they say in the motion picture business, "Dissolve to a scene now four years hence." In 1967—I am out of the White House. There was a problem in the Congress that concerned the movie industry, and I had hired some lobbyists to do some work. One of them came to see me and said, "Jack, we have this important Republican senator and he won't talk to anyone but you." I thought this was strange, one of the leaders of the Republican

Senate wanting to see me. When I got in his office he said to me, "Jack your people have talked to me about this. It really does not concern my state very much so I can vote for you. I am going to vote for you, but I want to tell you why." He said, "In this Nixon White House I cannot get anyone to answer my calls. No one gives a damn about me. I write letters and some third-level fellow answers them. But when you were in the White House, when Johnson was there, you people cared about me. You answered my calls, you did more for me in two years than Nixon will ever be able to do. I want to vote for you because it is my way of saying thank you."

I learned that Johnson was right. He understood with such clarity that people who man this government and the people who vote are human beings. They have egos, they care about their dignity, they want to be treated with kindness. But most of all they like to think that someone cares about them. Johnson believed that if you didn't attend to the human ego and you weren't sensitive to the human condition and the human spirit, you would be in big trouble. You cannot be aloof and give commands without knowing that you are dealing with human beings. Whether ordinary human beings or famous human beings, everyone wants to be treated with respect. That is something he did. He wasn't adverse to applying a little pressure now and then, but that was only the last resort when everything else had failed.

QUESTION: Does your experience and observation indicate that experience in the legislative branch, especially being a senator, is very important for the presidency? I am thinking of two people recently, Johnson and Ford. Johnson seems to have operated very differently than Ford when he became president. One of Ford's troubles was that he had been in the legislative branch so long he couldn't make up his mind. He was always looking at both sides and wasn't very forceful in going ahead on a course that he had set. Johnson, as you say, did; Ford didn't. So I am interested in your evaluation of legislative experience as a qualification for the presidency.

MR. VALENTI: I think that it would be a blunder to elect a man president who is not in politics. Second, I think it would be a mistake to elect a man president who has come from a small state as governor. I think Carter thought he was going to treat the Congress like the Georgia legislature and he foundered on that rock. I do believe that congressional experience is valuable but not all congressmen and senators, though they may be able parliamentary leaders, are fit to be president. It depends on the nature of the man. If you have within you the resolve and the energy and intelligence then you ought to be leader. On the other hand, I could also tell you it's very hard to figure that out in advance unless you do a real survey of a man going back to his childhood and see how he operated.

QUESTION: Mr. Valenti, you mentioned that President Johnson was capable of seeing six moves ahead on the chess board. With respect to Vietnam, did that capacity break down or did he see the debacle coming and couldn't do anything about it?

MR. VALENTI: One of the interesting things about Vietnam is that we are talking about events that happened beginning in 1965. It was in July 1965 that the crucial decisions were made. The Pleiku bombing began February 1965, but the seminal decisions were made 21 July to 28 July 1965. That's 19 years ago.

One must remember that Johnson was not a perfect human being. Almost anything you can say about Johnson has a glimmer of truth in it. The only thing that you could never say about Johnson was that he was dull. I do believe that you have to set yourself in the circumstances as they happened then. I sat in all of those meetings and I do not consider myself one-tenth the man of Johnson but I thought the decisions that were made then were right.

When Johnson became president there was 16,500 fighting men in Vietnam. At that time the *New York Times*, the *Washington Post*, Senator Fulbright and everyone and their brother was for the course of action that we were taking. How do you suddenly say, folks, I'm getting out, we are going to humiliate ourselves. I'm cutting my connections with the Kennedy commitment and we are leaving Vietnam because I don't think we can win. I don't think we can bring them to the table. That's what you have to keep in mind. Everyone writing books today is filled with retrospective wisdom.

Walter Lippmann would come in or Bill Fulbright or Scotty Reston or Joe Alsop, and they would fulminate about the world. Finally, the President would say, "Well, all right Walter (or Joe) I agree with you, you are right. Now tell me what specific order do I give at nine o'clock tomorrow morning because I have to make the decision." And then they would start backing and filling and say, "Well, Mr. President, you know I think yah, yah, yah." There were no specifics. And what do you do? Suppose I say this faculty needs a whole reorganization and I think we ought to have a new curriculum and do what they did at Harvard, the core curriculum. Everyone says that is fine, and then someone, the president of the university says, "Well, I think that's great, but now what do I do? What is my specific plan? What do I say to each member of the faculty, and what is it that I am to bring this university?" And then, you will see them scurrying for cover because that is very difficult to do.

That's a long-winded way of saying that Johnson was not prepared to risk what he thought was political devastation and the collapse of his Great Society—human justice, education and care for the old, among other things. The Republicans and the Right Wing would say, "We have a President who is a coward. It's the first time the Americans have ever lost a war, which is not even a war; we've been humiliated; we had to drag our tails behind us and why? You mean we cannot beat some little guys with rice bags on their back?" This is a terrifying thing politically. I'm giving you the other side and I'm sure that at the time the *New York Times* and the *Washington Post* hadn't been on the road to Damascus yet; they hadn't made their conversion, they hadn't seen the light. I think they would have denounced Johnson because there was no readily available reasons, revealed or otherwise, that said you are heading toward an absolute debacle.

I'm sure you have many people from the Johnson administration come and tell you, "I certainly was one of those who thought we ought to get out." Well, that's baloney! There was not one single member of the White House staff, either by word or

Jack Valenti

memorandum that felt that way, and besides George Ball and Mike Mansfield, there was no one in the government that felt that way.

COMMENT: In early September 1966, Cliff Case of New Jersey wanted me to serve on the bipartisan committee for his reelection, and I refused. I said, "You are already ahead by 500,000 votes." He said, "Five hundred thousand sixty three." I said, "How do you feel about the President's leadership and Vietnam?" He said, "I think Johnson is morally right in what he has been doing. Thus far I support him." He clearly indicated that he thought Johnson was doing the right thing in a moral sense.

MR. VALENTI: Well, the deterioration of the situation began to show its face in the latter part of 1966, about 14 months after these crucial meetings took place where the commitment to move in 125,000 troops was made. And then beginning on 1967 it was all downhill after that. Everyone was switching and this was when the antiwar protesters began to gain an air of legitimacy. It was not until close to the congressional elections of 1966 when we took a shellacking—I think we lost about 34 seats—that Johnson recognized it was the beginning of the end as far as his political support was concerned.

QUESTION: There was another option, I believe, that President Johnson could have had in Vietnam and that was to win the war. To take off all restrictions would have been very costly but it would have done the job. Why did he not take that option?

MR. VALENTI: That's a very good question. We did examine that option many times. The bureaucracy does option papers. An option paper gives four options and three of them are so absurd that there is only one left. And you say, well obviously option four is the one we ought to go for. The first one says nuclear war; the second one says let's get out; and then you get to the only one that you have a chance of doing.

Johnson had a fear of accidentally starting World War III. For example, there were military contingency plans to literally invade the North. Johnson believed that you could not win a war just on air power; you had to send troops in and occupy the territory. First, he conjured up the bleak vision of the Yalu River when MacArthur made that crossing. Suddenly there were 700 million Chinese turning him back. Second, he thought that if he started bombing North Vietnam into the Stone Age that the Russians were not going to allow it and there would be a Russian reaction. Three, to suggestions that we mine and bomb Haiphong, for example, Johnson said in one meeting to General Wheeler, "I just know I'll do that and then some fool aviator will drop a ton of bombs right down the smokestack of a Russian freighter with two members of the politburo aboard. By God, we would have World War III on our hands." It was the prospect of another war with China or Russia that haunted him, and that is why he never sought to win it.

Now Kissinger has said many times to me, "My, if you had done what we did you could have won the war." I suggested to him he may be right but I did not see any glorious ending to the Nixon-Kissinger plan either.

The point is that we should never have gotten in there in the first place. That was the fundamental mistake that was made. And once you make a decision it gets buckled to another decision and pretty soon there is a whole steel strapping plate that binds those decisions together and you cannot lop one off and go back and start over again. Each decision has a progeny and then pretty soon there is a legacy, and then there is a commitment, and there is a resolve. By that time you are in so deep you cannot get out.

QUESTION: It seems that President Johnson's administration really foundered on Vietnam, which was essentially an issue of foreign policy. We can debate till the day is over the value of the Great Society which is being repudiated today by some elements of the population. But that aside, his administration seems to have been somewhat successful. It seems to me that foreign policy is the issue that caused you the greatest difficulty.

We castigated Eisenhower for years because of his lack of skill in domestic politics. But he seems in retrospect to have had many opportunities to commit the United States to the kinds of blunders that we committed in Vietnam and he seems to have been very reluctant to do so. He seems to have brought to office a great deal

Jack Valenti

of experience in foreign policy and some strategic or geopolitical insight perhaps that his successor did not.

Could we then draw the conclusion that what we need today in our presidents is more insight into foreign policy and understanding of geopolitics and history rather than the kinds of expertise you have described in domestic politics?

MR. VALENTI: It's a very good question. There are no solid answers. First, I don't know what is an expert in foreign policy. I mean, who is that? If you want to get an expert I guess you would get a professor of international relations at Harvard, Yale, or the University of Virginia and make him president. Who is an expert in foreign policy? I don't know what that means.

Washington abounds with people who are experts in foreign policy. You get 26 foreign policy experts and you have 27 opinions. Who is right? It's like economists. I think Eisenhower's great asset was the fact that he had been the commander of the greatest coalition of disparate viewpoints the world has ever known—de Gaulle's, Montgomery's, Churchill's, and all of these people of monstrous egos all wanting their piece of the pie. He held it together, sometimes tenuously, but he did. Now it requires a man of capacious talents to be able to weld together such an unwieldy alliance. I think that was his greatest asset. He was used to dealing with people who were in conflict and he became expert at forging some kind of a consensus. That is what politics is about. Lyndon Johnson always thought that Eisenhower was a great President. I think history is revising its view of Eisenhower as a kind of an amiable fellow who blundered and whose syntax was horribly garbled to a view of him as a leader of the first rank. I don't think he knew foreign policy any more than the State Department, but he knew how to handle conflicts of interest among his allies and how to bring them to some kind of a consensus. That is a supreme political talent, and he had it.

I do not really care whether a president is a foreign policy expert or a domestic expert because I don't know what that means. A good president understands the process. He knows that you cannot bow your neck and say I want it all or nothing because you get nothing. Compromise is the grain and the meat and the mother's milk of politics. You must bring varying viewpoints to your side and finally decide on something sufficiently suitable to your aims that is also doable.

You are not going to discover the answer in this session and you are not going to discover it in any school that I know of because there is no training ground for presidents, no school for presidents. You never know how a fellow is going to act until he is president, until the dagger is against his belly. You never know how a person is going to act in a crisis until the crisis arrives. I don't know that you can choose a president by any means other than the way we do it now, which is visceral and not intellectual.

NARRATOR: I am sure all of you will want to read Mr. Valenti's book on President Johnson simply to expand still further your view of the presidency. We are always pleased to have him with us.

~ *Ten* ~

A SENATOR REFLECTS ON A PRESIDENT: LAXALT ON REAGAN*

Paul Laxalt

NARRATOR: During our discussions of the Reagan administration, one name has continued to be mentioned. Repeatedly we have been told that the one person we should ask to participate in our oral history of President Reagan is Senator Paul Laxalt.
 Paul Laxalt received both his bachelor's and law degrees from the University of Denver. He has been a district attorney, a city attorney, and both lieutenant governor and governor of Nevada. A fellow governor at one time with Ronald Reagan, he served faithfully and with great dignity in the United States Senate from 1974 to 1986. In addition, he was perhaps Ronald Reagan's closest friend and confidant, as symbolized in the historic trip that he made to the Philippines to discuss the change in government there with Mr. Marcos.
 There are many more things one could say—law firms with which he has served and honors which he has received. We count it a high privilege to welcome Senator Laxalt to Mr. Jefferson's academical village.

SENATOR LAXALT: Thank you very kindly, Ken. I guess many things could be said about Ken Thompson. From my own experience I would say he is a study in persistence. We have been attempting to put this together for at least three or four years, and

---

*Presented in a Forum at the Miller Center of Public Affairs on 19 October 1990. Reprinted from *Leadership in the Reagan Presidency: Seven Intimate Perspectives* (Lanham, Maryland: University Press of America, Inc., 1992).

A SENATOR REFLECTS ON A PRESIDENT

I must say my not having come earlier should not be interpreted as any reluctance to come back to this beautiful place. I've had occasion over the years, particularly when I was in the Senate, to come here and speak to some of your students. Many of them here, as well as many of the people throughout Virginia, constituted the base of the Reagan candidacies, starting back in 1976.

I am certain that people like Howard Baker and Ed Meese have done a good job in presenting the policies of Ronald Reagan as well as the Reagan presidency itself. Therefore, what I would like to do is give you the benefit of my unique perspective in having been very close to Ronald Reagan, both personally and politically, for a long time. I would like to talk about his California days, his 1976 presidential campaign, and the campaigns of 1980 and 1984. I would like to conclude with some general observations about the Reagan presidency, and then answer any questions you might have.

I first became exposed to Ronald Reagan on a personal and political basis in 1964. That was the time of the Goldwater presidential campaign—an exercise in futility in the minds of many people, but not in mine. At the time I was a very young lieutenant governor in Nevada and was the first public official in the West to publicly commit for Barry Goldwater. During the course of that campaign, I spoke at an event in California at which Ronald Reagan spoke as well. In my own mind at that time, Reagan had no public persona. He was a fine man and an actor whose work I enjoyed, but like many people at that time, I believed he was of questionable political substance.

It was during the Goldwater campaign, however, that he attracted national attention because of a speech he made in Los Angeles. It was a magnificent speech lasting almost half an hour; it was televised, and was probably the most exciting event during the course of the entire Goldwater campaign. Whether he realized it or not, Reagan had then come to the attention of many prominent political types in California—as well as throughout the country—who insisted in 1965 that he run for governor of California.

He had difficulty with that decision, because although he enjoyed politics, he hadn't really thought in terms of being a candidate. Many of his old actor friends tell me that in their acting days he constantly talked politics. Most of them weren't politically oriented so they considered this constant political interest to be somewhat of a drag and a bore. Nonetheless, Reagan persisted, and in 1966 he decided to run for governor; at the same time I decided to run for governor of Nevada.

We had parallel campaigns, kept track of one another, and were both elected. During the course of our governorships we had many problems in common, since our states adjoined. In particular, we had a huge problem in connection with Lake Tahoe, a magnificent area, which at the time was being overdeveloped. We were fearful of the adverse ecological effects which many ecologists said were probable if this overdevelopment on the lake continued. Consequently, if you can believe it, two staunch conservatives decided that the only way to deal with the problem was for us to create a huge metropolitan agency that would cover both states. We did that, and as a result we prevented the overdevelopment of Tahoe and have preserved it. Both of us are rather proud of that.

During that period of time, Reagan did many exciting things in California that brought him national attention. I would think then, as now, there are very few states that are as complex politically and have as many nagging problems as California. He approached these problems aggressively and, I thought, interestingly, because he approached them as a citizen-politician. He proceeded immediately to slash programs right and left. He incurred the animosity of most of the university structure in California; he wasn't exactly their darling during the 1960s. It wasn't all that safe to go with Ronald Reagan to any California campus. For that matter, it wasn't safe for many of the rest of us either.

He continued on that course, however, particularly on the spending side. He had at that time what many of us feel the President of the United States should have: the line-item veto. I saw him employ that hundreds of times and save the people of California literally billions of dollars. When he became governor of California, the state faced a very difficult fiscal situation; during the course of his governorship and thereafter, the state was actually sending refunds to its citizens. Absolutely remarkable!

After four years as governor of Nevada, I left politics to do other things, but Reagan continued as governor of California and was elected to another four-year term in 1970.

We remained in contact during those years, but we weren't all that close. In 1974 I decided to get back into politics and ran for the United States Senate during the Watergate scandal—a remarkable sense of political timing. Somehow I won, and as you all remember, in 1974 Gerald Ford succeeded to the presidency under the most difficult of circumstances and was doing an admirable job. At that time, many of the Reagan people and many of the conservatives throughout the country felt that while Gerald Ford had been a very effective caretaker president, he probably wouldn't be a strong enough candidate to get reelected. As a result, many people solicited Ronald Reagan for the purpose of considering a run in 1976 for the presidency.

You can imagine the heartburn that created in many circles, because to run against an incumbent sitting president in either party simply isn't done. It's tacky and is politically dangerous if you don't make it. I must say that when I went back to Washington in 1974 I had in mind that, while the Reagan people felt he should run for president—he did have an abortive run in 1968 in Miami which was very amateurish and which didn't go anywhere—he really wasn't in the presidential league. I must add, however, that the longer I was in Washington and the more I saw the so-called "big leaguers," the better Ronald Reagan looked to me. I found that for the most part, these big leaguers didn't have the charisma, the appeal, and the conviction that Ronald Reagan had.

At a dinner in 1975 at the Madison Hotel in Washington, there were four or five of us with Ronald Reagan considering whether or not he should look at a presidential run. I often think about that dinner because the Reagan presidency really began that evening. It illustrated to me what could happen in this politically complex and overwhelming country if you can gather a handful of people with enough conviction to even seek the presidency. Reagan decided that he would not commit at that time to run for the presidency. He wanted a feasibility study, which I suppose is a product of his General Electric days, so he commissioned several of us and asked me to lead the study. He wanted to know if a Reagan candidacy would be divisive to the Republican party. He didn't want to get involved in any effort that was going to be unduly divisive, because he believed strongly in the two-party system and

Paul Laxalt

had become a very dedicated Republican, particularly as governor of California. We took some samplings around the country and came to the conclusion that if the candidacy were performed in a positive way it need not be divisive. Eventually that report was made to him and he decided to run.

I think the 1976 contest for the Republican nomination between Reagan and Ford was probably one of the most civilized I have ever seen at any level. They are both gentlemen. There were no slashing personal attacks of the type that you see now since negative campaigning and negative advertising have unfortunately become vogue. They both presented to the Republicans of this country their various views of how the presidency should be conducted in the future.

We finally came down to the wire, as before the convention neither side had the requisite number to lock up the nomination and advance the convention. There were about 100 uncommitted delegates floating around who were eventually going to make the difference. I can remember being in competition with President Ford for those delegates, even though it really wasn't a fair competition; President Ford, utilizing the White House, as well he should, was inviting delegates there. He would have them picked up in limousines for visits to the Oval Office and the Roosevelt Room, and for receptions in the East Room as well.

Reagan was losing that battle for these delegates quickly because all we could do was call people and ask them for their vote. Therefore, we came to the conclusion that we needed to do something very exciting, lest the race be locked up. It was finally decided that what Reagan needed, and this was unprecedented, was a vice presidential candidate, preferably someone from the same area as the uncommitted delegates. In that particular year, as in many years, most of these delegates were from larger eastern and northeastern states like New Jersey, Pennsylvania, and New York. We finally decided therefore that we would solicit my seatmate in the United States Senate, Richard Schweiker from Pennsylvania, as a running mate in advance. He was shocked, but flattered, and in one of the more exciting press conferences I have ever seen in my life in the Capitol, it was announced that Richard Schweiker was going to be the vice presidential running mate for Ronald Reagan.

A SENATOR REFLECTS ON A PRESIDENT

Since Richard Schweiker had an image of being somewhat left of center, I think there was some consternation, particularly among my conservative colleagues. In particular, I remember Strom Thurmond saying, "But Paul, Schweiker is a liberal!" We proceeded, however, with that bold move to at least unsettle the situation so that these remaining delegates waited until the convention before they committed.

The Republican national convention of 1976 was by far the most exciting convention that I have ever participated in because it went right down to the wire; we were dead even. Both sides were fighting for every delegate; it was democracy at its best. We took a test vote in which we lost, narrowly, and I'll never forget what Dick Schweiker did the next morning. He said that he had examined the test vote and had come to the conclusion that the reason Ronald Reagan did not prevail was because of him. In particular Dick said that there had been some defections in some of the Southern states like Mississippi, and that he thought it would be better if he withdrew from the ticket to give Ronald Reagan a better chance. Without a moment's hesitation Ronald Reagan said, "No. We came on this together and we are going out together." This was a moment of truth which I thought reflected the character and integrity of both Ronald Reagan and Richard Schweiker. Finally, of course, Gerald Ford was nominated, and all of us pitched in to help him; as you recall, he was narrowly defeated by Jimmy Carter.

At this time Reagan was in his late 60s, and most people believed that at that age a person was no longer viable for any public office, particularly the presidency. I think the Reagans felt that they had had their chance and that was it. I implored them to stay loose because they had made a very positive impression, not only upon Republicans, but upon the country as well. I told them that politics was unpredictable and cyclical and that you never knew what would happen. Even though it is conventional wisdom that if a sitting president does a good job, ordinarily he will have eight years—and eight years would be out of the question for the Reagans—I asked them to stay loose.

I remember attending my first meeting as a senator with President Carter. It was several weeks into his presidency, and it

Paul Laxalt

was apparent to me then that as decent a man as he was and as competent as he was in some areas, he just didn't have it; he just didn't relate. He didn't even come close to relating to us as senators, not that this was the test. Therefore, that day after the meeting I called Ronald Reagan and told him that I thought I had just met a one-term president and strongly advised him not to make any public Shermanesque-type statements about not running for the presidency in the future. I thought that, depending upon future developments, the climate would be right so that Ronald Reagan would be a viable candidate in 1980. As you know, eventually he decided to run and conducted a tremendous campaign in 1980.

We had developed a team of pros in 1976 and kept them on in 1980. Some of them weren't tactically up to the 1980 race, however, especially in Iowa. Ronald Reagan, as many of you know, had his roots in the Illinois-Iowa area as a young man and spent much of his youth after graduating from college as a sports announcer in Des Moines. Therefore, some of our political pros felt that he didn't have to spend much time in Iowa, and that instead he should spend his time in other more important states. George Bush was running then, and he practically lived in Iowa for months. To the complete shock of the whole political community in this country, and particularly to the Reagan forces, Bush beat Ronald Reagan in Iowa. That loss awoke the Reagan forces, and a new strategy and new people were found so that the campaign could go forward.

I'll never forget a debate we had at a small school auditorium in Nashua, New Hampshire. George Bush, Ronald Reagan, and several other candidates such as Howard Baker and Phil Crane participated, but the stars were really Bush and Reagan. A parliamentary struggle developed as to whether Ronald Reagan or George Bush was to speak first, and the moderator turned off Ronald Reagan's mike. Because the Reagan forces had essentially paid for the cost of the whole event, Ronald Reagan grabbed the mike and said, "Mr. Green, I refuse to be turned off; I paid for the mike!" It was explosive! It showed a fighting spirit that Ronald Reagan had never before displayed. Psychologically, I think that little outburst completely broke the logjam as far as Ronald Reagan was concerned in New Hampshire and in the rest of the country. In New Hampshire he won a convincing victory over George Bush.

It wasn't easy early in the campaign because the people who had been running it had acted like political sultans. We had $18 million that we could spend on the entire campaign, but after New Hampshire, we found that we had already spent $12 million. Therefore, we had $6 million for the rest of the country to cover the remainder of the campaign, and George Bush was still a very viable and well-financed candidate.

In desperation, we went to a fellow by the name of Bill Casey. I had never known Mr. Casey, but apparently he had power in financial circles in New York and was well respected as a hardball man who could watch a dollar. He had also been in the Nixon administration and was considered to be a good political strategist. Out of desperation, and at the personal request of the Reagans, Casey was brought onto the campaign. He didn't really have a public persona, and you couldn't understand a word he said (in fact, when Bill was the head of the CIA we used to tease him by saying that he would never need a scrambler since no one could ever understand anything he said), but in my estimation he did a magnificent job.

He grabbed hold of that campaign, watched and nursed every nickel, used a minimum amount of television advertising, and I bet you that if you could somehow measure the expeditious use of presidential campaign money, nothing would have ever matched that campaign. We went through the whole rest of that campaign without wasting any money; we cut our work force, relied on volunteers—which is not in vogue anymore—and proceeded to have a wonderful race, an unprecedented landslide. On the evening of the election at about 5 o'clock California time, the Reagans were preparing to go to dinner with some friends when Jimmy Carter called and conceded.

In 1984 he ran against Mr. Mondale, with whom I served in the Senate—a magnificent man. He represented, however, an ideology which was not acceptable at the time to most Americans. Despite this, and despite the fact that Reagan seemingly had everything going for him (he was an incumbent president, had a strong political organization, and was at least on a par with Mr.

Mondale in the fund-raising area), he almost fumbled the campaign in one of the worst events that I have ever seen politically: the Reagan-Mondale debate in Kentucky. The debate was a total, unmitigated disaster. Ronald Reagan stumbled through it, he wasn't responsive, and his closing statement was abysmal. This could have immediately been very destructive because many people thought that while he was a wonderful man, he'd had four years and was now over the hill. Reagan's poor performance during this debate seemed proof positive of this belief.

Many of us examined what had happened and came to the conclusion that Ronald Reagan had been overtrained for the debate. He had been put into too many mock debates with people like David Stockman who would play Mondale and would be all over him and in his face, as the kids now say. Reagan's people loaded his head with numbers to the point that when he went into Kentucky he had a psychological straitjacket on him and performed miserably. Therefore, we decided that the second debate would be played differently; we didn't get into many debating sessions at all, but instead simply discussed issues in a general way, without stuffing any statistics into the President's head. The results of the second debate were quite different, as once again the old Ronald Reagan emerged and performed magnificently, and all that had been lost was retrieved.

Near the end of the campaign, when it was apparent that Ronald Reagan was going to win and win easily—every poll revealed that—we were flying over the upper Midwest, and several of Mr. Reagan's aides said they had received responses from Minnesota asking him to make a visit. To show what kind of gentleman he is, Ronald Reagan replied, "I don't really want to go into Minnesota because that's Mr. Mondale's home area and I'd rather not go in there at all." I'll never forget that, because this is after Fritz had already visited California, and with no trepidation whatsoever. On the weekend before the election, however, people in Minnesota were absolutely demanding that Reagan make a stop in their state, however briefly, so we threw together a brief airport appearance. One hour before we landed we put the word out through the radio that Ronald Reagan was going to come to this isolated rural airport, and as we flew in, I couldn't believe what I saw. There were trucks and automobiles coming in from every road from miles around, and on one hour's notice, 10,000 people had come to greet Ronald Reagan. He made a very gracious speech in Minnesota, and as you know, Minnesota was the only state that Ronald Reagan didn't carry—a very convincing victory to say the least.

I will leave the evaluations of the Reagan presidency for the historians because my views are somewhat biased. However, I think certain observations can be made. First, any citizen-politician, if properly handled and if in possession of the qualities necessary to become a candidate—even in these modern and sophisticated days—can realistically aspire to be elected President of the United States. That makes me as a citizen feel somewhat reassured, because from the beginning, Ronald Reagan was not a politician—not that I consider that to be bad—but he was basically a citizen who got into politics on a short-term, temporary basis. He also demonstrated that the power of the presidency, in terms of its being a "bully pulpit" as Teddy Roosevelt used to say, was absolutely awesome if properly utilized.

Having been inside the Reagan presidency, I was impressed by how limited a president is as a political force, because the plain truth is that the real power is in the administrative areas. It's almost irrelevant who the President of the United States is because the career bureaucrats run it. They see presidents come and go, and they do their thing regardless of who the president is and what philosophy he holds. By and large, that's not bad, because most of the people in the administrative areas are very qualified and dedicated.

However, in the areas where you really have to energize the country in dealing with Congress—the policy areas—the presidency can be an enormously effective bully pulpit, and this was Reagan's strength. I can remember in the old days that the Congress wasn't as recalcitrant as it is now. In the post-Watergate era, members of Congress are a new breed; they don't do something simply because the president wants them to do it, or because the leadership in Congress wants them to do it. They are motivated more by fear than by persuasion. Therefore, while Reagan very often couldn't convince the Congress of his position on major policy issues, the members knew that they had better not cross him because he would

Paul Laxalt

get on television and appeal to their constituencies and build up enormous constituent pressure. The mail and telephone calls that he was able to engender through his public appearances were absolutely awesome. On issue after issue I saw him change the complexion of Congress on key votes because he had that capability. Admittedly, toward the end of his presidency, that power diminished because of the Iran-contra situation; he did lose influence over the Congress after that. Overall, however, he did demonstrate how effective a president can be.

Lastly, I think that whatever you may say about Reagan or his record, and however you may feel philosophically, he had a basic adherence to several simple principles. First, he felt that the federal government was too big and too expensive. He believed that the size of the federal government, if it couldn't effectively be reduced, should at least be restrained to permit state and local governments to grow more. Second, he felt that the people are overtaxed and that we should have tax cuts, which would stimulate the economy and promote economic growth. Third, and most importantly, he felt that we were in a tenuous place in respect to the Soviets, and that the only way to deal effectively with them was to build an effective defense force. Reagan was convinced that if we did that, particularly with something like SDI, the Soviets would come to the negotiating table.

History will probably indicate that his basic principles at the time were valid and that he was effective enough to be able to carry them out. In addition, there are many who feel that with the events of the last several months, Ronald Reagan hasn't been given due credit for what has happened in Eastern Europe and in the Soviet Union. That may or may not be true, but as far as he is concerned, it's not a problem for him; he's basically an unselfish man. I visited with him recently in Los Angeles. He had just returned from a trip to Eastern Europe and Berlin, and I think he knows that the people there recognize and appreciate what he has done for them.

His staff tells me that in Berlin, and wherever he went in the Soviet Union, the people absolutely lionized him and gave him substantial credit for the fact that they had been liberated. They so indicated to him, and I have never seen him as appreciative of his efforts in public life as he is now. For an old friend and associate like me, that's reassuring, because very often politics doesn't turn out that way.

QUESTION: You spoke a few times about Mr. Reagan's age. Could you tell us what changes you have observed during your 25 years of acquaintance with Mr. Reagan in his memory, level of energy, and capacity for sustaining concentration and activity? If there have been changes, did they affect his ability to function as the chief executive?

SENATOR LAXALT: In terms of his physical energy and in terms of his alertness, I don't know that there has been any fundamental change. He is one of the few people I know who is virtually ageless. He does suffer from a hearing problem, which I think at times serves him well. There were times during debates or discussions in which he wasn't particularly interested when he would start to turn off and I knew what had happened. Essentially, Ronald Reagan was a delegator, so he didn't have to be a nitty-gritty type of person. During the time that we were governors together, I was absolutely amazed at how much he delegated out. I couldn't do that! I had to know what was going on in my shop. I don't know whether I was nosy or curious or if I just didn't have that degree of confidence. Thus, it wasn't required for him in terms of administration to have the degree of alertness that one normally would, although I'm sure that he did.

The same thing happened in the White House. He delegated almost everything out and never looked back, and for the most part it served him well. It blew up on him in the Iran-contra affair, because he didn't know what was going on in the basement, and he should have. In the last days in the Iran-contra period, I sensed that he was hurt because he received criticism from the people. He always had received it from certain quarters of the press, but to receive it from the people, who in poll after poll indicated that they didn't believe him, hurt him to the core.

As I said, however, I haven't seen any real change in him in terms of his energy. He is really energetic, even now. He was 80 years old in February 1991, and he is still positive, alert, and above all, I think, passive and serene; what a joy it must be after all the tumultuous years to be 80 years old and be at peace. He's actually always been at peace, because he has always been kind and gentle.

In the raucous and difficult world of Washington politics, I can remember many times when people really close to the President very often appeared to betray him. Yet, he was always able to look at the positive side of those situations and always able to give those people the benefit of the doubt. For example, when David Stockman went to the press to express his disagreement with Reagan's economic policies, there were many people close to the President, including myself, who felt that Dave should go not into the woodshed, but into oblivion. You can't tolerate that kind of behavior at that level, and yet Reagan still had a kind word for David. That demonstrates, I think, one of the more subtle qualities that made Ronald Reagan one of our most popular presidents.

QUESTION: It has been suggested by some that the Strategic Defense Initiative was the most important factor in convincing the Soviets to come back to the bargaining table. Do you think that this is an overstatement?

SENATOR LAXALT: No, I don't. I agree with it completely. I'm personally convinced that the Soviets would never have come back to the table in Geneva if it hadn't been clear that Reagan was going forward aggressively with SDI. I don't think you can overexaggerate the importance and the effect that SDI had in the geopolitical and strategic considerations of the Soviet Union. If there was a crowning point in the Reagan presidency in terms of security, it was probably SDI.

I'll never forget the first speech that he made in connection with SDI. He was criticized by the press and even within the Congress, and his SDI proposal was dubbed "Star Wars." Yet the people around him felt that SDI would demonstrate not only to the Soviets but also to Third World dictators that we were going to build our own protective defense against possible nuclear attacks. I would hope—even though the record of the Congress these last few days hasn't been all that reassuring—that on some kind of priority basis we continue to do what we can with SDI. Even though the Soviet threat is substantially diminished, I believe that in the years to come the greatest threat that we will face will be from nuclear proliferation in the Third World, for example, the possibility that men like Saddam Hussein may acquire a nuclear capability. We just can't leave ourselves vulnerable to those kinds of developments.

QUESTION: What is your opinion of the current procedure for nominating the vice president? Is it effective?

SENATOR LAXALT: I think that it's all right. While a case could be made that the election of the vice president should be separate from the election of the president—as is the case for lieutenant governors in many states—it seems that what is most important is that the vice president is someone whom the president feels is going to replace him well in the event that the unmentionable should happen. Also, the vice president should be someone in whom the president can have complete trust and confidence in terms of security and very confidential matters. If you throw the process open—which is appealing from a democratic standpoint—so that you have someone who is elected independently by the people, it could cause difficulties. You could end up having a team that would be basically incompatible, both personally and perhaps politically, and I don't think that would be good.

I would like to say something regarding the present situation. Danny Quayle is a friend and was one of my political protégés when I was still in the Senate. I remember well having dinner with Dan in New Orleans on the night before George Bush made his vice presidential selection. At that time, Dan was among those being mentioned. He approached me and said that he had heard that there was a possibility that he could get the nomination. Then he said, "Do you think I've got a shot?" I said, "Dan, no way!" In fairness to Dan, however, the manner in which that was handled really hurt him grievously from the very beginning.

The first impression that you make in this country—particularly on television—is critical, and once that impression is created it is almost impossible to correct it. Look at what happened with the Quayle situation. The Quayles weren't notified and they weren't conditioned. After he had been selected they had to find Danny and Marilyn, and within minutes he had been thrust into the national spotlight. I'm sure many of you remember his first television appearance after he had been selected. He was so cheerful and so enthusiastic that he looked like a cheerleader. I don't think it was fair to him at all. George simply was pandering to the press by trying to keep some suspense in the convention where you didn't have to. I think Danny should have been told the first of the week. He should have been conditioned and primed so that he wasn't sent up there cold as a candidate. I think probably that was not fair to him, and I think it has been a very important factor in determining why he has had the difficulties that he has had in this country. I proceed on a premise that he is basically competent, which I believe him to be.

QUESTION: As you know, the governor of Nevada and the governors in 42 other states have the line-item veto privilege. Do you believe that such a privilege will ever be given to the President of the United States?

SENATOR LAXALT: No, I really don't. I wish I could tell you that I thought so. The ironic thing about it is that the line-item veto was not harpooned by the Democrats, but instead by the Republicans in the United States Senate. The leading Republican opponent was not only a respected United States senator but also a former governor who in his state had the line-item veto and who exercised it many times, Mark Hatfield. Mark led the fight against it and did so very effectively. His position was that it's a lot different giving the right of the line-item veto to a governor of a state as opposed to the president. He said he would be perfectly comfortable giving that power and authority to Ronald Reagan because he didn't think that he would abuse it. He said, however, that he could think of presidents in recent memory whom he wouldn't want to have that power. One point Mark made was that with the line-item veto the president would have the ability to almost blackmail senators on legislation by threatening to veto their favorite spending projects in return for their support.

His argument convinced many of the undecided senators that as appealing as the line-item veto is, and regardless of how well it works in some states, perhaps it's a little dangerous on the federal level.

QUESTION: The media has begun increasingly to engage in instant analysis immediately after a campaign speech or a political debate. What is your opinion of this practice?

SENATOR LAXALT: I'm not a real fan of political people in television because I find most of them to be totally devoid of any substance, too often focusing on the sensational in how they cover and analyze an event. I don't know what you can do about it, however. They are a fact of life. I like to think that thoughtful people still basically control the process, and thoughtful people are not going to be swayed by "experts" who dissect a State of the Union speech in 30 seconds. I would also hope that thoughtful people are going to be reading periodicals and newspapers and engaging in discussions among themselves.

That was the case in the Reagan effort. The people who influenced policy in his administration were thoughtful people. For example, Jeane Kirkpatrick came from a campus and not from the television. It was because of her writing that she came to the attention of President Reagan and became a forceful factor in the administration. I think that most presidents recognize the distinction between entertainment and substance. Television gives you entertainment but not much substance, and most presidents, when making basic policy decisions, are going to be more substantive in their approach for advice. At least I hope so.

QUESTION: Why did Reagan agree to debate Mondale in 1984 when, as you indicated, it was obvious that Mondale had very little chance of winning the election?

SENATOR LAXALT: Many in the campaign felt that Reagan shouldn't debate Mondale because it would give Mondale additional media coverage. Ronald Reagan, however, believes in public discourse, and it was his decision to go ahead and have the debate.

There were also the so-called political "experts" in the campaign who had no faith in Ronald Reagan's ability to debate.

Paul Laxalt

They were afraid to let him out on his own, and they were afraid to let Reagan be Reagan. I used to fight with them over this because in debates and forums of this type, style is far more important than substance; and no one can beat Ronald Reagan on style. Even in the substantive areas, he constantly surprised us. The experts also had no faith in Reagan because they didn't consider him a professional politician, which is one of his greatest strengths.

We were in North Carolina in 1976 after Reagan had been defeated by Gerald Ford in New Hampshire. He blew that race because again, on the advice of political experts, he was told he had New Hampshire in his pocket. Therefore, the weekend before the primary Reagan left New Hampshire and went to Illinois because that's where all the votes were. He lost in New Hampshire by less than a thousand votes, lost in Illinois, and then lost in Florida. So in North Carolina it was do-or-die. One of the great conflicts we had within the campaign was whether or not Ronald Reagan should take advantage of his once being a film actor. The experts (I won't give you names, but you can guess who they were at the time, some inherited from the old Nixon effort) literally wanted to apologize constantly for the fact that Ronald Reagan had at one time been a film actor. They felt somehow that detracted from the seriousness that a presidential candidate should have. They prevailed until North Carolina. We were desperate to find something that worked.

Finally, we brought out a team of his old buddies, and immediately after Jimmy Stewart and the Hollywood crowd came on the scene of the Reagan campaign, the chemistry of the campaign changed. They added a dimension that otherwise you couldn't have had. What the political experts didn't recognize is that politicians per se and political events are dull, unless you are a political junkie. Starting in North Carolina and moving elsewhere, as soon as the Reagan friends were brought in from the film colony, it was unbelievable. As the campaign progressed in the Midwest, our events would draw 2,000 to 3,000 people in areas where normally you would have a few hundred and be happy to have them. This is proof positive that political professionals tend to be very myopic when it comes to seeing the total picture in determining the value of a candidate.

QUESTION: There is some concern about the budget deficits that Ronald Reagan bequeathed us. Did he ever recognize the magnitude of these deficits, and if so did he have any policy initiatives to counter them?

SENATOR LAXALT: If you asked him that question he would say that if the Congress had followed his budget recommendations, the budget would be in balance now; this is open to some questions, because others would say that if you took the Reagan budgets as submitted, we would still have huge deficit problems.

He honestly believed in supply-side economics. He believed that it was necessary to prevent the politicians in Washington from wasting more money, and that if you did that it freed more money for the private sector, and that would regenerate the economy. The fact that we have had the most historic run of economic growth in our history might be proof of that. However, the fact that we have these huge deficits presents the biggest problem in the whole Reagan era because we honestly felt that if we could exercise restraint on the spending side and combine this with tax incentives to raise revenues, all the ships would rise and all would be well. It simply didn't turn out that way. Our first problem is that we spent more on defense than anyone ever anticipated; defense costs burgeoned literally out of sight. Our second problem is that we were never able, for political reasons, to get the kind of cuts out of the Congress that we should have. I'm convinced that unless we get into a horrid depression, where everyone must really think in terms of sacrifice—particularly in the huge entitlement areas—we will never get the necessary budget cuts from the Congress; the political price is just too great.

The bulk of the spending that we have in this country now is in the so-called entitlement areas. This is where all of the big money items are, and they now account for 70 or 75 percent of government spending. For political reasons, everyone is afraid to touch them. The Congress has tried to realize some savings in the Medicare program before, but because of political pressures they have only been able to achieve modest results. Social Security is the biggest political graveyard in the history of this country. Fooling with Social Security will get you defeated faster than anything else.

If you don't believe me, just ask Republicans who lost in 1982. Unless we get some kind of dictatorial form of government, or if we just get into a total fiscal morass of 1930 proportions, I don't see how we are going to bring this thing into some semblance of balance. I'm afraid it's not going to happen.

I'll never forget when I returned to Washington as a naive young senator in 1974. I had been a balanced-budget governor—a constitutional responsibility—and had campaigned on the basis that we ought to be fiscally conservative. The very first budget that Gerald Ford submitted had a deficit of $23 billion, and I almost went into cardiac arrest! If we could only go back to those glorious days.

Coming back to the Senate chamber one day, I ran into Hubert Humphrey, whom I loved. Hubert Humphrey was a real political scholar and an honest liberal—right or wrong. I asked him about this budget deficit, and he told me not to get excited about things like that, and not to worry about balanced budgets. He said, "A lot of that money we owe to ourselves, anyhow. The real number to keep in your head always is what our debt is in relation to the gross national product." As a young, naive senator, I said, "You know I have all the respect in the world for you, Mr. Humphrey, but every instinct I have tells me that you're wrong." I still believe that, and yet today what are you hearing? You hear that these deficits really don't mean all that much. I have heard several times recently during the budget debate that what is important is what the relation of our deficit is to our GNP, just like Hubert Humphrey told me. I don't know what the answer is.

QUESTION: After Gerald Ford got the Republican nomination in 1976, why didn't Ronald Reagan endorse him?

SENATOR LAXALT: I am asked that question very often, but it's my distinct recollection that Ronald Reagan not only endorsed Gerald Ford, but also campaigned for him extensively. I know because I was on some of those trips with him. Unfortunately, there is this impression that Ronald Reagan backed away from Gerald Ford in that race, and it is simply not true.

A SENATOR REFLECTS ON A PRESIDENT

NARRATOR: We knew that this discussion was going to be inspiring, but we did not realize just how inspiring it would be. We are very grateful, senator, and we hope you will return to Mr. Jefferson's university soon.

~ *Eleven* ~

THE PRESIDENCY AND THE CONGRESS IN THE CONSTITUTIONAL SYSTEM[*]

Richard Bolling

NARRATOR: Some years ago Congressman Bolling wrote in Volume V of *Papers of Presidential Transitions and Foreign Policy*:

> As I look back and think ahead to seek ways of improving the effectiveness of governmental systems, divided, complex, and always in transition, I am convinced that it is a mistake to examine any one political phenomenon as if it took place by itself. There must always be an attempt to at least set the stage, to look at the past and to examine the short and long range consequences of a particular political event. Politics is not a series of separate events; it is much more like a seamless web.

Congressman Bolling served as congressman from the Fifth District of Missouri during the tenure of eight presidents, from the 81st to the 96th Congress. He occupied a number of crucial positions as chairman of the Select Committee on Committees of the House of Representatives; chairman of the Rules Committee; chairman of the Joint Economic Committee; a member of the Steering and Policy Committee of the Democratic Caucus and of the House Budget Committee.

---

[*]Presented in a Forum at the Miller Center of Public Affairs on 30 March 1988. Reprinted from *Governance I: The Presidency and the Constitutional System* (Lanham, Maryland: University Press of America, Inc., 1989).

THE PRESIDENCY AND THE CONGRESS

Lest you think that his background is exclusively that of the politician, he was Chub Fellow at Yale University and Fellow at the Center for Advanced Studies at Wesleyan University and taught and lectured in Kansas City. He was a Lieutenant Colonel in the United States Army and received the Distinguished Congressional Service Award from the American Political Science Association. He probably is the only person who will visit the Center who was ever elected to the *Sports Illustrated* 25th Anniversary All-American Football Team. He is the author of *House Out of Order* and *Power in the House*, which first appeared in 1968 and is now in a revised edition.

CONGRESSMAN BOLLING: I would like to talk a little bit about the last five presidents. I do not want to offend anyone, most particularly at the beginning, but I think that four of the last five presidents have been failures. They have been failures in utterly different ways. The one I do not consider a failure professionally is Jerry Ford, but that may be my prejudice because he and I were friends and still are, despite the fact that we disagree on virtually every domestic item one can think of. Still, we disagree in a way that is less than disagreeable. We disagree because we believe differently and we understand the political process. I had the opportunity to be very close to a few of the last five presidents, not very close to all of them, but I had the opportunity to observe all of them.

I didn't retire from Congress until after President Reagan's first two years as president, but he was not the reason I retired. Circumstances kept me from feeling that I had to stay. I retired relatively young for a congressman, but with no difficulties or political opposition. I retired because I thought it was time to do something else. Basically, it was to try and help all of the people in academia who have devoted their lives to studying how government works.

I thought that my responsibility as a congressman was to lead and to educate, and I thought education was the right role all of the time. I still feel that way, but I found it much more difficult to do what I had planned when I retired. The simple reason was that I still could learn. So I read a lot, particularly about the Constitution and constitutional history, and found it very difficult to come to a final conclusion. Fairly recently, I attempted a book and wrote a chunk of it and decided I did not like it. I am now on my fourth redraft, and you are going to get the benefit, or bear the burden, of hearing my conclusions.

I supported a candidate who is now out of the Democratic race for the presidency. I supported him to avoid what I believe were the reasons why four of our last five presidents failed. I shall tell you what I have as positive recommendations for any president in the future.

Lyndon Johnson failed because he wasn't balanced. He tried to do too much. I happen to agree with what he tried to do in almost all of the domestic cases. I think we were way behind on the things that needed to be done with the poor and the weak in society, but I think he overreached himself, and I think nothing could be done to stop him.

His successor, to my utter amazement, may turn up in history as professionally a pretty good president. Nixon was a crook and I always thought he was a crook; I despised Richard Nixon. To say that he might turn out to be a pretty good president in retrospect is a shock to me. Nixon did great damage to the republic. The fact that a president could be forced to retire hurt the political process severely.

Carter came to Congress with many pleasant and some very good ideas. He was very bright and very able, but wholly incompetent to be president because he could not deal with Congress at all, ever. From the beginning he failed with Congress and alienated his congressional allies, virtually from his first days in office. I think he would have been a good president, by the way, in the second term because he learned a great deal, but he was a terrible president in the first term. Aside from Congress, he turned off the American people and that didn't help.

I am going to say very little about Ronald Reagan, but I'll say something rather definitive, and I am going to say it right now: I think he is the worst president that ever served the United States of America.

There is one characteristic of all four presidents that I consider failed, and in some cases it goes against the myths of our time. For example, Lyndon Johnson was unable to creatively work with the Congress. The great myth is that Lyndon Johnson was a genius with the Congress; the fact is that he never was even a successful legislator. He was a successful politician in the House; when he was in the Senate and became Senate leader, he was a great manipulator of senators. He did not deal very well with any constituency except his own Texas constituency. He did that rather well, though in ways that I did not always admire. But that is beside the point.

When he became president, he failed to pay attention to anyone when he created his programs, unless they were going in the direction that he wanted to go. And everything he wanted to do, he wanted to do in the first year of his elected presidency. He succeeded Jack Kennedy in 1963 and served through 1964 and the election, but only after he was elected president did he become overwhelmed by himself.

By that time, his friends who had had the power to check him in the past were either dead or gone. Sam Rayburn died in 1961 and he was the only person who could really sit Lyndon Johnson down. His great friend in the Senate, Richard Russell of Georgia, was no longer there to influence him effectively, and he listened to no one. His imbalance made him a failure, not just in Vietnam but also in domestic policy and, in particular, in economic policies. He could not and did not work with the House, he just ran over it, and he tried to run over the Senate. He didn't learn from the institution.

Obviously, the same thing is true of Nixon. Nixon did a better job of working with the House, but he didn't work honestly with it. If you remember those days and if you watched events carefully, it was rather fascinating to see what happened. At first, the Committee on the Judiciary that dealt with the Watergate investigation was composed mostly of liberal Democrats who were concerned about Richard Nixon and what he had done. Then most of the moderate Democrats joined up, followed by the conservative Democrats. Eventually the most liberal Republicans were also swayed until virtually all Republicans were there as well. Even then some were still saying, that although they didn't really like him, they believed him. Still, there was a shift. The only time he really worked with Congress was the time when it was really working against him. He was never completely honest with the Congress; he never took advantage of all of the people that could have helped him in Congress.

Carter was hopeless. I am going to talk about this from the positive side. Carter had a legislative liaison team that honestly believed that the Congress of the United States was a little bit lower than the legislature of the State of Georgia. I grew up in northern Alabama, so I am not anti-Georgia or anti-South. The liaison team simply did not have any comprehension of what the House of Representatives was like; they did not even understand the constitutional sense of what the House of Representatives was supposed to be. They treated everyone as if they were slaves—people were supposed to automatically do what the president wanted. It was a disaster.

Mr. Reagan, on the other hand, was enormously successful with the Congress in the first year. You won't believe it because you don't see it in the press, but after that first year, he hardly ever won another fight. A few times he won on issues related to the Iran-contra affair, but on economic issues, like taxes in 1982, the Republicans in the Senate turned against him. We passed a tax bill that did exactly the opposite of what Ronald Reagan wanted until he accepted it. He swore for months that he would never sign a tax bill that increased taxes, yet taxes were substantially increased in 1982, primarily due to the efforts of Senator Robert Dole. That is certainly interesting considering the way things are today.

For reasons of politeness, I am not going into the rest of Reagan's eight years. I'm not sure that what I have to say would be completely balanced. I may not give him enough credit for cheering up the country. He did that. I may not give him enough credit for some of the things that have happened in foreign policy. Usually, it seems to me, good things happened *despite* him, but they have happened and they are very important.

So we have had, in my view, a disastrous breakdown in our system of separated powers starting after the death of Jack Kennedy. And in a system like ours, unless all of the players understand that they must share power, we do not get a government capable of governing the country. The only time a similar breakdown occurred was during the Civil War, and obviously there was no government that suited all of the people of the country at that time. That is the only time the political process has completely broken down.

The political process of this country is, in my judgment, the most difficult political process in the world. At least one can reasonably and honestly say, that we have popular government, free government, and democratic government with republican procedures.

We have a country so complicated that even when there were only 13 states, you wonder how it came to be. You wonder how those people were able to put together the Constitution, and more importantly, how the document was ratified. The wonderful thing about the Constitution is that is was ratified. There have been many constitutions written in many places. Our Constitution was ratified and we have managed to remain at peace with ourselves and to develop and grow. This was largely the result of the capacity of the Congress, the president, and the Supreme Court to have some relationship with each other on almost every major occasion. I am saying, in effect, that you cannot have an effective government, no matter how bright a president is or how well informed he is about the issues, unless he understands how to work with the Congress.

You may think that is fine as long as the Congress and the president are of the same party. We read a great deal about how our government has broken down because different parties control different bodies. Yet the greatest accomplishments of this country's federal government have been achieved with bipartisan support. Our victory in World War II was such an accomplishment. I guess there are a good many people who know that this war wasn't a cinch, that an Allied victory was not certain. There were, after all, two wars being fought, one in the Pacific and the other in Europe, and in each case there was a very good possibility that we were going to lose. Winning both wars was a bipartisan accomplishment, done with Presidents Roosevelt and Truman working closely with the Congress.

It is remarkable that even when Truman faced a Republican House, most of the important things he wanted to do in foreign policy and defense were done. The 80th Congress, which he used as a political whipping boy on domestic policy in 1948, was the Congress through which much of the great program went. On foreign affairs there was a residue of cooperative attitudes and an understanding that we had to work together. I am reasonably sure that at least in modern times, unless presidents are really able to work closely with members of the opposite party, they cannot implement programs which will last. I think Johnson pushed his programs so strongly that there was a backlash which undid many of those needed programs. This could have been avoided if he had been more moderate.

The key is that presidents must understand how to work with the Congress, and in particular the House. Why is the House so important? The House is so important because it is the only federal institution in which all of the concerns of the American people have a reasonable chance to penetrate. The House doesn't just represent the great issues; the House represents the issues of people in congressional districts and the small lobbyists. The people who don't have lots of money or numerical support have an opportunity to talk to members of the House. That makes the House more difficult to deal with than the Senate, especially because there are 435 members rather than 100. Its complexity, though, is one of the reasons the House is so fascinating. When you pass major legislation in the House, you are consciously putting all of the great interest groups of the country together, first in a contest and then in a cooperative effort. If presidents do not understand that, and don't work with the House on that kind of a basis, they cannot possibly work successfully with the government as a whole.

I could talk about the Supreme Court or the bureaucracy, and I am prepared to talk about a variety of other things if you ask me questions. There is one key point I want to make, and though I may just sound like an old, retired member of the House recalling how important his work was, that really isn't the point. I believe firmly that this country has forgotten the role of the House. By and large, it is true not just for presidents but for the whole country. The academic community has forgotten it because most academics don't like to spend the time necessary to understand the House of Representatives and how it works.

I will tell you an anecdote and then I'll stop. Years and years ago, the most distinguished of all of the journalists of his time, Walter Lippmann, invited me to lunch. He invited me to a club that I would not belong to for reasons that you may have detected in what I have said and what I will say. It amused me. It was a nice club and it was perfectly proper for him to be there, but it was not a group in which I was going to be involved for several reasons. We had a lovely, wonderful luncheon which lasted four hours. I couldn't believe it. The last hour or so I was trying to get away because I just did not believe that I should be taking up a great man's time. I didn't agree with Walter Lippmann on an awful lot of things, but I admired him. My press friends thought that he was a second coming of sorts. I don't mean to be disrespectful in saying that, but they really revered him. I didn't really know why he had asked me to lunch, but we spent a long time talking about nothing but the House. He asked the questions and I answered quickly and briefly.

For a long time I did not hear anything from him and I simply did my job in the House. Finally I heard, as I knew I would hear in time, why he wasn't picking up on anything we had spoken about, and why I did not hear from him again. Lippmann is supposed to have said, "You know, the young man was really very interesting. He said all kinds of things that I knew to be accurate and was giving me a really wonderful description of the institution. But I have decided it was just too complicated for me to get involved in, and I am not going to do anything more about it."

I will submit to you that this is what all of the media people have decided, with the exception of a few, and too many others have decided the same. Further, I would submit to you that if that isn't understood by either the people or the presidents, our system is going to break down. It is not going to work unless we have presidents who understand that they have to work with the House and how to work with the House.

Jack Kennedy died having had the greatest congressional relations team there ever was. The Republicans in the Eisenhower administration and in this administration have had consistently good congressional relations. We shall need better congressional relations with the president if we are going to make the policy decisions we must make.

QUESTION: Congressman Bolling, you have indicated how important it is for an incoming president to be able to work with the Congress. Is there anything on the other side, something that Congress needs to do? What do you see, particularly in the transition between the election and the inauguration that might be accomplished?

CONGRESSMAN BOLLING: I think Congress needs to do a number of things to improve the transition. I think there should be more money made available for a newly elected president, whether it is George Bush or some Democrat. There should be the opportunity to do some things very quickly, and it takes money to do that. The Congress already has a burden, in my opinion, to improve the formal transition—the approach to the transition. The Congress has to have a sense of responsibility to the president.

I don't think I exaggerate in saying this: The *president* more or less determines how partisan the Congress is with his own behavior. I'm talking about Congress as an entity, as an institution. If the president is friendly and sticks to his word, and tries to be cooperative with both individuals and institutions, he will ultimately get a pretty good reaction. If he is confrontational and determined to make political hay out of situations, it can get pretty ugly. But the president also has the power to cool down those situations.

It got pretty ugly in the 1940s, in Truman's time. But Truman never lost the people with whom he had to work effectively in foreign policy and defense to get results. He would blast the Republicans on domestic policy and fume about the no-good 80th Congress, yet he maintained his relationships with Vandenberg and people in the House who were equally important. In order to get things through the House, he had to have the support of some Republicans.

I think the president has the initiative because he is, after all, the most powerful politician there is, and the most powerful legislator. Everyone forgets that the president is a legislator, though it is odd that they do. He is a legislator because he has a veto, and all he has to do is veto something and he raises the ante almost out of sight. Getting two-thirds of the votes in the House, or in the Senate, is very different than getting the majority. That veto is a tremendous source of influence. I am not trying to put all of the burden on the president. I would be shocked if a Democratic speaker did not respond to a legitimate, nonpartisan request from the president.

I don't know how it looks from the outside. The media deal with things as they wish (though I don't mean to be a media-basher). I worked with them very closely for many years, and the media just did not give Congress much of a chance to be understood simply because they did not have enough people covering it. There are probably only a half dozen papers in the United States that have real coverage of the House. The media cover what is relatively easy to cover. You can cover the president very easily. Sam Donaldson could cover the president by himself, and he will be able to supply the whole network with news about the president reasonably well. It isn't hard to keep up with the Supreme Court either; that also can be dealt with by one person. Similarly, one person can deal remarkably well with 100 senators, partly because the Senate is run entirely differently. But when you get to the House, you are dealing with complexity. I do not know how to solve that problem, but I think that's *the* problem.

I cannot conceive of a House Speaker in this era who would be an affront to the president. It has happened to other presidents, Lincoln, for example, who was accosted by the radical element of his own party. Roosevelt too, had an incident or two when his leadership in the Senate resigned on him because he bad-mouthed a senator for what he had said about the wartime tax bill. Roosevelt was dead right; it was a lousy tax bill, but he should not have made it known the way he did. In any event, that's all they could get and they had worked very hard on it. Alben Barkley resigned in a huff, and Roosevelt had to beg him to come back. I recognize the problem. If Robert Michel [House Minority leader] turned out to be the Speaker and a Democrat were elected, he would be just as worried about being good to the president as I would, or anyone else who was on the Democratic side.

Richard Bolling

COMMENT: To carry on the same line of thought, the House seemed to be easier to understand in the days of a very strong Speaker and a half dozen strong committee chairmen with whom the president might have rapport and considerable contact. The reorganization of the House seems to present, at least to the public view, the presence of a considerable array of power centers. Therefore, the institution is harder to understand and deal with. Looking at it from the inside, how is the House mobilized into effective majorities?

CONGRESSMAN BOLLING: That is hard to answer because you have to recognize a number of myths first. Some of you may know that I worked very closely with Sam Rayburn for the last ten years of his life. Sam Rayburn had very little power compared to the institutional power of Carl Albert, Tip O'Neill, or the current Speaker. Most of the time he was defeated by the committees. Sam Rayburn could only do what was possible, given the committee system. For the most part, the committee system of Congress was controlled by a coalition of conservative southern Democrats and almost all of the Republicans from 1938 until 1961. The Democrats from the South were conservative, the Republicans from the Middle West were conservative, and of course conservatives came from other places too.

The truth of the matter is that Roosevelt completely lost control of Congress from about 1939 on. Sam Rayburn was sort of his emissary who tried to do something with Congress. Rayburn had great power to change a few votes. He had gathered up his chips in the classic way. His power lasted the longest in the history of the House. He had been a committee chairman in 1931 and then Speaker until he died in 1961. I don't know of any other political career that was like that. I happen to believe that Rayburn was the greatest legislator of all time. But he did not have all of that power usually attributed to him.

The *institutional* power of the present Speaker is substantially greater. Rayburn looked powerful because on the surface he stayed out of the committee problems. He controlled two committees and dominated one. He controlled the majority of the Ways and Means Committee on a crucial item—taxes—in a way that I did not agree with, especially taxes on oil and gas. He also controlled it in a way I did agree with in regard to trade, but he didn't really control it beyond that. He didn't control the Rules Committee for most of his career. Howard Smith of Virginia was more powerful than Sam Rayburn in the House of Representatives regarding the flow of legislation, and so were some other committee chairmen. Sam Rayburn was for a Tennessee Valley Authority in another part of the country, in the Northwest. It was blocked by a committee chairman who was powerful enough to defy Rayburn and, as a matter of fact, defy his committee and defy the House. So there are all kinds of myths that one needs to get rid of.

Nevertheless, Rayburn was a great legislator. If the Eisenhower people came to him, or if Eisenhower himself had him down for a drink and a chat, Rayburn would tell them the truth. I have listened to Rayburn on the telephone, saying, "But Ike, you can't do that." So Rayburn was up there telling them what they could and could not do, and they would work things out so that they wouldn't try to do the impossible, unless they wanted to do it for political purposes. You had an entirely different view of what was really going on; Rayburn was getting whipped over and over again.

You are, however, absolutely right that the legislative process has been seriously impaired by the increase in subcommittees, and probably by the increase in subcommittee staffs. I am not sure about the impact of the staff increase, but I am sure that the subcommittees have damaged the legislative process. The reason I am sure of it is because the only way you could deal with it was through the Rules Committee. You had to be able to have a debate on the floor that was coherent, and the only way you could take four, five or six different committees and make their product coherent, sensible, and fair was by a rule of debate that was very intricate and complicated. If we had not been able to do that, the House would have collapsed in a general chaos, and it still could. It very badly needs to be reorganized in terms of committee jurisdictions.

As you probably know, I chaired a committee at the time when we adopted the Budget Act that failed. We got many other interesting things done but not the crucial thing, which was to reorganize the committee system. I am all for modification of the committee system regarding seniority, and I am all against the subcommittees. I think we need a president to help us on that, by the way, but he [President Reagan] never says out loud that he is for anything.

QUESTION: I am thinking about your Lippmann anecdote and the fact that no one wants to hear about the House. I wonder if you can allay my fears about the negative attitudes toward Congress and specifically the House which have developed in our culture.

There was a moment last summer during the Iran-contra hearings when I thought that Brendon Sullivan [Oliver North's lawyer] was saying, in coaching Oliver North, "The way we can win this thing is to make it a battle of North against Congress; a solitary military hero and patriotic figure against congressional characters, many of whom are old crocodiles." That played pretty well. To me it showed that the understanding of what this institution is all about wasn't there. Let me formulate it this way: the attitude contained more than boredom or disinterest; it contained a certain animus against Congress. This President can say, "All North did was not tell Congress everything; I do that myself," and get a laugh. There is a lot of negative imagery surrounding Congress, and specifically the House. I feel that it has increased, and there was a moment last summer when the negative image of Congress became very strong. I hope you can tell me that I am wrong.

CONGRESSMAN BOLLING: No, I do not think you are wrong. Part of the reason is that Congress needs very badly to reorganize itself, the House in particular. I am not sure about the Senate because I simply don't understand the Senate as well as I do the House. But the House desperately needs to have a reorganization that makes it work somewhat better. I think reorganization is possible with the help of a very well organized set of lobby groups on the outside to assist in convincing individual members of the House of the need to reorganize and work with a president who is not hostile.

Some legislation with which I was involved and which would have reorganized the institution very substantially was not a cinch to lose. It did not get passed because we made a few mistakes, because of bad luck, and, unlike the issue on which the Budget Act rode into being, because it did not get good press. We had reasonably good support from a variety of places, but we didn't get good press. While I think it is absolutely essential that the Congress do that, I don't think it will happen without a president who is understanding of Congress.

One of the bad breaks that we had on that Select Committee of Committees was that Ford, who helped set up the committee, left the House. Carl Albert consulted with Ford, when he was still in the House, on setting up the Select Committee on Committees. It would have helped us if Ford had been there, and it would have helped institutional reform if he had remained in the presidency because he was friendly. We need a president who understands the House and who is clever enough to be able to convey his sympathy, though he cannot afford to go public with it. If he goes public with his support, he automatically creates opposition among representatives who fear that the president is trying to interfere in their districts. That simply isn't so. Jack Kennedy was in on the fight we had in 1961, which gave the power to control the flow of legislation back to the Speaker as opposed to Howard Smith, but he never acknowledged this publicly.

Maybe there is another thing that we ought to talk about on this. Much of what happens in Congress has to be secret in the preliminary stages. There is no way on earth that you can work out a very difficult political issue unless you do it in secrecy. That does not mean that your acts in a committee or on the floor should not be recorded. Everyone's votes should be known. But when you begin to work on a very difficult problem like the Marshall Plan or the first Civil Rights Act, you have to have secrecy because the people, who represent districts and interest groups, have to have a chance to go back with a plan to consult with at least some of their constituents on what will work. When you get into the process, you have to go completely public. So you need secrecy in the conceptual stage. The best example of that is of course the Constitution. They had to have secrecy initially, or they never could have gotten this document passed that won state by state by very narrow margins. When you are fighting with narrow margins politically, you simply must have the ability to put together your piece without public knowledge. All bipartisan efforts are done that way. Part of the problem, then, is that Congress cannot defend itself.

QUESTION: I have two questions. One is rather general and the other is more precise. The first one has to do with your view that President Johnson was a failure. I am interested in how you would contrast him with Kennedy. And more specifically, my recollection is that Johnson secured the passage of legislation that Kennedy could not get through Congress. Is that correct?

CONGRESSMAN BOLLING: That's right.

QUESTION: As I understand your view, it is that despite Johnson's civil rights legislation and his war on poverty, he was a failure because he disturbed relations with Congress and because some of his legislation went too far.

CONGRESSMAN BOLLING: No, each of these presidents was different. Johnson passed all kinds of legislation that Kennedy could not get through. You don't have to look very far to see why. Kennedy never had anything like a friendly Congress. Johnson passed very important civil rights laws. I happen to know a great deal about them as I was involved in the details, including when Johnson shifted the priorities from the tax cut first—which was Kennedy's approach—to civil rights. Johnson used the sympathy for Kennedy to do something dramatic about civil rights. It was magnificent. I think Johnson was a great president, as well as a failed president, because of that.

Incidentally, the civil rights legislation had already passed the House under Kennedy. Johnson, however, reversed opinion in the Senate by using the power of the presidency. That deserves a great deal of credit. On the other hand, he not only ran over Congress, but also ignored advice from Congress. He had always taken it when it had come from Rayburn's mouth. Later, there was no one there that he would listen to, not a soul. He made excessive demands because he never argued the case for how much should be done later on.

THE PRESIDENCY AND THE CONGRESS

In 1965 when all of the great programs that should have come up in 1945 came up in smaller measure, he received an overwhelming majority, which he then misused. We never did achieve anything substantial about the District of Columbia because he overreached himself. He didn't maintain a balanced approach, although some of the things he did were wonderful. Nevertheless, he didn't handle the economy well; he caused inflation to start. Also, of course, I do not think he dealt very well with the Vietnam situation. But I don't want to make an issue out of that; I just think he overdid it. He pressured congressmen rather than worked with them.

I am trying to say that Congress produces some wisdom as well as some clowns.

QUESTION: It looks like the budget touches right on that subject. Could you give some examples of legislation that, in your opinion, he went too far on? My second question concerns your view of the recent proposal that the president be given a line-item veto.

CONGRESSMAN BOLLING: Well, I am one of the very few Democrats who is basically for the line-item veto, and this is why: I think it will take away some of the power committee chairmen should not have, such as getting a number of pet projects passed when they aren't really justified.

I served as chairman of the Rules Committee for a number of years, and I had too much power. No one should have that much power. In the last six months of a two year term I had more power over legislation than the president. I realize that is an awfully strong statement, but I had life or death power on virtually any piece of legislation unless it had unanimous support. That power of congressmen needs to be curbed. I shall even name such a congressman. Jamie L. Whitten has taken such good care of Mississippi that it is amazing to me that there is anything wrong in Mississippi. I don't think people should be allowed to do what Jamie L. Whitten did, and I think only a line-item veto can do it.

This raises many problems, of course, and if it goes through, it will go through on a great, big, complicated deal where power is shared in different ways. Perhaps it will go through on a complicated lousy deal, which is related to the legislative veto. I don't know, but that is how things get done in the real world. It may turn up, for all I know, in the modifications of the Budget Act which very badly needs to be modified. I am not giving you a very optimistic answer. It is going to be a tough piece of work.

Regarding the examples of excessive demands made by Johnson, I think the example of the Office of Economic Opportunity (OEO) is the saddest one, and at the same time the most important bill among those that should have been done moderately. The OEO should have been started out relatively small with a good many of the principles included, but he kept it growing like Social Security. He wanted to get constituency for it and keep it there. I do not pretend to be able to list all of these bills without going back and looking them up. Generally speaking, the ones that Nixon knocked out are the ones that went too far, and the ones that survived Nixon's attempts at elimination are the ones that were done right. That is a very pragmatic explanation, but it is fairly accurate. If Nixon could not get rid of them, then they were probably pretty well accepted.

In other words, legislation should not be acceptable only in a partisan sense, but it should be sustainable in a broadly gauged national sense if it is to last. The legislature and the president, in my view, have a responsibility for not putting too much on the table. Johnson's program, if looked at in economic terms was nuts, although I loved all of the ideas it contained.

QUESTION: Is a bipartisan foreign policy possible? If so, would you please address U.S. policy toward the Soviet Union in this context?

CONGRESSMAN BOLLING: Yes, we can have a bipartisan foreign policy. This is one of the areas, however, in which I cannot be polite about President Reagan. My main criticism of President Reagan is that he doesn't do his job; his job is not to be a cheerleader, but to be the master of our foreign and defense policy and to maintain a society that is stable. For a society to be stable it has to be relatively at peace with itself, which makes necessary all of the social legislation I have talked about.

I don't think President Reagan has ever known enough about the realities of foreign policy to be a president. I don't think he has ever tried to know enough. I have been scared to death of his lack of knowledge about the defense establishment. I am not against the defense establishment as such; I think it is crucial that we have a strong defense. While I have been against some weapons systems, I have supported others. Generally I am thought of as a hawk, at least by my critics. But I don't think we need to have the kind of military base we have been building. We have been throwing money at the military in a way Johnson threw money at domestic programs. I think that is madness and that we have a real problem.

For years we tried to put together a bipartisan consensus in Congress to reform the defense establishment. It began after I retired in 1981-82. I was fascinated to watch it. Perhaps it was a reaction to what I consider Reagan's excess, compared to the reasonable increase in defense undertaken by Carter. (I mean the first time Carter increased defense spending, not the second time when he seemed to sweeten the pot and perhaps was playing politics as he left the presidency.)

In any event, Senator Sam Nunn and a variety of other people, not all of whom I know very well, are very busy trying to rationalize our defense establishment and defense policy. Behind that, of course, is the need for a rational foreign policy and behind that is the competition with the Soviet Union. My view on the Soviet Union has not changed an iota. I have been almost a professional anti-Stalinist, although Stalin has been dead for a long time.

Despite that, I feel that at all times you have to be in communication with the Soviet Union as much as with China. Presently I am a little bit less of a hard-liner than I was. But I'll probably be more of a hard-liner in the next years for the reason that the American people will be in one of their euphoric phases when they think of the Soviet Union as a friend. I won't be. I think we have to have a balanced defense; I think we have to be careful about our commitments; I think we have a major responsibility in the democratic world. Part of that requires an aggressive effort to get along with the Soviet Union and reduce the piles of weapons for which we really do not have much use. We ought to keep the ones we need.

QUESTION: I wonder what would happen if we had an ideological and stubborn president who could use the line-item veto and deny the House the right to override? Wouldn't he be able to destroy months or years of legislation?

CONGRESSMAN BOLLING: That is a very good question. Superficially the answer probably would be that he could. But the fact of the matter is that when you get into these struggles the people who turn out to be ideological fanatics are relatively few in number. Nevertheless, today we are facing for the first time in my experience a significant number of people who have decided that near-fanaticism is the only way in which the Republicans will regain the House. So you have some very bright people, including a man from Georgia named Newt Gingrich, who are very far to the right and insist on being confrontational.

I don't think they are going to succeed. I think so because I have met enough Republicans in meetings where we were not conferring as partisans but as people who wanted to get things done. The last thing we need today is the confrontational approach taken by a few Republican fanatics. What we need, with our economic difficulties, which in my opinion are enormous, is civility. Even though we still have a remnant of euphoria about the economy, at least in some parts of the population, I see problems ahead. I hate to use the word that some people think indicates weakness, but "civility" is one of the things that we very badly need in the times ahead.

Let me just engage in a short discourse on the problem of civility. At this moment we are in the election process. That is the time to fight. If possible, you ought to do it in a way that is educational, but now is the time to do it. When everyone is elected and has become part of the government, that is the time to work together. It isn't very smart to play party electoral politics year-round. You ought to be able to confine your party politics to election time, and regardless of whether you win or lose, be civil about the outcome.

Take those people who supported the Constitution. Those people had been at each other's throats on previous occasions. Jefferson and Hamilton, for example, had violently differing views.

But they knew they had to work together once the controversy about the Constitution was settled. In the same way we have somehow to get the American people and the Congress to work together, and the president has to learn that first. Then we will not have to worry about the line-item veto and legislative conflict.

If Harry Truman could get Vandenberg and company, who comprised very large numbers in the House and Senate, to consent to a bipartisan foreign policy, why can't anyone else?

NARRATOR: One of the legitimate criticisms of social science and academic work is that often it is too far removed from the patient in the bed and does not deal with the real issues. Dick Bolling's service in the 81st to the 96th Congress amounted to some 34 years in which he was very close to the patient in the bed, and he is quite willing to diagnose the condition of the patient. That is why it is so important to have him here today to speak about a very neglected problem in American political history and political practice. We are all extremely grateful to him for coming.

V.

PRESIDENTS AND THE FUTURE

~ Twelve ~

THE PRESIDENCY AND THE FUTURE[*]

David Broder

I am very glad to be back on this campus and to be a part of this series under the auspices of the Miller Center. We have been adopted Virginians now for slightly over 25 years and I know that leaves us still very much in the category of newcomers in this state. We feel a close bond to this state, however, and to this great institution of our state.

I recently spent several days at the Capitol, watching a Democratic House of Representatives responding to a Republican president who had been in office for all of a 108 days as of yesterday. The House passed a budget bill that was urged by the president and that mandates the elimination of about $36 billion worth of permanently authorized programs, plus billions of dollars of additional appropriations for the coming fiscal year, in effect, reversing about 48 years of domestic policies. Those committees are now required to report their specific cuts to the floor of the House of Representatives within the next 30 days.

I came home last night and started working on the notes for this talk, and I picked up Joe Califano's new book, *Governing America*. As I leafed through it, I came across one passage discussing the presidency, looking at it both from the Carter perspective and from his earlier experience with Lyndon Johnson. The following passage struck me: "The time it takes to get something done underlines the necessity for persistence. It's rare to get a bill passed in a two-year Congress, much less a one-year

---

[*]Presented in a Forum at the Miller Center of Public Affairs on 8 May 1981. Reprinted from *The American Presidency: Principles and Problems* (Washington, D.C.: University Press of America, Inc., 1982), Volume I.

session. Most legislation percolates for years until interested groups believe they understand all of the consequences and have extracted whatever protection or advantages they can. Three of every four dollars in the federal budget must be spent unless legislation is passed amending already existing laws. Changing the course of the federal budget, therefore, takes time."

Now I say this, not intending in any way to poke fun at my friend, Mr. Califano, who has written—as many of you know—his own excellent book on the presidency called *Presidential Nation*, but rather to make the point that sweeping judgments about the character of the presidency or the powers or the infirmities of its incumbent are subject to fairly rapid change and revision. Arthur Schlesinger's book *The Imperial Presidency* was published in 1973, the year before the first president in our history was ridden out of office on a rail. And so it goes.

As a journalist, I find this a somewhat consoling thought, even though I suppose if I were an academic student of the presidency, it would drive me up the wall. I find it very difficult, myself, to arrive at any great certainties about the condition or the future of the presidency as an institution. Therefore, I tend to be cautious and even skeptical about those who would make a particular analysis of the presidency and its condition serve as the foundation for fairly sweeping proposals for what they regard as the improvement or the reform of that office. For all that we have come to know and all of the good studies that have been done of the institutional presidency, it remains a highly personal office. The contrast between the last two presidents, Mr. Carter and Mr. Reagan, certainly demonstrate that fact.

On the face of it, both Jimmy Carter and Ronald Reagan looked like rather exotic creatures to be coming to the White House. Neither Annapolis nor Eureka College had previously produced a President of the United States. Nor could the trade of acting or peanut processing boast any alumni in the White House. Both men were outsiders, devoid of Washington experience and equally devoid of any broad knowledge of world affairs. Yet, how different their presidencies seem—at least at this point. Take a look at the staffing and the structure of the White House, which is a matter of the discretion of the president. Jimmy Carter operated without a chief of staff the first 30 months that he was in office, and in some respects he served that function himself. He was extremely reluctant to delegate significant decision making to others on his staff. Ronald Reagan came into that same office and delegated responsibility so thoroughly that when he was shot and seriously wounded after ten weeks in the presidency, the White House functioned during his convalescence almost without missing a beat.

Look at the area of congressional relations, on which all of the scholars of the presidency have focused as a critical institutional problem. Neither Carter nor Reagan had ever served in the Congress of the United States, and yet Jimmy Carter's relations were almost foredoomed to disaster. He offended the Speaker of the House of Representatives; he offended the chairman of the Senate Finance Committee, the chairman of the Senate Budget Committee, and the chairman of what was soon to become the Senate Energy Committee, Senator Jackson. He had Congress's institutional back up so high that it never really came back down again.

Ronald Reagan operated with exactly the same tools at his disposal, the same supply of cuff links in his desk drawers, the same number of seats in the presidential box at the three theaters of the Kennedy Center, and the same size congressional liaison staff. However, he tamed Congress to submission. How did he do it? He did it by being sensitive to personalities and the human needs of the members of Congress.

If you will allow me just one anecdote, there is a story that I heard from a member of Congress himself that struck me as being so typical of the change in attitude. On the Friday before the President was shot, he gave a luncheon at the White House for members of the Baseball Hall of Fame. There were two members of Congress who were invited to that luncheon. One was Bob Michel, Republican minority leader of the House of Representatives, who was for many years the star pitcher of the Republican baseball team in the annual Republican/Democratic softball game. The other was a young man from California whose name is not known to many people, even in Washington. His name is Tony Coelho, and he is a second-term member of the House of Representatives.

THE PRESIDENCY AND THE FUTURE

The thing that was strange about Coelho's being there was that he was the newly elected chairman of the Democratic Congressional Campaign Committee. Coelho told me that as he looked around the room, he could not figure out why he would have been chosen as the only person from Congress other than Bob Michel to be a guest at that luncheon. When the President got up to speak, however, he mentioned having played the part of Grover Cleveland Alexander in a movie, and he said he had been so moved to learn that while this great pitcher had been vilified in his own lifetime as a man who had a terrible drinking problem, the truth was that Grover Cleveland Alexander had been an epileptic and had never felt he could admit it to the public or to the team owners because they would have ruled him out of the game. Tony Coelho said, "Then I knew why I had been invited to that luncheon. I'm an epileptic, and I've never made any secret of it as far as my constituents or anybody who has wanted to discuss it with me are concerned. I've been very up front about it." All of the staff people from California probably knew that, and Coelho said, "In fact, I'd been discussing it once with Mike Deaver in a kind of a casual conversation," Deaver being one of the President's top three assistants.

Coelho also said, "I have no complaints about Jimmy Carter. He was very good to me, as a freshman Democrat in the House of Representatives." Carter's staff, however, when they came to talk to members of Congress always wanted to talk about HR 1144. The White House staff, according to Coelho, understood that we thought about things other than HR 1144, and they knew how to reach us and talk to us in terms of the other parts of our lives and not just as legislators who have a vote that they may want. He told that story in a newsletter to his constituents, and you can imagine the kind of message that carries back to the Democrats, particularly, who read that in his own district.

Another aspect of the presidency that all students of the office have focused on is communication to the public. Among the many hats the president wears is that of the "Commander in Chief" of the United States. Particularly since the advent of electronic broadcasting and now television, this has been a great weapon in the hands of those presidents who knew how to use it. Carter threatened even before his inauguration to go over the heads of Congress when it was balking him. Tip O'Neill told the President that it be a great mistake, and he was right. Carter lost his audience almost as quickly as people tuned in for the first broadcast. Reagan, using the same media more sparingly than Carter, has moved public opinion time and again, and thereby altered the political climate for decision making.

To be fair and somewhat balanced, there are similarities in the performance of the two men. Both learned early on in their presidencies that there is cost and pain in the effort to try to have Cabinet government. They have learned the basic point that Elliot Richardson, who has occupied half the chairs in the Cabinet, makes about those Cabinet jobs. He says, "You can do the job of running the internal affairs of your department in about an hour a day because the interesting problems in government are always the problems that cut across departmental lines."

Jimmy Carter learned the cost of having an energy secretary who was perhaps too smart for the job. Ronald Reagan has learned very quickly that there are also costs when the occupant of that particular Cabinet post perhaps has an opposite problem.

The institution, however, is really a reflection of the man. We ought to ask, when bold prescriptions are announced for rescuing the presidency from whatever outsiders believe at any moment is its plight, how permanent is this condition that is being remedied; when did it really begin to afflict us; how long has it endured; and is the nature of the ailment such that it cannot be cured by the result of the next election? This is particularly true when the remedy suggested is a constitutional change. We ought to be cautious and conservative, as we Virginians are supposed to be, in that regard.

In recent years, many of the wisest men and women in this country have come to the point of endorsing what I would regard as rather radical changes in the constitutional structure of the presidency. Lloyd Cutler and Stuart Eizenstat, two men who are perhaps among the wisest of the old and young men in Washington and both with an intimate exposure to the workings of the presidency, have said that we need to change our system constitutionally, to move it much more in the direction of the parliamentary system, blurring the separation of executive and legislative branches.

Mr. Cutler has been joined by many other *very* able and worthy people, including some of the former presidents of the United States, in recommending a constitutional change that would give the president a single six-year term. That particular idea strikes me as perhaps the most distinguished and powerfully endorsed bad idea that has come forth in a very long time. My own feeling is that rather than try to remake the presidency as a kind of temporary constitutional monarch, we want to instead tie the president more closely to the other parts of the political and governmental system, not separate him from it. Nothing ties a president more closely to the political system than the threat or the possibility of running in the next election.

There are a couple of practical reasons why I shrink from that particular recommendation. It seems that there is a tendency among our presidents, even now, to tire of the dirty work of grubbing around in domestic policy-making, dealing with the Congress and the interest groups, and getting their hands soiled in that kind of arena. As soon as they go to their first international summit conference and deal with other leaders of government and heads of state, they discover a world that is far more appealing to them than that grubby world of Washington and domestic politics. I seriously believe that if we had a president serving a single six-year term, his one goal in life after the first year in office would be to win the Nobel Peace Prize. He would find it far more appealing to spend his time up there at the summit than down in the trenches of domestic policy-making. In fact, if we had this constitutional amendment in effect, we would be lucky to get the president back to Washington once a year to deliver the State of the Union Address.

There are other less theoretical problems with this recommendation. Would we really be better off as a country and as a society if the American people, who according to the polls that Pat Caddell took early in 1980 had decided by a two-to-one margin that they did not want the leadership of Jimmy Carter, had to face an additional two years of Carter's leadership? Would we be better off if we had a Ronald Reagan who, at the age of 74 or 75, having experienced the rigors of the presidency plus the effects of the wound he suffered ten weeks into office, was forced to stay in office for another two years beyond what is now the normal term limit? My inclination is to be very cautious about that kind of change, and equally so about jumping to conclusions regarding the permanency of the changes we see from year to year and almost from month to month in the institution of the presidency.

It will not surprise you to learn that, less than four months after Mr. Carter left the White House with people saying that the presidency had lost most of its leadership clout, there were nascent worries in Washington about the extent and the sweep of presidential power. I give you one example from the area of regulatory reform. By the stroke of a pen, as the saying goes, President Reagan signed an executive order that gave the Office of Management and Budget the right of review of all executive branch regulatory agency edicts, on the rationale that OMB could conduct an independent evaluation of the cost and benefits of any new regulation. The man who is administering this program for the President was quoted as saying that when he worked in a similar position in OMB under the Ford administration, he tried, as others have in that job over the past decade, to impose greater central control over government regulation. "Quite frankly," Mr. Miller is quoted as saying, "when we were in the Ford administration, the only weapon we had was ridicule." Today, any of the executive branch regulatory agencies must come to the OMB, which is part of the executive office of the president, before it can carry out what it sees as the mandate of the statute it is to administer. It must get approval from OMB before any of the new regulations can go into effect.

Another example of presidential power is in the area of budgetary policy. Dave Stockman went far beyond what most people thought were the limits when he imposed budgetary reductions on the government's so-called untouchable programs. These were not appropriations, not the annual money bills, but permanently authorized government programs that under the mandate of the budget resolution had to be scaled back or eliminated. Unless that was carried out or a waiver was granted by the House or Senate, no legislation or appropriation in that area could come to the floor without being subject to a point of order by a single member. It was the first time this kind of specific mandate had been put into the first budget resolution of the year, the spring resolution. The Senate, in fact, went further than the House, forcing a vote on the reconciliation instructions, these reductions in categorical programs, even before it passed the first budget resolution.

There are people who say that by doing this and by allowing the executive branch, in effect, politically to set the limits and terms of that first budget resolution, the Congress gave away much of its historical leverage. The test of strength with the executive branch, as you know, was played out in those confrontations in particular committees between the legislators who were experts in that area of jurisdiction and the executive agency officials who were carrying out those programs. Looked at from the other side, or the president's viewpoint, this change in procedure means that instead of having to fight a hundred wars on a hundred battlefields in a hundred different subcommittees of the Congress, each with its representatives and senators having a fairly narrowly focused interest and constituency, the president can wage the budget fight once before the whole Congress and the whole public and then let Congress itself discipline the committees.

This is a real shift of power whose meaning, frankly, is only now beginning to dawn even on most of the members of the Congress itself. How permanent this shift will be, whether Congress will now respond to the realization of what is happening by changing its own procedures again with the new budget, remains to be seen.

I am sure there will soon be warnings about a new imperial presidency emerging in Washington. There are some significant differences that we should not lose sight of, however, between Ronald Reagan and the men who gave birth to that term, Lyndon Johnson and Richard Nixon. Where Johnson was a pervasive, unrelenting force, a man who my colleague Phil Geyelin had said, "really had the unspoken motto, 'We shall overwhelm,'" and Richard Nixon was a kind of secretive and sly and scheming person, Reagan is much more open and relaxed. Yet, there is a much more important difference between Reagan and those two strong predecessors. Johnson and Nixon attempted to build their strong presidency on weak political party structures. By pushing the presidency beyond its tolerable limits in order to compensate for the weakness of the underlying political party structure, they brought down upon themselves and upon that office very serious consequences.

Lyndon Johnson distrusted the Democratic party because he saw it as a source of infectious Kennedyism. Richard Nixon distrusted the Republican party as a political incubus with strong right-wing tendencies that would keep him from carrying out some of the programs and policies that he wanted to pursue. What may sustain and stabilize the Reagan presidency is that its strength now rests on a financially, organizationally, and politically strong base in the Republican party. Mr. Reagan has shown a good deal of readiness to embrace that strength and draw on it.

With the advantage of hindsight, I suppose we could say that the Republican party got a real break in 1976 with the defeat of Ronald Reagan for the presidential nomination at a time when it would have been hard for any Republican to win the presidency, and also with the defeat of Bill Brock in the Senate race in Tennessee. When Brock came to the Republican party chairmanship at the beginning of 1977, he said it was his purpose to try to rebuild the strength of that party not from the top down, or from the presidency down, as had been tried so often, but rather from the grass roots up. He inherited a rather strong financial base, and he broadened that base to the point that in the fall of 1980 there were about one million individual contributors in the Republican party. He used those funds and the staff that they provided to build the organizational base of the Republican party at the grass roots level, recruiting candidates for local office and legislative office, and training the technicians who could run the campaigns at all levels.

He did one other thing, which to my knowledge had not been done previously since we entered the television era of politics. He put the Republican party on television with an institutional advertising campaign. The ads were rather clever. The basic message, stated over and over again, was "If you're unhappy with what you see going on in Washington, D.C., please remember, dear voter, who has been running things in Washington all these years."

As it happened, this message from the Republican advertising campaign dovetailed nicely with the message Mr. Reagan was prepared to give as the Republican nominee in the course of the fall campaign of 1980. Reagan's focus was obviously on the White House, but he was not nearly as selfish a candidate as many other recent Republican nominees and presidents have been. Wherever he went, he made a point of saying, "Don't send me to Washington alone." It was through this kind of party and personal campaign that the Republicans won not only the White House but also their first majority in the Senate in 26 years, and they managed to reduce the Democratic margin in the House of Representative by more than half.

Does this mean that everything is secure and safe with Mr. Reagan in the presidency? I don't think so. I do wonder, however, whether Lyndon Johnson would have heeded the early warnings of growing dissent within the Democratic party over Vietnam had he not been so aloof from the party and whether there would have been a Watergate incident if Richard Nixon had not turned his back on the Republican National Committee to instead create his own campaign organization, the Committee for the Reelection of the President (CREEP). We don't know the answers, but I do see instances now in which it is clear that Ronald Reagan's presidency is being stabilized and wisely guided by his relationship with the Republican party.

In the spring of 1981, Howard Baker, the majority leader in the U.S. Senate, said in very clear terms to the Reagan White House, "This is not the time to put forward a proposal for selling this kind of military aircraft and equipment to Saudi Arabia. That action needs to be postponed and considered more fully in conjunction with the Republican members of the Senate and House of Representatives." The White House heeded that advice. It is quite possible that similar advice now coming from the congressional Republicans on the budget and tax program may cause the President to move away from his rigid stance. He could move in a direction that would reassure those people on Wall Street who are currently taking the exact opposite actions from those needed for the President's economic program to have a chance of success.

David Broder

In summary, I feel that at the moment we are in a rather healthy stage of development for the presidency, if not for the presidential selection system. The latter is another topic for another day's discussion. Today's condition is almost certain to change tomorrow when we are talking about the presidency. With an office as powerful as the presidency, it is probably wise always to keep your fingers crossed about what may be coming next month.

~ *Thirteen* ~

THE SETTING: MORALITY, POLITICS, AND FOREIGN POLICY*

George F. Kennan

NARRATOR: George Kennan once referred to Reinhold Niebuhr as the father of all of us in political and moral theory, and the relationship between the two of them was close. In a somewhat similar way, one could refer to George Kennan as a father of international political thought—in a dual sense. For any well-tested parent, it will be understandable if we speak of Mr. Kennan as father both of those who have worshiped at his feet and concurred with his thinking and those who have challenged his teachings. There are at least two other reasons for his enduring influence. One reason certainly is whether his "children" agreed or disagreed with what he said, they knew what it was he was trying to say. James Reston made reference to that fact when in reviewing *Russia, the Atom and the West*, he observed that "Mr. Kennan had an idea and he could write. He had not been living in a university community long enough but almost long enough to smother his ideas in clouds of academic jargon." The other reason is that in every one of the great debates on public issues and foreign policy, Mr. Kennan, sometimes reluctantly, and sometimes deliberately, has found himself at the center of those debates. This has made him, for those who agreed and those who disagreed, a force to reckon with in American public affairs.

Two subjects are of paramount concern to the Miller Center. One undergirds and surrounds everything we are doing: the

---

*Presented in a Forum at the Miller Center of Public Affairs on 9 April 1979. Reprinted from *The Virginia Papers on the Presidency* (Washington, D.C.: University Press of America, Inc., 1979), Volume I.

THE SETTING: MORALITY, POLITICS, AND FOREIGN POLICY

question of morality and purpose as they relate to public policy. For almost every aspect of policy, the issue of right and wrong is raised and debated. It is on this issue that Mr. Solzhenitsyn has once again drawn Mr. Kennan back to the center of controversy in the discussion of purpose, morality, and policy. Rather than quoting from Solzhenitsyn's 1979 Harvard University Commencement Address, I will assume that Mr. Kennan will make reference to it, but if not, the speech has been widely reprinted.

Another issue that is central to the Miller Center is the question of the president and the Foreign Service or the president and America's diplomats and ambassadors charged with carrying on foreign affairs. This topic is also the subject of a rather intense and strongly worded piece in *Foreign Affairs* for spring 1979 by Mr. Laurence Silberman who takes issue with Mr. Kennan, claiming ambassadors should have a direct political relationship to the president and speak as partisan political envoys for him in contrast with the opposite view of ambassadors as part of a career service dedicated to the pursuit of the national interest and the protection of Americans abroad.

Mr. Kennan truly needs no introduction. These references to intellectual debates may help to place his presentation in context. His concerns fall at the center, not on the periphery, of the present and future work of the Miller Center.

MR. KENNAN: Thank you. The statement of Mr. Solzhenitsyn to which you referred was this: He referred, first of all, to certain well-known representatives of American society who say that we cannot apply moral criteria to politics, and as a consequence of this, he added people such as myself—and he referred to me by name—"mix good and evil, right and wrong, and make space for the absolute triumph of absolute evil in the world." It is hard for me to comment on this statement except to say that it is perhaps somewhat exaggerated if the two absolutes are taken away, but even then I don't know where he got this idea. I think it comes from lectures that I gave at the University of Chicago 30 years ago in which I referred to the tendency of American statesmen to be carried away by moralism and legalism in judgment of the policies of other governments. I was thinking at that time particularly of

Japan around the time of the Open Door episode. My reference was an observation about history; I have no idea who interpreted it to Mr. Solzhenitsyn or gave him the impression that he has of my views. It opens up, though, something that I think is really one of the most difficult subjects in the whole realm of political science: the connection of moral principles with the conduct of foreign policy. I can only grope here in various ways with the question, but it is probably useful to do so.

When I think of the question of the relationship of foreign policy to moral principle, I am always inclined first to think of what morality is *not*, what many people seem to think it is, and what I think it is definitely not. I won't bore you by dwelling on that, but merely indicate what sort of thing I have in mind.

I think it is not preaching to other governments nor striking high-minded moral poses because it makes us feel virtuous and because it makes us look nice to ourselves in the mirror. It is not reproaching people for doing things that we ourselves do—something that Americans have done very liberally and generously in recent weeks and months in the case of the Russians. I don't want to take time to go into examples, but the United States has warned the Russians not to interfere in Iran, this at the end of 20 years, if one wants to be honest, in which we have entered into every phase of Iran's national life. The United States has warned them not to send arms and military instructors to various countries, something that America also has done on a scale far greater than they have. I could go on with this. In a number of instances, Americans have put pressures on other people not to do things that they actually have done themselves.

Morality is not criticizing others for reasons of domestic policy to appease individual pressure groups and lobbies within this country and then claiming that one is criticizing those governments on the basis of high principle.

I do object to the selectivity in our moral pronouncements abroad. In numbers of instances the United States criticizes other governments and makes demands on them in the name of high moral principle. In others it simply doesn't. Dozens of dictatorships scattered around the world have treated their people very harshly in recent years, and the United States has said nothing about human rights in those particular countries. But we speak very loudly about human rights in countries where violations happen to be of interest to some pressure group within our own government. That is all right, except then I think the United States should not claim that it is speaking in the name of high principle.

I think it is not morality to urge courses of action on other people when one cannot clearly see the probable results of the particular course of action and when one is oneself not going to have to live with the results, but someone else is. I think in many instances when America is pressing one course of action or another on other governments in the name of high moral principle, we really do not know and have not thought very much about what might be the consequences if they accepted our advice. We are quite content to have given the advice because this action puts us in a high moral posture. Americans are not the ones who are going to have to live with it, however.

A very painful and sensitive example is that of the Rhodesians and the South Africans. I would not like to be misunderstood; I have no sympathy for the apartheid of the South African government. I think the circumstances of the Rhodesian government are a somewhat different matter, but I am not defending its policies. I am merely saying this: Both of those governments have gotten themselves into a royal jam in which no present course of action they could take is likely to have results favorable to them, nor possibly even results favorable to the people over whom they preside. This *is* possible. Governments *can* involve themselves as a result of a long series of mistakes in tragic dilemmas where their only alternatives are ones all of which involve heavy disadvantages and threaten to raise new troubles. One can say that had they done the right things years ago, they would not have been in this position; very well, but they are in it today. Is it desirable then, since almost any course that they are going to follow is problematic and full of trouble, to give advice to people in such a situation? You invite upon yourself a portion of the responsibility for whatever unfortunate consequences flow from their taking your advice, if they take it, and, of course, it is they who have to live with those consequences and not yourself.

George F. Kennan

I question whether this is morality. I think sometimes morality consists precisely of keeping one's counsel, reserving one's judgment, leaving responsibility where it belongs, and especially not giving advice in situations where one cannot influence the implementation of that advice, because that area is also very dangerous.

All of these things, I would say, are *not* the observance of high moral principles in government. But does this situation mean, then, that there is no such thing as morality in politics, or that the exercise and the conduct of foreign policy is unaffected by any moral limitations or moral principles whatsoever?

I think that question too has to be answered in the negative. I do think that certain moral principles are applicable to American foreign policy. I won't attempt to speak for the foreign policies of other governments because I do not share the responsibilities of citizenship there.

Before I go on to that question, I would like to point out something else that is very hard to explain to people but seems to go right to the heart of the issue. One ought to remember that the conduct of foreign policy by a government, in this instance the U.S. government, is a process or a function that does not reflect essentially a moral purpose. The purpose of the conduct of foreign policy by the American government, as I see it, is to assure the security and promote the reasonable interests of the American people in a world where those interests impinge on the interests of others. Now these functions don't strike me as being moral aims. They are simply functions that flow from the very fact of our existence, not from the virtue or morality of our existence. They flow from the fact that Americans are a people who occupy a given portion of the surface of the globe. Other nations have recognized that in this quality as a people, Americans have certain interests that flow from the workings of our society. I hope that these interests will always be reasonable ones—ones that others can respect without detriment to themselves, but I do not see them as having much to do with morality. I do not think that the existence of this country was the reflection of any sort of moral action or purpose. The United States has been created by historical

THE SETTING: MORALITY, POLITICS, AND FOREIGN POLICY

circumstances. Here we are, and someone has to conduct our relations with other people.

It seems to me that in essence, then, that function is not in itself a moral one. It is affected, however, by certain moral principles and certain injunctions of a moral nature that play upon it. They affect for one thing, or ought to affect, the style and quality of American diplomacy. They ought to dictate, it seems to me, a certain courtesy, considerateness, and generosity in the treatment of other nations and peoples in this world, particularly smaller ones. This also means, I think, that we as Americans have an obligation to use our great weight and strength as a country in such a way that we try not to bring hardship, suffering, or detriment to the interests of others. We ought to be careful not to step, whether inadvertently or not, on other people's toes, but rather to treat them with respect for their interests and with consideration. We do have, as I see it, an obligation to use our great strength in ways that are conducive to the prevention of major war and the preservation of a reasonable degree of peace and stability, particularly among the main industrial powers of the world.

Here again, it is possible to carry things too far. Maxim Litvinov used to say that peace is indivisible. (His pronouncement of the word *peace* almost always brought amusement to the people who heard him.) I think this statement is carrying it much too far. Peace is not indivisible. There will always be localized wars. Sometimes they can be tolerated without detriment or danger to the world as a whole. On the other hand, wars today among the great powers, particularly among the superpowers and nuclear powers, cannot be tolerated without detriment to the world as a whole. I think the United States is faced, in this respect, with a necessity, or perhaps a moral principle, but in any case a necessity. The United States does have to use its power in such a way as to try to prevent the catastrophe that now lies very near at hand. The mere existence of these massive quantities of destructive power in the hands of mere men who are fallible, weak, and often misguided is a tremendous danger.

The United States, as the greatest of these powers, certainly has an obligation to use its strength in order to avoid a major war. But these are requirements that I would regard as duties to ourselves and not to others. I think it is very important to recognize this. They are duties that result primarily from what the United States is and what Americans think of themselves. People are the heirs here in America to certain traditions and ideals that have marked this country and certain concepts of right and wrong that are prevalent among the American people that we like to think we are preserving. These inherited values lie at the heart of American's image of themselves, their self-respect, and their sense of the uniqueness and the historical significance of American civilization. Of course, we have a duty to respect these values and even to place them at the heart of our conduct as a nation among nations. But these are not really what Americans owe to other people. They are simply what we owe to what we ourselves are.

I would like, more by way of illustration of what I have said than as a continuation of it, to take a different path and start by saying something that now concerns the substance of the policy. I have often been accused in this recent period of being an isolationist; in a limited sense, this accusation is quite true. I say in a limited sense because I do feel strongly that the United States ought to be faithful to the various solemn obligations of alliance that it has undertaken, especially to the Western Europeans and the Japanese. Even here, of course, the United States does not have an absolutely unlimited commitment; it must be faithful to its allies to the extent that others reciprocate. That always is a limitation.

I acknowledge all of these things. Beyond that, however, and when it comes to the whole great portion of the world that is vaguely referred to as the Third World, I think our sense of what our obligations are toward these countries is greatly exaggerated. The greater part of U.S. involvements there, what we are trying to do there, could just as well be omitted. In this sense I would term myself an isolationist.

Two objections are immediately going to be raised to such a view. First of all, it has been said that this view means abandoning the Third World to the Soviet Union. That, of course, is a big subject in itself, and I can expand on it only very briefly here. I will merely say that I do not see the evidence of this objection. I think such a view vastly overrates the capabilities both of the Soviet Union and of the United States for manipulating the reactions of

THE SETTING: MORALITY, POLITICS, AND FOREIGN POLICY

people in other parts of the world. I am not very worried on this score. I don't think the Soviet Union is any greater than any of the major colonial powers who have lost their colonies. In fact, I think they are a good deal more clumsy than most of the rest of the world. It seems to me that their record to date is not such that it should strike terror into our hearts. They have tried in many instances to dominate other countries in one way or another from a great distance, often through puppet groups of one sort or another, and they have a record of a spectacular series of failures. One has only to think of Egypt as it was six or eight years ago to see what can happen.

So I personally am not afraid of Soviet triumphs in the Third World. When one stops to think of it, the places where the United States has involved itself most heavily, as in the case of Vietnam and Iran, have been the places where things have actually worked most badly for the United States and most favorably for the Soviet Union. I don't really think much of that argument.

One of the silliest reactions occasioned by these exaggerated fears of Soviet penetration and domination of the rest of the world is the suggestion, which many have heard often in recent weeks, that wherever such dangers of Soviet penetration and domination seem to exist, the obvious answer would be the dispatch of American armed forces to the region in question. I stand in amazement at these suggestions. I have to ask myself: Against whom is it conceived that American troops would be fighting? Outside of the areas of Eastern and Central Europe that fell to the Russians with our blessing at the end of World War II, the Soviet government, in contrast to ourselves, has not sent its forces beyond its own borders at any time since 1945, and, I think, has not intention of doing so today. This means that if the government were to send American forces to any of these areas that worry us, whether it is South Yemen, Afghanistan, the Horn of Africa, or wherever, American troops would be fighting not Russians but natives, and everyone ought to know what this means.

I really wonder sometimes, when I read these suggestions, whether Americans have learned anything whatsoever from the whole Vietnam misery of recent years. The lessons seem to have passed completely out of people's minds. Many are suggesting that the United States start it all over again. These people have never understood that in Vietnam, it was not just the question of Americans and Russians or Americans and Chinese. The United States faced a native people there who also had something to do with it. One could not fight the Russians by just fighting the Vietnamese; and one cannot fight them by fighting the South Yemenese or other native peoples either.

The second objection that will be raised to the principle of America minding its own business in foreign affairs, or in other words, to a limited isolation, is that it would be immoral because Americans have a moral duty to give aid to underdeveloped nations and that this situation too means an unavoidable involvement in their affairs.

Here again, I think anyone who looks closely at the historical record of the last two or three decades will have to recognize that this thesis has been extensively refuted by experience. Americans have learned, or should have learned, a number of unpleasant lessons. We should have learned that there is no form of economic aid to another country that does not involve some degree of undesirable interference in the life of that country. When one gives aid to another government, there are always some people who benefit by it and usually some people who decidedly do not benefit by it. When the United States introduced the modern plow in India, it weakened a great body of people whose livelihood came from making the old wooden plows.

It is very difficult to benefit everyone in the new countries. You are interfering in what is essentially a competitive political situation, and it is very difficult to benefit all of the competitors alike.

Beyond that, Americans should have learned that the true causes of underdevelopment are usually ones that cannot be corrected just by outside aid alone. They lie in such things as overpopulation, deficiencies in resources, climate, habit, political immaturity, and other circumstances that no outside force can remedy in any short space of time.

I would not say that there would never again be a time or a place where economic aid on a small scale would be indicated for this government and would be justified. There will always be exceptional situations, particularly ones connected with natural disasters and calamities of one sort or another. But I do think it would be a very good thing if Americans could get it into their heads that they are not the answer to everyone else's prayers, that what it would take to straighten out many of these countries is not really the sort of thing that Americans are able to give; even if it were, it is doubtful that in its present state the United States would have the resources to spare for these purposes.

Finally, it is urged and argued that Americans have a duty to promote the spread among other nations of the principles of liberal self-government, human rights, majority rule, and so forth, and that Americans ought, as a people, to quote one proponent, to "speak out on these questions." This is a vast subject, but I have great trouble with such a thesis. I have trouble with it for several reasons. One is that I do not think the United States has the capacity to influence all of these people that way. I am inclined very much to doubt that democracy is always a suitable or possible form of government for all of the peoples in question. It seems to me that democratic self-government is a form of government that had its origins on and around the shores of the North Sea and has thrived there and in such other parts of the world as were populated initially with people from that area. I think democracy is the exception rather than the rule for this world. Looked at against the whole span of world history, it is rather an abnormal form of government and has many deficiencies. I prefer it for this country, but I would not be prepared to say that it would be a feasible or even necessarily a more desirable form of government for certain places that I can think of in the rest of the world. Other objections to Americans pressing human rights also exist, to which I will refer shortly.

I would like to make this one fundamental point about such things as our duty to spread democracy and human rights. Everyone knows from the experience of personal life that it is almost invariably by example and almost never by precept that one influences other people. And so it is in international life. People can talk all they want about the virtues of democracy and human rights, but what is really going to count in the last analysis for other countries is the impression they have of things in American lives that they admire and advantages that they wish they had. They are not going to be slow to get the message. They are going to imitate those things they respect and want to imitate. If they see discreditable and depressing things when they look at our country and things that appear to be in contradiction with the high moral principles about which Americans like to talk, all of our words and good advice are going to be for naught.

This brings me to my last point. It seems to me that there is one dictate of morality that applies to the substance of American foreign policy. It is the duty to recognize one's own limitations, not to undertake more than one can fulfill, not to bite off more than one can chew, not to advance unfounded pretensions, and not to arouse false hopes either in others or in one's own population; but rather, to be aware of the limitations of one's own ability to contribute. It seems to me that if the United States expects to be of any great use to anyone else in this troubled world, the first thing Americans have to do is to put our own society in order and keep it there.

It does seem to me that we have not been doing very well in this respect since World War II. I know this is a complex subject, and there are many examples of good and bad in American national life. But it seems to Americans that we have certainly not mastered in this recent postwar period a number of the great problems that are creeping over our society and that threaten serious consequences if they are not mastered. America has not mastered the problems of growing crime, cynicism and corruption in public office, moral dissolution and pornography in its cities, declining standards at various levels of education, environmental deterioration, inflation, and above all, the specter of an energy problem.

If this last problem is not taken in hand very soon, I cannot state how seriously I would view the possible effects on this country. The United States is a country addicted to the use of motor fuel in a way that reminds me of a narcotic addition. It could not be broken suddenly without withdrawal symptoms of a social nature throughout the country. Yet the United States had the clearest conceivable sort of warning in October 1973 in the oil embargo. Since then we have done nothing but fritter away time and have actually allowed the importation of foreign oil to rise rather than decline.

This discussion does lead to one last point that is very old and controversial, and I put it forward tentatively. It seems to me questionable whether what one want in this world is really a maximum of interdependence, particularly for a country such as this one. I wish more energy resources were available in this country. I wish the United States was not so dependent on other countries, and I will explain why. If our pipeline is broken off and there is an interruption of supply from the other end, the United States will then be not only tempted but almost compelled to resort to force to guarantee its economic security and well-being. I speak of this possibility with some feeling because 25 years ago in a series of lectures at Princeton I pointed to America's growing dependence on other countries for fuel and raw materials. I also pointed out that if someday these other countries interrupted their supply to us, they might put America in a painful position, and the country would be moved to resort to force to assure the maintenance of the supply. In that way, the United States would start all over again and re-create a new sort of 19th-century colonialism. This might, in other words, be a beginning of a new colonialism for this era, long after everyone thought that sort of thing was over. I have not failed to note recently the number of people who have written in the press about the possibility that the United States might have to go into Saudi Arabia with armed forces to assure the continuation of our energy supply if a dissolution of society were to take place there comparable to what has happened in Iran.

Therefore, I would question whether it is really moral to let oneself be drawn into a situation where one can save oneself only by taking violent action against other people. I think it might be more moral to proceed with great vigor and determination now, at least to recover enough command over the resources of the American economy so that the country would not be tempted to intervene.

To sum up, in general, my plea would be that Americans stop being so self-conscious about the problem of morality; that we stop looking at ourselves in the mirror and asking how good we look and how beautiful our postures are in this or that image; that we stop giving moral advice to others as to how they should behave; that Americans stop casting ourselves in the role of the lady bountiful professing to have the answers to everyone's problems. My plea would be that we give a little more attention to the cultivation of our ideals right here at home, and that if we want to recommend those ideals to others, we do so not by preaching at them and not by injunctions to them about how they ought to behave themselves. Americans have been very liberal with this in recent times. Rather, I would urge that by the power of example, which is the most powerful force Americans have, we hasten to put this country back on its feet to assure both its internal vitality and the tone of its life as a society and its external economic independence (at least to a reasonable degree) and recognize our commitment here at home to the ideals of decency and moderation our ancestors bequeathed to us. It seems to me that morality, like charity, begins at home. It begins really with what one does to oneself and the way one shapes one's own society. You have to approach it that way before you can really do much for others. You cannot be more to others than you are to yourself. It seems to me that if Americans would set their steps resolutely on that path, they would not have to worry so much about the ultimate morality of their behavior as a nation among nations. It would flow of itself from that line of conduct.

~ *Fourteen* ~

THINKING AND WRITING ABOUT THE FUTURE*

Paul M. Kennedy

NARRATOR: Paul M. Kennedy graduated from the University of Newcastle with first class honors and received his doctorate from Oxford. He taught in England before coming to this country as J. Richardson Dilworth Professor of History at Yale. He is a fellow of the Royal Historical Society, visiting fellow of the Princeton Institute of Advanced Studies, and has also been a fellow at the Humboldt Institute in Germany. He lives in Hampton, Connecticut, where he coaches soccer; he is a man of many talents.

His latest book, *Preparing for the Twenty-First Century*, has aroused great attention in its discussion of the impact of progress and technology upon areas such as the agricultural economy. The rise of biotech foods and food substitutes will likely reduce jobs and employment. Kennedy also devotes a portion of his book to robotics and the increased automation of manufacturing. The book is full of revealing, if not terribly encouraging, statistics and data that bear on such problems as population and the environment.

MR. KENNEDY: I would like to begin by offering some provoking thoughts on the topic of thinking and writing about the future. Let's start with some definitions. First, when you think or write about the future, whose future are you talking about?

In May 1993 I talked to a group of high school juniors and sophomores at Hampden High School, and when I looked at them, it was clear that their thoughts about the future were. Would they get through the long semester and make it to summer vacation?

---

*Presented in a Forum at the Miller Center of Public Affairs on 16 September 1993.

Their parents' thoughts about them were: Are they going to get good grades? Will they attend a good college? Will they have a good career? Likewise, businesses must continually think about the future and plan for the future. Otherwise, they usually go out of business. A number of companies like Exxon, for example, will have a 20-year plan with respect to global energy resources and energy supply.

You may also think or write about the future from the perspective of a country. I was recently in Canada because a separate edition of my new book was published for Canada. While there, I was confronted by several journalists who, having gone to the index to see what was there under Canada, protested, "Professor Kennedy, you have nothing about Canada in this book." I replied, "It isn't a book about Canada's future, but about global trends. If you accept the message about these global trends, then you can fit Canada into that larger context."

When you think or write about the future, it is not only a matter of defining whose future but also what time frame. Is it just tomorrow? For the past few months, President Clinton's thinking about the future has been driven primarily by questions of whether his proposed budget will pass in the House and Senate. That is a narrow focus for thinking about the future, but a practical one nonetheless.

Some think about the future in terms of a two-year or five-year span. The future of Europe, the debate on the Maastricht Treaty—issues such as these that were in the press a few years ago have this sort of time frame. It is interesting to observe how the Euro-phoria of only three years ago has now changed. You can see how a mere two or three years can vastly change the thinking about a particular region. This is not, however, to say that projections should have a two- or three-year limit. Others think in much longer time frames. The *Economist*, for example, recently invited a number of people to think 150 years into the future in various elements of politics, technology, society, and education for a special pull-out section in celebration of its 150th anniversary. In my own work and in writing *Preparing for the Twenty-First Century*, I projected trends as far ahead as the year 2025.

Paul M. Kennedy

In thinking about the future and especially in writing about it, a third question to consider is what sort of language should be used. In the past five years I must have gone through thousands of books and articles by futurologists. Many of the writings I found, especially by the journalists or pundits, were extraordinarily confident and predictive. For instance, such titles as "The Coming Crash of 1997" describe how this crash is going to happen. As you read it, you think, "How does he know? How exactly does he know what is going to happen?" I think that sort of language should be avoided.

I introduced my new book with a reference to the famous late 18th-century English clergyman, Thomas Malthus. Malthus looked at population trends in his native England and at the way population seemed to be growing much faster than the available food supply. In his famous *Essay on Population*, which resulted from these examinations, he stated that there would be in the future "a giant inevitable famine." The word *inevitable* is one that historians and most social scientists are trained to avoid. Death is inevitable; taxes are inevitable (you know the old joke); but apart from death and taxes, there isn't much else that is inevitable. One must be more careful and more conditional with the language used.

Only a few years ago, all of the economists were predicting that through the 1990s the Japanese economy was likely to grow at a compound rate of 4 percent a year. In contrast, the U.S. economy would grow at only 2 percent a year due to lower savings rates and less investment per capita in new industry. I must confess that I bought the argument and put it in a footnote in my new book. I wrote that if this trend continues, by the end of the decade the Japanese economy will have inched nearer and closer to that of the United States. As it turns out, while the U.S. economy isn't doing that well at the moment, it is growing at a rate of approximately 1.5 percent a year. It looks as if the Japanese economy is going to contract this year by around 1 to 2 percent.

Population trends, upon which I focus heavily, can also be amended over time. Since the early 19th century there have been many kinds of future projections of the population size of the United States. Time and again these have been wrong because there were different patterns and new variables emerging that had to be considered. The population projections for Africa, the fastest growing area of the world demographically, are currently looking toward a near trebling by the year 2025. These may need to be substantially amended, however, because of the pandemic of AIDS. When I first began researching for my new book in 1989, the World Health Organization estimated that there were about 10 million people worldwide who were HIV-positive. By 1991, because of evidence coming from India, Brazil, and elsewhere, that estimate had been increased to 40 million people worldwide. By the time my book was going to final proofs at the end of 1992, a Harvard study had estimated that these numbers were still far behind the curve, with probably 100 million people worldwide (entire families in Uganda and Zaire) HIV-positive. Certainly that factor will affect the demographic projections.

Despite all of those caveats, despite the caution, I still think there is an argument for thinking about the future and for writing about the future. I think it gives us some perspective. It gives us a broader picture of global or national developments. It allows us to ask the question, What is happening to our world as a whole and in general?

For those who feel that talk of the future must be reduced to future trends or contemporary broad developments, there are probably two of chief importance. The first is the technology-driven future, those technology-driven forces for change that we sometimes describe as modernization. Modernization is chiefly occurring in advanced economies like the United States, Japan, and Western Europe. An example is the increasing automation of the factory and the workplace, which I discuss at length in a chapter on robotics and the future of manufacturing.

Currently, in Japan, due to labor shortages and a desire to not import so many guest workers, there are entire factories where sophisticated field robots move around all day and night. They are able to work at night because sensors mean they don't have to see anything. These robots assemble less sophisticated robots, which are then sent to automobile assembly plants. It is a strange experience to go to the Fanuc factory near Mount Fuji, wherein one sees few people but many yellow, sophisticated field robots moving around, assembling less sophisticated robots.

Paul M. Kennedy

Biotechnology is also examined, especially regarding its implications for food and agriculture. Genetic engineering now allows us to create plants that are frost-resistant at temperatures as low as minus 12 degrees, are resistant to particular bugs or diseases, or in the tropics will produce rice that can withstand daytime temperatures of over 100 degrees. The element of most interest and concern, however, is the creation of artificial foodstuffs in vitro. These are created in biology labs and are substitutes for naturally grown produce. Artificial cocoa and artificial citrus fruit are currently under experiment. We already have some examples of this: When you enjoy your vanilla ice cream, do not think it comes from natural vanilla. In actuality, it is factory-created vanilla.

The world of computers is continually evolving, and the implications for the future are many. We must now consider how active computers, networks, satellites, and fiber-optic cables have increasingly integrated the world of science, communications, and finance. Every night when we go to sleep, billions or perhaps half a trillion of our so-called sovereign U.S. dollars are being traded in the middle of the night on the Tokyo, Singapore, and Hong Kong currency exchanges. There is little you, I, or even the U.S Treasury can do about it. Approximately $1 trillion in international currencies per day lurches around the globe in a 24-hour, computer-driven system, over which no one has control. When I ask my banker friends who is now in charge of world financial flows, I get two answers. One is that no one is in charge. The other is that the system is controlled by the 200,000 individuals who sit looking at a computer screen, watching, for example, Japanese yen futures as they flicker across the screen, individually deciding whether to buy or sell, and then tapping that decision into the keyboard. What does this potential financial volatility mean for the world?

One should not overlook the benefits of modernization. There are many new high-level jobs and cutting-edge technologies that come as a consequence of this global technological revolution. Despite such advantages, the labor market nonetheless seems to suffer. The World Labor Organization estimates that each year we should be creating 45 to 50 million new jobs for our young people, especially for those coming out of developing countries. The reality in this country, it seems, is the new phenomenon of jobless growth, which bewilders our economists. Many other countries have seen the creation of a certain number of new jobs due to modernization, but only for those people with postdoctoral training in areas such as communications or biotechnology. At the same time, automation has meant the elimination of a large number of traditional jobs. Relocation is also an issue. Assembly plants in high-labor-cost areas are being closed down and relocated to areas such as the U.S. southern states, Mexico, and Thailand, leaving perhaps entire communities without their main employer.

The second great force transforming our globe is demographically-driven developments—that is, changes in our global population. I am particularly thinking of the forecast increases in the overall size of our global population. In the 1980s, while we supposedly saw an increase in our own standard of living, we added 950 million additional mouths to our global population. The annual addition continues at about 95 million. Our global population is now at 5.5 billion, and the forecast suggests that we will reach 8.5 to 9 billion in 2025, after which we may "stabilize" at 10 or 11 billion in the middle of the next century. Some gloomy estimates have placed this last figure as high as 14 billion. The interesting thing is that this is not a uniform increase. In fact, in many of the more mature societies in Europe and Japan, populations are actually declining. Of the forecasted increases in global population, 95 percent will occur in poor developing societies, which are not well equipped to handle such an explosion. India, whose population is now at 860 million, is forecast to overtake China as the world's most populous country, reaching 1.5 billion in 2025 and then possibly two billion somewhere in the course of the next century. India grows much faster than any of its neighbors, including China, as a result of a fertility rate of nearly 4.2.

Other countries that will see vast increases in population are China, Indonesia, Iran, Nigeria, Mexico, Brazil, and probably the whole of the continent of Africa. Let's think through some of the implications. Within these poorer societies we are seeing a massive internal migration from poor, depleted agricultural regions toward gigantic shanty cities. By the end of this decade, Mexico City will have a population of 24.5 million people; San Paulo, 23 million; and Shanghai, 22 million. What is to be noted, however, is that cities do not fit the old European conception of the city—centers with an urban professional middle class, much culture, many theaters, parks, and various other features one notices and expects when visiting Stockholm or Copenhagen. On the contrary, these are gigantic shanty cities with vast sprawling suburbs and attached shanty towns, and they are unlikely to be able to provide the infrastructure that the traditional city offers.

The population explosion also brings the risk of environmental damage born from desperate subsistence living. At the beginning of this century, 50 percent of India was covered by forests. This has now fallen to 14 percent and is heading rapidly toward the mere 2-percent forest coverage currently found in Ethiopia and Haiti. Local environmental damage is now found on a significant scale, with rapidly vanishing supplies of water, fuel, and wood. This in turn perhaps contributes also to the process of global warming.

As the population so rapidly expands, think of the consequences for social and political instability. How does one deal with hundreds of millions of frustrated young people, especially energetic teenage youths, in societies unable to educate them or to give them jobs? Historians can cite examples such as Elizabethan England or Napoleonic France to show that fast-growing populations of young men with little to do and a great deal of ambition and energy are often followed by great expansion or social implosion. What does one do when these various peoples of different ethnic groups or religions press upon the same shared water supplies or grazing supplies? Some pundits think that if there is to be a conflict in the Middle East in the next 10 or 15 years, it will not be over oil. It will much more likely concern shrinking water supplies in the Euphrates, Jordan Valley, and Litani Valley as populations double.

A final thought to consider is migration. What happens when you have large numbers of poor, jobless peasants who are determined to find work? They move to areas where they see hope, where they see employment prospects. Right at this moment there are approximately 21 million individuals being held in transit camps or ships who were en route from poor, war-torn, or resource-depleted countries to what they hoped were richer countries. We don't quite know how many illegal immigrants come over the Rio

Grande each year, but some estimate it to be about one million. Last year, two million refugees entered Europe alone. The long-term implications demand consideration when one looks at the demographic figures. The forecast population growth of the five southern European countries from Portugal to Greece over the next 25 years suggests hardly any increase at all except in Greece. The forecast population increase of the five countries on the north African littoral from Morocco to Egypt is, by contrast, estimated to be 108 million. Many of those people already have a cousin in Barcelona, Marseilles, or Frankfurt, whom they will eventually try to join. The Spanish and French navies are now on daily and nightly patrols across the Mediterranean trying to turn back these immigrants. One can see the consequences in the newspapers each day: the angry backlash in France with the Le Pen movement, the neo-Nazi activity in Germany, the shameful treatment of legal, as well as illegal, immigrants in northern Italy. It is interesting to note the aspects of globalization—the globalization of finance, capital, and production—that have been so warmly praised by, for example, the *Wall Street Journal*. The freedom of labor, however, is another matter. According to laissez-faire philosophy, we are eager to allow the freedom of all of the other factors of production—investment flows, capital production, and raw materials—but we say no to labor. That is rather ironic and contradictory.

I began my book *Preparing for the Twenty-First Century* with the historical metaphor of Malthus looking at the fast-growing populations of northwest Europe, including England, 200 years ago and forecasting terrible things ahead. I haven't been very optimistic to this point in my remarks, and I sometimes get described as Malthus come again. The *Wall Street Journal* had a kindly headline about me earlier this year: "Yale University's Professor of Doom Strikes Again." In actuality, I used the metaphor of Malthus's look at population growth in Europe 200 years ago precisely to point out that he got it wrong. He couldn't foresee that there would be certain new technologies, especially those of the industrial revolution, that would create jobs, raise productivity levels, and increase standards of living for the entire British population, not just the mill-owners and bankers. We can now see the many variables Malthus did not take into account, variables that might have altered his thinking and his forecasting about the future.

I conclude my book by asking several pertinent questions: What is there to be done? Are there variables to be considered? Can we use new technologies to help us deal with our global demographic revolution? Will we, in fact, not do that? Will we not think about the future? Will we not take preparatory steps? Will we not think about how to handle the demographic explosion and the technology explosion until they interact in a way that provides political and social dissidence? Those, I think, are the big challenges for us as we think and write about the future. We have to condition our language. We have to understand that we are not going to get everything right, but we must nevertheless be forward-thinking. We have to encourage our citizenry, congressmen, and political leaders such as the president to take a day or two off from their busy schedules and spend some time thinking about and planning for the future. Then, perhaps, they might start doing some things to give us, our children, and our grandchildren a better future.

NARRATOR: I reviewed both your book and George Kennan's book recently, and I was struck that Kennan put such emphasis on tradition and continuity. You are a distinguished historian who is well aware of that trend. Are there lessons to be learned from the past? You certainly mentioned several of them.

MR. KENNEDY: I think there are. I also value tradition when it is good tradition. I am not a root-and-branch radical. Nevertheless, I am concerned when we cling to our traditions without heeding those new circumstances that might call for new actions: a new policy, a second look at a constitution, a new way to run our budgets, or new ways to educate our children. I would argue that many educational institutions in this country, including Yale, are not really thinking about the curriculum that prepares our children for the 21st century. We have a great deal of serious work to do, which is true for the schools as well. Tradition and history are fine, but they need to be used and respected in a particular way.

THINKING AND WRITING ABOUT THE FUTURE

Very often politicians and journalists use history and tradition as a grab bag for slogans. You find a wonderful Winston Churchill quote and repeat it when you are giving a presidential address, for instance. History as a grab bag is an insult to the discipline and an insult to the past. We ought to understand the past empathetically—to see the human condition of people under pressure, not unlike those under pressure today, and try to learn something from them. Don't believe, however, that history is always repeating itself. That is another fallacy. It is true that there is an element in history which is cyclical—that things come around again and again—but history is also linear and developmental. You may say, "This is just like 1932, with the breakdown in trade talks," and so on; but things are in existence in the world today, in the 1990s, which were not in existence in the 1930s, or in the 1890s, or in Malthus's time. If we can understand that we should use history as a dialogue between the past and the present, as my remarks suggest, we will be more informed in thinking about the future. There is a way of blending tradition with innovation, of blending the better things of the past, which we want to preserve, with the need for change.

QUESTION: What effect do you think wars, crime (especially intercity shootings), and weapons manufacture are going to have on population growth?

MR. KENNEDY: They are not going to have much effect at all on, for example, Sweden, where there are about 19 homicides a year in the entire country and where there is not much intercity crime. Furthermore, the Swedish tradition of international neutrality means that it is unlikely to be sending its troops into the Bosnian mountains, to Macedonia, or elsewhere in the very near future, except under the United Nations blue-helmet auspices. On the other hand, in Kashmir, where everyone has at least two or three rifles, where the tensions and rivalries over territory and ethnicity are massive, and where the proneness to war is great, there will continue to be a Malthusian "check" on population growth that cuts into the most energetic and economically productive part of society—the young people.

Paul M. Kennedy

If with your question you were thinking of American inner cities and American society, then we are looking at a combination of drugs, crime, and the breakdown of education and, in some cases, societal norms in these gang-strewn inner cities. Yale University is approximately one-half mile from one of the worst such gang areas in the country. It seems fairly certain that they will continue to shoot at themselves and at others—our national homicide rate of 19,000 a year (which does not include the large number of people who are injured or crippled by guns) is unlikely to decrease. We have a national propensity to stock more weapons per head than any other advanced civilized nation by a very large margin. By a rough count, there are 220 million private firearms in this country. Such figures will ensure that not every 17-year-old now living in the inner city will be there at the end of the year.

COMMENT: Malthus wasn't wrong; he was just ahead of his time. There was a great deal of empty space in what was then the British Empire to absorb excess population. America as well had the west in which to expand, so those problems of population were merely postponed. Malthus's thesis is much more relevant today than it was in the 1790s. After reading your book, I have been thinking of the possible solutions to overpopulation, and it seems to me that there really is no solution; those extreme measures that would be effective in curbing population are unlikely to be enacted under a democratic political structure like that of the United States.

MR. KENNEDY: You make a wonderful point, and I could have spoken more on the use of Malthus as a historical analogy. Yes, Malthus was wrong because, first, there was an agricultural revolution in England that kept feeding people during the 19th century; second, there was a technology revolution that kept creating jobs; and third, there was a transport revolution that meant 20 million people could leave England and Scotland during the 19th century and escape to the West (Canada, Argentina, or Australia, for example). Consider, though, how Malthus would react some 200 years later, if given today's numbers. He was terrified at England doubling from seven million to 14 million in the next 25 years. To be told that we would have global increases of 95 million a year would have been extremely shocking to him.

The technology revolution today does have some job-creating potential for people with doctoral degrees in biotechnology, but the automation of the factory and the creation of artificial foodstuffs is actually undermining large numbers of potential jobs in manufacturing, assembly, and agriculture. While in the past there was much empty space to absorb the impact of population growth, in the present there is not much inhabitable empty space left in our world of the late 20th century. Furthermore, the movement we see now is not from advanced nations into less advanced open-space societies; it is rather from poor societies toward rich societies, and the rich societies don't like it. The challenge today is even greater because we have less room. I think we also have less time because the absolute numbers are so much larger, and the technology change now is so much faster than in the early stages of the industrial revolution.

QUESTION: Based on the population figures and forecast you have given, could you comment further on the political consequences of the resulting migration? We have in this country, particularly in the west, some immigration restrictions. At the same time, we have under consideration the North American Free Trade Agreement (NAFTA). Are we headed for the global war of the fat against the lean?

MR. KENNEDY: Let's constrict the answer, as you have, to our western hemisphere and to the future of our relationship with Mexico. There are a certain number of "demographic fault lines" across our globe. There is one across the Mediterranean, separating the fast-growing populations of North Africa and the stagnant populations of Europe. There is one between the Slavic Russian peoples and the non-Slavs, again with one side growing four times faster than the other. In North America, the Rio Grande, in a way, is another such demographic fault line. The population increases, or fertility levels, in Mexico are significantly higher than those within this country. Further, if you deconstructed our own fertility levels and distinguished between Caucasian fertility levels as opposed to black and Hispanic, you would again see that some parts of society, some ethnic groups, are growing much more rapidly than the other. That factor, together with a constant inflow of migrants from the south, is leading to what some scholars calla the "re-Hispanicization of the southwest," which is a profound historical irony.

Such an event will clearly shape the long-term internal politics of this country. It will change voting patterns. If you were running for mayor in San Antonio now, you would probably see a race between various types of Hispanic-American politicians. It will change the allocation of congressional seats over time and may change attitudes toward the south. We have traditionally looked east to the Atlantic because our politicians looked east. Later, we looked west to the Pacific. Perhaps now we will be spending more time in South-focused politics in the international sphere rather than Israel-focused or German-focused politics.

This perceived change in focus also leads to the big question of the political, not economic, implications of NAFTA. Politicians are scared to discuss this question openly because they think they will be accused of being racist. You could argue that it is difficult to deal with the current social problems of American society, even with our present population. Therefore, an ingress of 15 million people a decade is too much, despite our tradition as a melting pot society that welcomes immigrants. On the other hand, we need to listen carefully to the arguments of the Mexican government and finance advisers. I had a debate with some of their trade ministers at the World Economic Forum in Davos, Switzerland, at the beginning of this year (1993) when NAFTA was one of the items on the agenda. An economist of the Mexican government said, "You are criticizing the move of assembly and manufacturing south of the border to cheap labor. We can either export goods and manufactures to the United States, or if you raise tariffs, don't negotiate for NAFTA, or keep fiscal and customs borders, we will export people. Our population is forecast to go from 85 to 150 million in the next two and a half decades. We either create jobs for them here, south of the border, or they will go north in search of jobs." You could say that this argument is one of the more interesting ones in favor of NAFTA, but the further implication is that we will be a different society in the course of the next several decades, and that will profoundly affect our politics.

QUESTION: In view of the tremendous problems stemming from present and future growth in population and search for jobs, what will it take to make the world start reducing birth rates? Will it take greater crises such as widespread starvation or the complete loss of civility? In the present age we are lengthening the lives of old people and reducing infant mortality rates, which is contrary to this whole subject. There must be a way, even with some of the religious barriers that exist, to reduce population growth in the world.

MR. KENNEDY: In traditional, pre-industrial, peasant-based societies there are high fertility rates. The average number of children born to a woman in such societies would be between six and ten; but due to high infant and child mortality rates, many of those children do not live beyond the age of two to five.

The pre-industrial balance between high fertility and mortality levels can be altered in two ways. One would be to change the overall circumstances in which those families, especially the women, live. If the women have access to education, marry later, and are urbanized rather than living on a farm, they may have fewer children. Peasants typically want to have many children because children are cheap and can perform all of the chores they have been doing for thousands of years. In the cities where there are higher standards of living, family size shrinks. If the women of a society are educated, family size shrinks. It is possible to change the overall conditions in which families expand.

Another way to change this crude balance between mortality and fertility rates is to reduce mortality rates. That, ironically, is what is behind the great surge in population since the 1950s in Africa, India, and elsewhere. We transferred what we thought were beneficial Western inoculation techniques and vaccination medicines, enabling us to vaccinate many young babies. The result was a dramatic reduction in mortality rates. It is a wonderful example of what theologians or logicians would call "the unintended consequences of a beneficial action," because the population exploded. In Kenya, it went from six million to 27 million in about a quarter of a century. Can we do something about it? I think we can.

If you look at UNESCO statistics in all of the developing countries, with some exceptions in the central Asian republics, and examine figures for the average number of children born to women denied access to education, the figure ranges from five to seven, eight, nine, or more. Yet in the same society, the average number of children born to women *with at least seven years of education* drops dramatically to about 2.8, 3.1, or 3.5. Perhaps it is utter utopianism to think the condition of women in central China, India, or Africa could be transformed, but the single most stunning reform would be improvement in the condition of women in the developing world.

There is yet an even quicker means to reform than education. According to the World Health Organization, there are about 200 million women in developing countries who would like access to benign, inexpensive contraceptives. (I'm not referring to abortion or forced sterilization.) These women are unable to get contraceptives because of the cost. They have two or three children already and would prefer to look after those two or three children. The cost of providing contraception there is about the price of a B-1 bomber. There is also, however, the extremely sensitive issue of how that conflicts with personal or religious beliefs. In no way could these programs be forced or authoritarian means of implementation be used as China does. On the other hand, however, a number of theologians think there is a higher morality in the definition of human dignity. They argue that once a family has reached what it considers a desirable size—whether it is two, three, or four children—then they should have access to benign forms of family planning, allowing them to bring up their children in a dignified manner and allowing the woman to have some degree of human dignity.

COMMENT: If you look at the progress of Southeast Asia during the last 50 years, in the face of the potential population increases in India and China, it seems ridiculous to worry about NAFTA in the context of Mexico.

THINKING AND WRITING ABOUT THE FUTURE

MR. KENNEDY: East Asia, like Korea, has in three decades gone through the demographic transition that took 100 years in Malthus's England and has become more prosperous. In regard to the idea of preparing for the future and thinking about the future, how did East Asia do it? What lessons from Asia's development could be applied to other societies? One chapter in my book called "Winners and Losers in a Developing World" plays off the fact that in 1955 South Korea had the same standard of living as West Africa, and yet now it has 15 times the standard of living that West Africa has. Was it a matter of culture? Was it Confucian education, better politics, or investment rates? We have to study more.

China is trying to curb its massive population, but like India, it is in many ways simultaneously a first-world and a third-world country. It has a great deal of technology and assembly and extraordinary economic growth in the coastal provinces. Inland, however, it has a poor peasant demographic explosion. India has 100 million middle-class people, with Bangalore starting to look like Silicone Valley. At the same time, India has 750 million poor peasants and is adding to their population by 18 million a year. If we could get India and China on a South Korea or Singapore track and then think through the environmental issues (which is the other difference between 200 years ago and today), there is a chance for hope. We needn't leave this room today saying, "I need a really stiff drink after listening to Kennedy." We might say, "I'm provoked, and I want to think more about the future."

NARRATOR: We thank you for a most enlightening and provocative analysis of issues that no one can afford to ignore. I hope you will visit us often in the future.

VI.

AN EPILOGUE

~ Fifteen ~

PRESIDENT CARTER ON
URGENT CONTEMPORARY PROBLEMS[*]

President Jimmy Carter

MR. THOMPSON: President Carter, we have asked former University of Virginia President Edgar Shannon for a word of welcome on behalf of the University and the Miller Center Council on which he serves. It was President Shannon who was "present at the creation" in the earliest discussions with Mr. Burkett Miller that led to the establishment of the Center. President Shannon.

MR. SHANNON: Mr. Carter, it is certainly a great pleasure to welcome you here. I wish that Governor Linwood Holton, who is the chairman of our Council for the Miller Center, could be here. I am standing in for him today, but as Ken Thompson has said, I have been involved with the Center from the very beginning, when it was just a notion in Mr. Miller's mind and a gleam in his eye. It has been a great pleasure to see the fruition of that idea and it is particularly heartwarming to welcome you here. You have worked with us extensively and we are so grateful for that. It is a very exciting and happy occasion to have you here at our Center in person to see the kind of work that is going on here. I am sure all of these people have lots of questions that they will want to ask you, and I think you will have an enjoyable time in the interchange. So on behalf of the Miller Center, the University, and the Council, we thank you for coming and welcome you here.

---

[*]Presented in a Forum at the Miller Center of Public Affairs on 9 February 1987. Reprinted from *The Carter Presidency: Fourteen Intimate Perspectives of Jimmy Carter* (Lanham, Maryland: University Press of America, Inc., 1990).

MR. YOUNG: I will say a word very briefly. The presidency of Jimmy Carter was a first in many respects. Mr. Carter was the first president to be elected from the deep South since the Civil War. He was the first true outsider to be elected president since Woodrow Wilson, and there were many firsts in policy and in operating style. The first that counts perhaps the most for us here at the Miller Center, however, is that he was the first president to open his presidency to intense, sober and objective examination by scholars before his library was opened. President Carter and almost 50 members of his staff, with his support and cooperation, gave very generously of their time to sit down around this table and other tables to reflect on their experiences in office. So it is the first presidency that has left behind a record of its reflections in a study for future generations so that we all may learn from that experience.

A Conversation with President Carter

QUESTION: In light of recent events in the Reagan administration with respect to Iran, and in light of your own experience of disagreements between your national security adviser and the secretary of state, can you share with us any reflections on your view of the proper relationship among the National Security Council, the national security adviser, and secretary of state?

PRESIDENT CARTER: Yes. In a totally objective way, I think that the relationship that I had in my administration was the proper one. I made the decisions on foreign policy and defense policy when I was president. I don't think anyone would question that, including Secretary Vance, Secretary Muskie, or Mr. Brzezinski. Because of that fact, I wanted a very strong, evocative, and innovative national security adviser. When I was elected president, I had the whole nation from which to choose and Brzezinski, by the way, was the one that Secretary Vance recommended for national security adviser; Vance was the one that Brzezinski recommended, conversely for secretary of state. I would say that 95 percent of the time, or even more, they were completely harmonious in their policy recommendations, but there is an inclination within the press in

President Jimmy Carter

Washington to exacerbate the differences that do exist. I did not deplore the differences.

Brzezinski had a tiny staff, relatively speaking, including 35 or so professionals. The State Department is an enormous bureaucracy by contrast and is extremely lethargic; the inertia of the State Department is almost overwhelming. Once it gets started going in one direction, you cannot change it and when it stands still, you cannot get it to move. I can't recall a single exciting or innovative idea that ever came out of the State Department during the four years that I was president. That is the nature of the State Department—it's an anchor.

Brzezinski and his staff, on the other hand, would come up every week with several innovative, bright ideas, 90 percent of which might ultimately have been discarded or modified. Whenever I made a decision, I would always have it thoroughly "vetted" (to use a State Department phrase) by the State Department, the Defense Department, and perhaps other departments. I never acted unilaterally on a recommendation by Brzezinski that involved international policy. So I looked upon the national security staff as my own personal staff to give me ideas, but then I very carefully made sure that the National Security Council, in some form, helped me make the final judgment. I made the final decision and always took the responsibility for it.

We had a regular weekly meeting of at least two hours on Friday mornings with Brzezinski, Vance or Muskie, Brown, the Vice President, and sometimes others. We discussed every item that anyone could think of that might be pertinent during that week, and Brzezinski took notes. He submitted his notes to the Defense and State Departments to make sure that they were accurate and then the notes came to me for my files. On Wednesdays Brzezinski, Brown, and the secretary of state had a luncheon meeting where they discussed matters that did not require my presence. So there was a "melding" of the group. There were some obvious differences of opinion between Brown and me or between Brzezinski and me, but I didn't deplore that. I thought it was okay.

One thing that ought to be done is to retain that core of ideas and that possibility of cooperation. The bad thing that has happened recently, of course, is the coalescence within the White

House of a small operational group which actually carries out a decision contrary to the sound advice of the State Department and the Defense Department and apparently—though I don't know—without even the knowledge of the President. This is a horrible derogation of responsibility, and possibly laws have been violated in the process. The president needs a strong, vital national security staff without operational characteristics, unless the National Security Council itself specifically has a finding, signed by the president, and certified to be legal by the attorney general. Then, on rare occasions, they might carry out a mission, perhaps just one or two times in four years at the most.

QUESTION: Could I ask one question as a footnote? If this is the pattern, then is there any danger in that the role of the NSC adviser as custodian and coordinator is difficult to sustain? There are several forthcoming books, one of which we have been reviewing recently, that make the argument that it was very difficult for Brzezinski to be both advocate and custodian.

PRESIDENT CARTER: Brzezinski's advocacy role was strictly limited by me. Some of you know Brzezinski, and he is an evocative, outspoken person. He would like to be a lightening rod. Whenever anything went wrong, Brzezinski was eager to take the blame. I never knew him to duck and say, "Well, I didn't really want this; the President wanted it," if it were a mistake.

Secretary Vance, a fine, gentle person, had extreme loyalty to the State Department. He looked upon himself as a descendent of Thomas Jefferson, as a secretary of state more than he did as an aide or assistant to the President. Vance was very loyal to the State Department and he was very cautious about what he said. Sometimes I wanted a public statement to be made or I wanted a small group of key columnists in Washington to be briefed privately. For instance, I would sometimes request that Secretary Vance make a public statement concerning Cuba, Angola, or China; quite often he would not do it if it were controversial, or perhaps, if it violated what the State Department thought was best. There were no violent differences. He would absolutely refuse to let a small group of distinguished columnists like Scotty Reston and others enter his home or enter the State Department dining room. On occasions like that, after I waited a few days for this to be done, I would tell Brzezinski to go ahead and make the statement. I might tell Brzezinski, "It's okay for you one Sunday afternoon to be on 'Meet the Press,' if Secretary Vance continued to disagree with my decision. But when Brzezinski did anything of that kind, it was with my approval as an alternative to a precise, pointed, and perhaps pithy remark that I felt was needed to shape public opinion.

QUESTION: Mr. President, looking at the Defense Department, the fundamentals of the national defense, and the interservice rivalry, for a moment, what are your views on the growth of the Defense Department and the services today?

PRESIDENT CARTER: When I came into office we had had a dramatic reduction in defense budget expenditures in real terms over the previous eight years. This was not because Nixon or Ford wanted to see this done, but because the Congress was exercising restraint on budgetary allocations primarily as a reaction against the Vietnam experience. Therefore I decided quite early with Vance, Brzezinski, and others to have an inexorable and predictable increase in the defense budget every year. Our goal was a 3 percent increase above and beyond the inflation rate and we basically adhered to this. Every year when we prepared a defense budget, it was prepared by me, the secretary of defense, the joint chiefs of staff, the National Security Council, and the Office of Management and Budget. Also quite often, when there was a particular question to be answered, I would call in the key members of the House and the Senate Armed Forces Appropriations Committees to make sure that we had some degree of compatibility. It was an organic evolution of the budget. Whenever they wanted a new weapons system, I required Secretary Brown to decommission an obsolescent or obsolete system to stay within the budget restraints. We built up the rapid deployment force in this way. We had to build up our forces, as you know, in the Indian Ocean and the Persian Gulf region later on. But I felt that at that time the Defense Department was well under control.

PRESIDENT CARTER ON URGENT CONTEMPORARY PROBLEMS

When President Reagan ran against me in 1980, he repeatedly said that the Defense Department had been going to hell under my administration and that the budget had gone down; this was erroneous as I pointed out to him subsequently. He recommended something like a 13 percent increase above the inflation rate in the first year and an 11 percent increase above the inflation rate in the next year. The Congress went along with President Reagan's recommendation in the first two years. I think Weinberger has been eager to take any money he could get for the Defense Department and they have not decommissioned any old systems. Almost every new idea that came along about a weapons system has been endorsed heartily, and the public has been convinced that each was vital to our national security. The resurrection of the B1 bomber is the most vivid demonstration of absolute and total waste on a weapons system that will have no efficacy even after it is finished and which will not perform its putative duties.

The result has been a reaction in the Congress against this uncontrollable spending, and for the last two years, as you know, there has been a zero increase in the Defense Department budget, which means the budget is like a roller coaster. There is an outpouring of profligate spending for a couple of years and then no spending increase in the next year. There is no careful planning and no involvement (or very little involvement) of the joint chiefs of staff. Now we are seeing a Defense Department that is suffering because of these altercations over alterations in budgets.

QUESTION: Mr. President, one of your major achievements was the formalization of relations with China. Taiwan, of course, has remained an issue. Would you care to comment on Peking's demand for the U.S. to at least set a date for termination of its arms sales to Taiwan?

PRESIDENT CARTER: Yes. I covered this, fairly well I think, in my memoirs, *Keeping Faith*, which you might want to read. I must say Deng Xiaoping was a very tough negotiator. After I was elected, I made it clear to the members of the House and the Senate at a meeting at the Smithsonian Institution that I intended to normalize relations with the People's Republic as one of my

President Jimmy Carter

major goals as president. I also discussed plans to conclude a Panama Canal Treaty, move towards peace in the Middle East, and certain other things at that gathering. But Deng Xiaoping insisted that we not provide any more military assistance to Taiwan. I would never agree to that. I insisted that he make a public announcement that the differences between the People's Republic of China and Taiwan would be resolved peacefully. He would never agree to that publicly. Those, then, were the two things on which we did not agree and, in effect, we just kept our own positions and went ahead with normalization. As you know, I continued to sell Taiwan military supplies of a basically defensive nature.

The treaty concluded between us and Taiwan was honored meticulously. It had a provision in it for a one-year notice prior to termination, and we honored that one-year notice of termination. In addition to that we agreed not to recognize Taiwan as an independent nation, but we established a trade mechanism within Taiwan based on the Japanese example. I would say that our commerce with and our visitation to Taiwan has probably increased dramatically ever since we recognized the People's Republic of China. So we reserved the right to continue to sell defensive weapons to Taiwan on my terms, but not including weapons with which they could attack the mainland of China from Taiwan. China insisted upon its right to call for and accomplish the termination of the difference with Taiwan in any way it saw fit. I wanted them to say, "We guarantee that it will be through peaceful means." Though they never would say that, I think China will never try to resolve the differences with Taiwan through other than peaceful means. I cannot imagine a military effort.

I believe that China's present role in Hong Kong is being carefully orchestrated from Beijing to show the world and the people on Taiwan that there can be an area in China—that is Hong Kong—where the people can preserve their own way of life and have access to Western ways. As you may know, since then Deng Xiaoping has offered Taiwan its own independent army and a very large degree of autonomy. I do not know what will ultimately happen, but my presumption is that we will continue to make sure that Taiwan can defend itself. On the other hand, China will try to resolve its differences with Taiwan through peaceful means.

PRESIDENT CARTER ON URGENT CONTEMPORARY PROBLEMS

QUESTION: Mr. President, as we all know, this is the bicentennial of the Constitution and a prominent group in Washington came out with proposals two or three weeks ago on how to change the Constitution. I am wondering how you would change the Constitution on the basis of your experience, if you had a free hand to do so? I am thinking particularly of the relations between the Congress and the president and the question of terms of office.

PRESIDENT CARTER: First of all, I would hate to see us have a constitutional convention because I think it would be an uncontrollable body that might dramatically modify the existing Constitution, which, in general, is all right. There are two specific things that I would like to see changed if I could unilaterally change them.

First, I would prefer to see a single one-term, six-year presidency. This is the case, as you know, in a number of foreign countries, and it works very well. I could have done a better job in six years than I did in four years; I would have not been stigmatized when I did something of a dramatic nature that seemed to be politically oriented to get me reelected. Also this would have precluded many of the public positions President Reagan took, for instance, when he was basically running against other Republicans like Rockefeller, Nixon, and Ford. In his earlier life while seeking the Republican nomination, Reagan took positions on things like China, human rights, and arms agreements with the Soviets that later proved to be a great handicap for him. I don't think he would have done those things if the incumbent president could not have run for reelection. One six-year term is one change, then, that I would make.

Another thing I would change would be the two-thirds majority required of the Senate to confirm or to ratify a treaty. This seems illogical because a third of the members of the Senate can now block the legal implementation of an international agreement consummated by the president. Perhaps it ought to take a two-thirds majority of the Senate to override what a president has concluded by agreement with a foreign nation, or at least a majority ought to be adequate for ratification. Because about a third of the members of the Senate now, including Strom Thurmond, Jesse

282

President Jimmy Carter

Helms, and others, will hardly support anything that has international scope and especially anything that deals with the Soviet Union, it is difficult to ratify any treaty. There is a presumption that if something is good for the Soviet Union, if they agree to it, then it inherently is bad for us.

So those would be the two basic changes I would make. I would not recommend that we go to a parliamentary system of government or dramatically change our system, nor would I recommend that we change the basic relationship among the president, Congress, and the Supreme Court. I think that system has basically proven to be very well advised.

QUESTION: President Carter, having been in the Justice Department of your administration, I would assume that perhaps you are not totally in agreement with Attorney General Meese's policies. I would like to ask you what effect you think his policies are having on the country, and, assuming a Democratic victory in 1988, what would be necessary to rectify those policies for the next administration?

PRESIDENT CARTER: As you may know, when I was president I appointed more than 45 percent of all of the federal judges in the nation in the brief period of just four years because it happened that we expanded the district and circuit courts. Over a period of eight years, President Reagan will probably appoint about half of the federal judges at the circuit and district court level and several Supreme Court justices. That gives a great deal of stability to the policies of our country. I have seen my own appointees, without any influences from me, carry out the basic principles of environmental quality, civil rights, and so forth in opposition to what the Reagan administration has proposed as the cases have been brought to them. I think, to answer your question then, President Reagan's remaining influence will carry over into the next administration, but will not exceed the influence that my own administration has had through my appointees to the district and circuit courts. Reagan's policies will have minimal adverse impact.

My guess is that the next administration will revert back to the basic progressive policies of the four or five previous administrations. For instance, on environmental quality, on civil rights and other matters of that kind, Gerald Ford's, Richard Nixon's, Johnson's, and Kennedy's policies were similar to mine. I look upon my policies on those matters as being quite compatible with those of my predecessors. The radical departure has been under the Reagan administration.

QUESTION: Mr. President, I think there is general agreement that Camp David was a very valuable achievement but that its aftermath has been quite disappointing. I wonder how much of the failure to follow up and expand on the Camp David agreement—to produce a full-fledged settlement in the Middle East—is attributable to the United States government and how much is attributable to Israel and to the Arab states?

PRESIDENT CARTER: I have written a book about this called *Blood of Abraham*, and I'm going back to the Middle East next month for another three weeks of quiet conversations. I will see not only the incumbent and opposition leaders, but also the scholars in the great universities of Damascus, Cairo, Alexandria, Tel Aviv, Jerusalem, and so forth, just to bring myself up to date on it.

I think that the Camp David accords provide a sound basis for any future progress on regional peace. The principles expressed within them are quite compatible with UN Security Council Resolution 242. They are quite compatible with President Reagan's speech of September 1982. They are quite compatible with the Fez statement that was a regional response. So from the Arab side, from President Reagan's side, from the United Nation's side, from the Camp David side, there is a lot of compatibility among those documents. This offers some hope for the future.

President Reagan has a basic aversion to using diplomacy and negotiation to resolve regional disputes. I don't know of any real negotiations that are ongoing now, for instance, that would resolve the problems that the world faces. For example, in Central America the Contadora process could very well succeed—in my opinion it would succeed—if it had a modicum of support from the Reagan administration. But we have blocked progress on the Contadora process and are trying through this administration to overthrow the Sandinista government.

There has been a dearth of practical American involvement in Middle East affairs at the diplomatic level. We sent troops into Lebanon, resorting to force in the midst of what I consider to be a civil war, and in the process, many people were lost; about 200 marines died in addition to the thousands of people who were killed as we bombarded the hills around Beirut. I think we have become pariahs in many parts of the Middle East because of that military action, which I thought was unnecessary.

There is no way, in my opinion, that the United States can play a strong mediation role through the use of an ambassador, no matter how well qualified or how distinguished. There are a couple of exceptions. If President Reagan were to call on, say, someone of the stature of Henry Kissinger to be his personal representative, that might pay dividends. It almost has to be a secretary of state or the president to get concessions and ideas from the leaders there who might want to take the next step toward peace. I think most of the nations involved, even including Syria when I talked privately to Asad, see the United States as an integral player in the future progress, when and if the time comes.

That does not mean that all of the blame for lack of progress falls upon the United States. The Palestinians are divided and speak with multiple voices; King Hussein waxes and wanes in his degree of enthusiasm; Mubarak has been playing a game to get back into the Arab fold—very successfully, I might say. I think that this is what Sadat would have done.

But there are always potential opportunities for progress, and sometimes the progress has to be quite incremental in nature. The Camp David accords are there and they are intact. The only tangible result of the Camp David accords was the treaty between Israel and Egypt that came six months later. With only tiny deviations, that treaty's terms have been observed by both sides in a meticulous way in spite of terrible challenges to its integrity—the invasion of Lebanon, the death of Sadat, the withdrawal of Israeli people from the settlements and the Sinai, and the multiple changes in the Israeli government. The treaty is still there, is still intact, and is still a model for what can be done in the future.

PRESIDENT CARTER ON URGENT CONTEMPORARY PROBLEMS

So I would say that our country has helped to prevent any progress because in the past, when Kissinger was secretary of state under Ford and Nixon or when I was in office with my secretaries of state, anyone in the Middle East, including the Palestinians, Sadat, Begin, Hussein, Asad, or anyone else who had the slightest desire to move forward, knew that he would have an immediate ally and partner in the White House if he wanted to take a tentative step. That has been totally absent the last six years. I think and hope that with a new president we will have a reinstitution of well-known, dependable, and persistent involvement in the Middle East in order to take advantage of any opportunity toward peace.

QUESTION: Mr. President, you had a marvelous track record anticipating what would work for the nomination and election in 1976. Query: what will work in 1988?

PRESIDENT CARTER: I think the identity of the nominees will be more important than anything else. Let me add quickly, however, that I think that President Reagan's *policies* are basically unpopular. *Personally*, he is still quite popular but, as you may know, almost two-thirds of the American people disapprove of aid to the contras, not to mention the $200 billion annual deficits, the doubling of the nation's debt, the farm crisis, the lack of progress on civil rights, the abrogation of even existing nuclear arms agreements. Those kind of things are not popular with the American people, so I don't think that someone is going to inherit Reagan's policies and find that they have an automatic platform on which they can be elected president. I think the likely nominee on the Republican side, at this time, is George Bush. He is President Reagan's choice, and even though Robert Dole or someone else might be coming on stronger and might ultimately prevail, my guess is that it is Bush's nomination to lose; he might hold on or he might lose it. I think additionally that Bush will not overwhelm the Democratic nominee with charisma; his record in elections is not very notable.

So that brings us down to the question of whom the Democrats will choose and I do not know the answer. There are some notable people whom the Democrats could choose that I would like to see in the White House. Someone like Senator Bill

Bradley from New Jersey would be good, but I do not think he will run. Mario Cuomo might show some popularity in the South—it would surprise me if he did, but he might. He is an intellectual. He has proven to be a successful, tough Italian infighter in the street brawls of New York politics and he is an evocative speaker. Joe Biden is a candidate. There might be a governor somewhere that is as unknown as I was at an equivalent time who will come forward. Bruce Babbitt might very well show success.

My own personal choice, if I could select a nominee, would be Sam Nunn. First of all, I think Sam Nunn would be a good president. His credentials on social matters are very good. I would say they are compatible with mine which by definition makes them good! He is strong on defense but he is also very critical of wastefulness in the Defense Department, and he is looking now at overall defense policy, which is good. I think Sam Nunn could carry the South and mathematically it is almost impossible for a Democrat to win the presidency without the South. Nunn would be the most successful in insuring that the Democrats would sweep the South. So he would be my choice, but I am not publicly endorsing him. I have talked to him about it and encouraged him to run and so have many other people. I have no idea whether he will run yet. So I think the Democrats have a good chance provided they choose the right person. That is where the winnowing process comes in with the long and tedious primary season, which I think is good. I don't deplore it; it is good for the candidates to learn about our nation and it is good for the nation to learn about the candidates.

The unpredictable element, which I am sure some of you are studying, is the massive southern primary. We had "Super Tuesday" in 1984, which I helped to initiate before I went out of office as governor, but the impact of 13 to 15 states having a simultaneous, early primary in the South is still to be determined. Clearly it does escalate the importance of the South. So I feel good as a Democrat about our prospects in 1988, but a lot can happen between now and the election.

MR. THOMPSON: About a month ago, Senator Nunn spoke at this table and he promised to come back. More recently, a leading popular newspaper announced, "He's back," and then explained it was not Nixon but Jimmy Carter to whom it referred. Ray Price pointed out in an article recently that it took Nixon only ten years to come back, whereas it took Truman 20 years and Hoover 30 years. Well, it has taken Jimmy Carter only about six years, and we hope his coming back with a 55 percent popularity rating in the country, with three of his associates elected to statewide office, and with resurgence in many areas will symbolize a willingness to come back to the Miller Center and the University of Virginia.

PRESIDENT CARTER: I hope you will all remember my invitation to come to the Carter Library and Center if you are passing through Atlanta. I think you will be pleased with the time you might spend there, and I am very grateful again, not only for a chance to come here, but for the very significant work you have done and the honor that you all have paid my administration by working on the oral history. Thank you again.